THE
COMPANY
TOWN

*Architecture and Society in the Early
Industrial Age*

Edited by
John S. Garner

New York   Oxford
OXFORD UNIVERSITY PRESS
1992

Oxford University Press

Oxford   New York   Toronto
Delhi   Bombay   Calcutta   Madras   Karachi
Kuala Lumpur   Singapore   Hong Kong   Tokyo
Nairobi   Dar es Salaam   Cape Town
Melbourne   Auckland

and associated companies in
Berlin   Ibadan

Copyright © 1992 by Oxford University Press, Inc.

Published by Oxford University Press, Inc.,
200 Madison Avenue, New York, New York 10016

Oxford is a registered trademark of Oxford University Press

Library of Congress Cataloging-in-Publication Data
The Company town :
architecture and society in the early industrial age /
edited by John S. Garner.
p.   cm.   Includes bibliographical reference and index.
ISBN 0-19-507027-5
1. Company town architecture—History—19th century.
I. Garner, John S., 1945–
NA9053.C57C66   1992   307.76'7'09034–dc20   91-35627

2 4 6 8 9 7 5 3 1

Printed in the United States of America
on acid-free paper

Preface

This book owes its existence to a growing interest in the history of industrial landscapes and the vernacular buildings that defined them. It is also the result of good timing. In April 1990 I chaired a session on the subject in a meeting of the Society of Architectural Historians held in Boston. Joyce Berry of Oxford University Press attended the session and suggested that I edit the papers. The outcome hinged on the uncertainty of whether the participants could expand their papers into chapters, and whether I could round out the collection to produce a useful volume. I hope that we have succeeded on both accounts.

My thanks go to Mats Ahnlund and Lasse Brunnström, senior lecturers in architectural and landscape history at Umeå University in Sweden, who traveled far to participate in the session. Richard M. Candee, professor of American and New England Studies at Boston University, had only to travel across town to share his knowledge of New England. A complement to his chapter was offered by Margaret Crawford, assistant professor of architecture at the Southern California Institute of Architecture in Los Angeles. By contrast, Bruce Thomas, assistant professor of architecture at Lehigh University in Bethlehem, Pennsylvania, shared the results of his studies in South Wales.

In addition to the participants in the session, Leland Roth, professor of architectural history at the University of Oregon, attended the Boston meeting and brought to bear his considerable knowledge of resource towns in the American West. His research was assisted in part by a grant from the National Endowment for the Humanities. Roth's counterpart on the subject of resource towns is Olga Paterlini de Koch, professor of architecture and urban planning at the University of Tucumán, Argentina, whose research was also known to me.

Finally, I acknowledge a debt to the Fulbright-Hays program for a senior research award to France, and to the University of Illinois, where I am professor of architecture, for a sabbatical to pursue my interest in French villages. Jane Cook, also of the University of Illinois, kindly typed the final manuscript.

Urbana, Illinois   J. S. G.
January 1992

Contents

The Company Town

Introduction

A company town is a settlement built and operated by a single business enterprise. Most company towns appeared between 1830 and 1930 during the early industrial age, an age that Lewis Mumford called the "paleotechnic era." Technology was primitive and the operations performed in these settlements can be characterized as primary and labor-intensive. The towns flourished in countries that embraced capitalism and open-market trading and belonged to industrialists whose early businesses contributed to the "takeoff" phase of the Industrial Revolution. To Mumford and others, it was a period of environmental decline; an age of plunder, pollution, and despoliation; of unbuilding, or *Abbau*. In many instances, the company town came to symbolize the wrecking of the environment, at least in places associated with extractive industries such as mining and lumber milling. *Production* and *profit* are the words that best describe its purpose. That it was built over a shorter period of time with large capital outlays made it distinctive. It stood apart from other communities.[1]

The term *company town* is of recent origin. It was coined in America in the late-nineteenth century and applied first to mining camps and smelters in Appalachia and the Monongahela Valley. It was always used pejoratively and has carried a stigma that has not gone away. In his *History of Manufacturers in the United States*, Victor Clark quotes an early description of "mill and furnace industries":

> Such works were generally under the personal direction of their owner, who exercised absolute dominion over a large tract of territory. He cut the fuel for his furnace, mined its ore, and quarried its limestone upon his own lands. . . . The cottages of his employees, grouped about the works and belonging to the proprietor, formed a settlement often remote from other communities. The iron master's feudal sway over lands, farms, furnace, forge, mill, store, and tenements might embrace even church and school.[2]

To Mark Twain, the coke towns of western Pennsylvania suggested "hell with the lid off." In time, "company town" would be used to describe other single-enterprise towns, including those engaged in manufacture—places earlier referred to as mill towns or industrial villages. The term does not carry quite the same connotation as the Swedish *bruk* or the Belgian or French *cité ouvrière*, nor did Europeans view such places in quite such negative terms.[3]

Some company towns were preplanned, but many were not. Rather like Topsy, they just grew, expanding as their enterprises matured. In a company town, virtually everything associated with the settlement, including the houses, store, school, and even the chapel, was subordinate to the business enterprise. Factories or mines, "the works" to which the British refer, dominated the site, and there was a sameness to the houses and other ancillary buildings. According to Mark Girouard, these places were "all of a piece," and when we stumble on them today, however fragmentary the remains, their singularity of purpose still takes us by surprise. In writing about them, our intent is not to retell the story of the Industrial Revolution or to focus on community and labor relations but rather to revisit the sites themselves and to explore the industrial settings of places overtaken by time and now largely abandoned, forgotten, or engulfed by urban sprawl.[4]

The towns described herein derived from iron smelting, mining, lumber milling, and the manufacture of staples such as textiles and foodstuffs. Because they were dependent on resource sites, either for materials or for water power to operate their mills, their architecture and environmental setting exhibited a special character. Most towns were quite small, with populations rarely exceeding a few thousand. The workers who lived in company towns, who conformed to the circumstances imposed on them, created subcultures of their own. Social order derived from labor routine, isolation, and company-imposed rules or policies. Unlike that of the industrial city or corporation town containing more than one enterprise, even when devoted to the same industry, most property in company towns was owned by an individual, family, or partnership. In some towns the workers themselves shared in the ownership, but these were rare exceptions. Mining camps, lumber camps, or mill villages could develop into company towns if in time a single enterprise prevailed.[5]

A model company town was one in which the paternalism of the owner extended beyond the bare-bones architectural requirements of factories or mines. Well-designed houses, parks, schools, libraries, and meeting halls, all set within an attractive landscape, represented an unusual degree of interest by the developer. But equally exceptional were the social programs that extended to the families of employees. Some resident industrialists took a genuine interest in the welfare of their work forces, and attempted to provide a model environment. Although their interest in local affairs could also be meddlesome or oppressive, more than a few industrialists undertook paternalistic measures to recruit or retain skilled labor as well as to maintain their financial investment in buildings and grounds. Some attempts were made to manage resources and to preserve or protect the surrounding environment. The best of these places contributed to ideas later set forth in the planning of Garden Cities and New Towns, as Walter Creese has shown. Parker and Unwin, the architects who laid out Letchworth, England, for Ebenezer Howard and his collaborators, had earlier designed the company town of New Earswick for the chocolate manufacturer and Quaker Joseph Rowntree. Port Sunlight and Bourneville, England, have often been cited as Garden City prototypes. English observers of industrial villages and apologists of the factory system, such as James Hole in the 1860s and Budgett Meakin in the 1890s, visited these industrial villages and remarked on their pleasing environments and efforts at "social upliftment." Later, the American prophet of scientific management, Frederick Winslow Taylor, chose the site of the National Cash Register Company and its model village near Dayton, Ohio, to conduct experiments in labor efficiency through time-motion studies. Despite its architectural and economic success, the company town failed in a political sense. Most had no form of government, no elected officials, and no municipally owned services, and many remained unincorporated. Residents had no say in local affairs, no investment in real estate, and ultimately no long-term affection for the place in which they lived and worked. Even in the best model company towns, strikes occurred and resentments were harbored.[6]

The image of the company town has been largely shaped by the exposés of social reformers and the reports of labor investigators. Towns devoted to industry did not escape the eye of outspoken Victorians. Charles Dickens, Benjamin Disraeli, Elizabeth Gaskell, Octavia Hill, Harriet Martineau, and Florence Nightingale all called attention to the social upheaval brought about by industrialization. Friedrich Engels's report on the condition of the poor in Manchester in 1844 reveals the abject misery of Irish immigrants uprooted from their native farms and left to the mercy of English landlords in the large industrial city. Dickens's portrait of Coketown in *Hard Times* lays bare the mean conditions of factory workers and their avaricious landlords. And although his account was fictional, there was sufficient evidence of human suffering in Lancashire, Wales, and elsewhere in Britain to trouble British society and to launch efforts at labor reform. Similarly, the human wreckage portrayed by Victor Hugo, Honoré Balzac, Louis Blanc, and Émile Zola set the stage for investigations into industrial conditions in France by René Villermé, Émile Muller, and Émile Cacheux. Housing reform represented a tangible goal of those seeking to improve the lives of industrial workers. The Housing Congresses initiated at the Paris Exposition of 1889, which culminated in Europe in the great municipally financed housing estates of the 1920s, first drew upon examples of model housing in company towns.[7]

Despite the way in which industrial developments were depicted in the nineteenth century, with smokestacks proudly sending forth curls of black soot as symbols of productivity, references to the company town were guarded. Instead of the hubris that might otherwise attach to a modern type of settlement, it summoned the image of a "medieval, feudal barony"; in North America, where company towns numbered into the hundreds, they were assailed as "un-American." Their occupants were "held in thrall" as "serfs" or machine-enslaved "automata." The captains of industry who built the towns were labeled "robber barons." Reformers and muckrakers, such as Richard T. Ely, Edith Elmer Wood, Graham Romeyne Taylor, and Lawrence Veiller, called attention to their unwholesome character. That labor exploitation occurred frequently is a matter of record. And the last refrain of the song "Sixteen Tons," written in 1947 by Merle Travis and later recorded by Tennessee Ernie Ford, exaggerates only in degree. "I owe my soul to the company store" had a popular ring to it, especially in the South and West, where company stores abounded, but in reality industrial workers were far less dependent on credit than agricultural workers. In both lyric and literature, the hardships that really did occur have been romanticized.[8]

In North America, and to a lesser extent in Northern Europe, skilled labor was relatively unfettered. Workers unsatisfied with their situation could pick up and leave. Locational mobility ran high. The fact that laborers had few worldly possessions and rented instead of owning their homes increased their mobility. Another exaggeration is that workers represented a proletariat in the classic meaning of the term. Conditions of labor in the period 1830–1850, especially during times of economic recession and unemployment, were unquestionably terrible, especially in larger cities where overcrowding occurred. Quality of life declined as mortality rates increased. Child labor and workdays that extended well beyond ten hours were among the more odious conditions that prevailed. But such conditions were prevalent before the onset of the nineteenth century. The textile workers of Renaissance Tuscany and Flanders would have welcomed workdays confined to hours determined by the clock, and they would have been amazed by the personal freedoms and material goods the later age afforded.

What made the nineteenth century so terrible was not just the exploitation of labor but the perfection of machines that would accelerate human tasks and thus endanger lives, prematurely age men and women, rob children of their youth, and—even worse—threaten to put them out of work. Such legitimate fears sparked violence in nineteenth-century Europe and twentieth-century America. But the popular uprisings of 1831 and 1848 in Europe did not harden divisions among social classes, nor did they sound the clarion call of revolution as Marx and Engels had predicted. If anything, during the second half of the nineteenth century workers embraced the tenets of capitalism and espoused bourgeois values. A surprising number of workers in company towns opened savings accounts, indicating that wages offered more than a hand-to-mouth existence. Although their lives were hard and their homes spartan, workers were not forced to grovel. By the early twentieth century, the hardships brought about by layoffs, which occurred frequently in the textile industry, were probably less dire than that confronted by marginal farmers or sharecroppers in America who had suffered a failed crop. Because of the very nature of a company town, where all suffered the same fate, employers occasionally accepted losses to make work for those who might otherwise leave. One grievance of the Pullman strikers, who had been among the better paid workers in Chicago, was the reduction in wages resulting from commissions on piecework during the depression of 1893–1894. But to have paid regular wages, according to George Pullman, would have been "a piece of business folly."[9]

Pullman, Illinois, founded in 1880, is by far the best known company town, and its story remains the most infamous. Its notoriety stems from the Pullman Strike of 1894, in which the American Railway Union under the leadership of Eugene V. Debs championed the cause of the car builders at Pullman on Chicago's South Side.

Introduction 7

Because of the depression, some workers had been laid off, were put on reduced work schedules, or were paid by piecework. Despite the exigencies under which the workers were forced to subsist, company management did little to relieve their plight. Rents, for example, on company houses were not reduced. When workers appealed to George Pullman to arbitrate their differences, he rebuffed them. Partly as a result of the town's location and partly because of the Haymarket riot of 1886, George Pullman could not escape organized labor and the heated political climate that surrounded him. Although he weathered the strike and the workers eventually returned to their jobs, the negative publicity attached to the event would have lasting repercussions. The town survived less than ten years as an unincorporated holding, and by the time of the strike, it had already been annexed by Chicago. To the extent that the model town failed, it failed in its relations between management and labor. In Ely's exposé of 1885, written before the strike and before the image of the town had been tarnished, he signaled the trouble to come, the resentment fostered by the paternalism of the company, and the fuss it made about maintaining its premises. Ida M. Tarbell, whose investigative reporting exposed the Standard Oil cartel, would later describe the paternalism of Pullman as a failed opportunity: "Men want to putter about their homes; Mr. Pullman insisted on doing the puttering himself. Women like to hang their clothes in the yard, Mr. Pullman provided an enclosure. But Mr. Pullman gave this country a standard for building and landscape gardening which was a revelation to many of us, and he gave, also, a valuable lesson in what not to do." In architecture and planning, Pullman represented a decided improvement over most industrial towns. Carroll Wright, who became the first U.S. commissioner of the Bureau of Labor in 1883, applauded the example of Pullman and strongly endorsed the standards envisaged by its founder. Expenditures for gas lighting, water supply, sewerage, garbage collection, and landscaping—amenities only the most affluent suburbs of the period could afford through property taxation—were borne by the company. After the Pullman Strike, Illinois's Governor Altgeld launched an investigation into Pullman's holdings and eventually brought suit against the company under state antitrust laws. By 1908, the Pullman Company had been forced to divest its residential and retail properties. The condition of the housing declined rapidly once it reverted to individual ownership. Without the company's subsidy, the arcade and market buildings also succumbed. The park with its street lights, benches, and carpetbed gardens gave way to weeds and vandalism. By the 1930s, Pullman had become just another blighted South Side neighborhood.[10]

Paternalism was Pullman's undoing. The tenets of noblesse oblige had been set out toward the end of the eighteenth century by, among others, Jeremy Bentham, who espoused a philosophy based on utilitarianism. Moral reform could be brought about by an improvement in material conditions. Those fortunate enough to better themselves could ensure their gains by putting the less fortunate to work in model factories. Bentham would have remanded the poor to workhouses in much the same manner as he had earlier suggested incarcerating criminals. Robert Owen carried forward Bentham's philosophy within the industrial setting of Lanark, Scotland, the textile mill founded by David Dale and Richard Arkwright in 1783 and purchased by Owen in 1799. Within a few years, Owen had launched a campaign to reward his workers for good work habits and to provide an education for their children. In 1813, Owen published his program, the "Institution for the Reforming of Character," and then went on to test his ideas by addressing audiences at home and abroad. Yet his attempts to further his ideas in the utopian scheme of 1825 for New Lanark, Indiana, foundered.

In America, paternalism, to the extent it existed, differed inasmuch as it did not seek to reform the laboring classes or correct social evils but served instead as a ploy to attract and retain workers. Kirk Boott, agent for the Merrimack Manufacturing Company of Lowell, Massachusetts, founded by the Boston Associates in 1822, promised wholesome living arrangements for the "mill girls" he recruited from surrounding farms and villages. Their boardinghouses were prim utilitarian boxes, neatly set in rows and superintended by matrons. Chapel service was required, and a literary society founded to provide a diversion from work. Lucy Larcom and her fellow mill hands could recall the early years at Lowell with affection. However, the model conditions encountered by visitors, including William Scoresby from England, lasted but a short time. In 1836 the mill girls staged a strike to protest the inequities in compensation for work performed. Until then, industrial labor in America had been treated as a special commodity, but such deferential treatment ended with the waves of European immigrants who began arriving in the 1840s to compete for jobs. The architectural historian John Coolidge has written, "The first twenty years of Lowell's history had been an era of profitable paternalism. The succeeding period, by contrast, was one of nepotistic mismanagement." For Bentham, Owen, Boott, and others, paternalism was a secular matter. But for the Quakers, who embraced paternalism with a religious fervor, it played a part in their vision of a new society.[11]

John Grubb Richardson and Rowland G. Hazard were two Quakers who placed paternalism at the very center of their industrial experiments. Although William Penn was probably the first Quaker to take a paternal interest in those who settled his colonies in the seventeenth century, he never carried his proprietary interests to the point of building homes in Londonderry, Northern Ireland, or Philadelphia. Nor was he a resident landlord. Richardson built the town of Bessbrook, near Newry, Northern Ireland, in 1846 for his linen mills. Open space in the form of a village green and generous allotments for vegetable gardens echoed Penn's insistence on a "green country town." A community hall, school, dispensary, savings bank, cooperative store, and houses built of granite completed the layout.[12] The number of services to employees approached that of Marquette, France, where the Scrive brothers, also manufacturers of linens, provided a similar array of buildings and services (Chapter 2). Hazard, whose family had occupied land near Kingston, Rhode Island, since the beginning of the century, began developing the village of Peace Dale around his woolen mills after the completion of a new factory in 1847. He greatly expanded his works in 1856, and by the 1880s, Peace Dale had reached a population of 1,200; of a work force of 450, nearly two-thirds were foreign-born and two-fifths women. "The Hazards have their homes in Peace Dale and make its material and moral prosperity their concern. Their residences are unpretentious, offering no occasion of envy to their employees." Because Hazard was a Quaker, he attempted "to make his business a blessing to all connected with it. His influence lives in the policy of the company and in the economic prosperity and moral well-being of its workpeople."[13] Edwin L. Shuey, who was Budgett Meakin's American counterpart, described the Hazard Memorial Hall as a community building that furnished a "moral, social, and educational advantage" to the town. Shuey rationalized, "It is good business for the manufacturer to make factory life as attractive as is consistent with steady work. . . . A stretch of green lawn and a few flowers . . . clean paint, instead of grimy interiors; none of these things costs much money, but they go far toward making life worth living for the man of work. They give him a pride in the plant, and help to make him enthusiastic for its success."[14] Hazard corresponded with John Stuart Mill and wrote a number of small books in which he expounded on his theory of work and social reward.

Company housing formed a bond between the employer and employee. Apart from the factories or mines, it accounted for a sizable investment in the town and was always a source of contention. Industrial housing in developmental tracts predates the company town and can be found in settlements of various descriptions. An argument can be made for suggesting that it was an ancient solution to a problem of workers' housing. In Egypt during the Middle and New Kingdoms, planned orthogonal tracts of houses for artisans were laid out at Kahun, Deir-el-Medina, and Tel-el-Amarna. These were not towns but rather subdivisions of larger cities, and it is unknown to what degree the crafts performed by their occupants were carried out in the dwellings or elsewhere thereabout. During the late Middle Ages and into the Renaissance, tracts of houses for textile workers were constructed by merchants or guilds in established cities such as Ghent in the late 1300s and Augsburg in the early 1500s. Jacob Fugger built two-story row houses in Augsburg in 1519 for his weavers, who wove cloth at home. Each unit or flat consisted of two rooms and a kitchen, and one of the rooms usually contained a loom. The development became known as "Fuggerei," and some of the houses survive. Arkwright's row houses in Cromford, England, erected in 1776 and still occupied, established a precedent in vernacular design that continued well into the nineteenth century. The history of low-cost housing for working families has been addressed by several studies in Europe and America. By the beginning of the twentieth century, large-scale housing estates developed to serve industry had become a subject of considerable interest. However, only a small portion of this housing was constructed by companies for their employees. Given the alternative, companies preferred not to build houses and left the responsibility to private landholders. For most, company housing posed a liability—the return on investment was low, it required periodic maintenance, and it could involve the company in domestic and ethnic disputes. In isolated locations, companies had little alternative but to build housing, lest workers build shanties that were unsightly and risked health hazards. In many instances, immigrant and itinerant laborers could not afford to rent nonsubsidized housing, and in a number of places company housing was used as an incentive to attract workers who might choose to go elsewhere. For rents charged, housing by companies was usually superior to that of private developers.[15]

Planning was a part of any business venture, but the layout of a company town often appeared haphazard. Camps and villages occupied the leftover spaces adjacent to the works. When site planning did occur, it often progressed in stages and not all at once. However, there were also examples of planned towns, whose architects and landscape architects became well known. Two eighteenth-century examples were Nuevo Baztán in Spain and Arc-et-Senans in France. Nuevo Baztán was designed by José Benito Churriguera for Juan de Goyeneche, a royal banker and patron of Charles II. Constructed between 1709 and 1713 and laid out on a grid, the town lies southeast of Madrid near the Arroyo de la Vega. Occupying the center of town were the *plaza major* and a baroque Churrigueresque church. But instead of the barracks of a military garrison, a glassworks dominated the town.

In contrast to Nuevo Baztán was Arc-et-Senans, the royal saltworks at Chaux, near Bescançon. The purpose of Arc-et-Senans, obscured by its Neoclassical architecture, was the extraction of salt from deposits in the Forests of Chaux. Water carried by wooden pipes took the salt from mines to a sluice outside the arc of the village, where the saline solution was precipitated, boiled, dried, and placed in tubs for shipment. Claude Nicolas Ledoux created the plan for the town, which was based on a circle, although only half of the plan was actually carried out (1775–1783). On the diameter of the circle were the director's and clerks' houses and factories, and on the perimeter of the outer curve, facing center, sat the houses of the workers—each built for several families and each with its *petit jardin* behind. Had more attention been given the saltworks and less attention the fatuous tar-tufferie of Ledoux's cultural pavilions, designed for the workers' leisure, the operation might have overcome its technical deficiencies. Both of these planned developments suffered from the economic and political turmoil of their time, namely, the Wars of the Spanish Succession and the collapse of the ancien régime. At least the architects of Nuevo Baztán and Arc-et-Senans conceived plans that recognized the place of the worker in a new industrial order.[16]

Each of the following chapters addresses the building of company towns within its own industrial and geographical setting. Some thought was given to grouping the chapters according to type of industries described, whether extractive or manufacturing, but in the end it was decided to group them according to location. The first three chapters describe places in Wales, France, and Scandinavia, and the remaining four chapters focus on North and South America. Although the perspective offered is broad in scope, it is by no means comprehensive. Each contributor sets out a framework of several towns and describes at least one in some detail. Economic and social histories of industrial cities are more easily found than descriptions of what they looked like. But in this collection, architecture is emphasized. Although it may be inferred that the company town was an early type of industrial settlement that has all but disappeared, in truth company towns are still being built in Latin American and other developing countries. Whereas in Western Europe and North America company towns can now be viewed as historical types, a few continue to operate in Scandinavia, Canada, and the western United States.

No industry transformed a landscape more than iron making in South Wales. Bruce Thomas describes the ironworks villages of Merthyr Tydfil, whose earliest foundries date to the 1760s. Although Abraham Darby's works at Coalbrookdale on the River Severn in western England touched off a revolution in iron manufacture by producing iron in quantity and with the efficiency of new fuels, the locus of iron making quickly shifted to Wales, where mineral resources—especially coal—abounded. The once-isolated and peaceful valleys of Merthyr became a roaring inferno "whose intense flames turned nighttime skies into glowing orange sunrises" (Chapter 1). Nowhere was the specter of the Industrial Revolution more awesome. Merthyr's incredible furnaces and smelters also produced incredible squalor. It used up its environment with voracious intensity, so much so that by the 1860s, it had exhausted itself to the point of decline. Merthyr shocked visitors with its appearance, which provided an apparition of things to come. In France, although iron making had had an early start at Creusot, textiles had long been an important domestic industry. Some of the earliest model villages and planned residential quarters, *les cités ouvrières*, grew up around the mills and are described in Chapter 2. France was also known for its export of wine, cheese, and chocolate. The Menier chocolate works at Noisiel-sur-Marne was a model company town with an exceptional monument to industrial architecture, the turbine building of 1871–1872. Noisiel-sur-Marne not only predates such towns as New Earswick, England (1897), and Hershey, Pennsylvania (1903), but prefigures, in the simplicity of its plan and social program, a model of a *cité industrielle* that would be greatly amplified by the architect and planning visionary Tony Garnier after the turn of the century. Mats Ahnlund and Lasse Brunnström complete the first part with a brief history of company towns in Scandinavia. The largely resource-based settlements, devoted to the mining and smelting of iron ore and other metals, the milling of lumber, and eventually the harnessing of hydroelectric power, provide a comprehensive array of planning layouts and buildings. Had company towns been built only in the Scandinavian countries and nowhere else, they would deserve a place in the writing of urban history. In Sweden, alone, tremendous emphasis was placed on building in remote and hostile environments, which challenged the country's leading architects.

Mill villages of the textile industry sprang up throughout New England during the first half of the nineteenth century, in part through the efforts of such proponents of industrialism as Tench Coxe and such British immigrants as Samuel Slater during the 1780s and 1790s. As a direct result of Jefferson's trade embargo against England (1807–1809), textile manufacturers gained a foothold in a very competitive market, and by the beginning of twentieth century, mill villages had begun to transform the economy of the American South. In Chapter 4 Richard M. Candee traces the development of those villages that stemmed from the "Waltham system" and emerged as company towns. He describes four towns of the Piscataqua River Valley in New Hampshire, their factories, houses, and topographic settings, and the families of manufacturers who risked investing in them. Isaac Wendell and Stephen Hansen, fellow Quakers, would build Dover, Great Falls, and Newmarket during the 1820s. Margaret Crawford follows with an appraisal of the company town in the Piedmont region of the South. Southern textile manufacturers not only borrowed from the earlier villages of New England but enlarged on their technologies and paternalistic practices. The landscape architect and planner Earle Draper, who trained in the office of John Nolen and emerged in the period 1917–1925 as a designer of company towns, attempted to strike a balance between the requirements of the manufacturer on the one hand and those of his employees on the other. Chicopee, Georgia, embraced many of the planning attributes that Draper would later apply in Norris, Tennessee, built for the Tennessee Valley Authority after 1933.

Leland M. Roth and Olga Paterlini de Koch carve out vast regions in the American West and the badlands (*los mala tierras*) of Argentina and Chile in their descriptions of company towns devoted to resource-based or extractive industries. The mining and lumber milling towns of these less-settled regions, occupying the frontiers of their respective countries, share much with the company towns of Scandinavia. Within Roth's taxonomy of plan types, those that were laid out by such professional landscape architects and architects as Warren H. Manning, Bertram G. Goodhue, George Kessler, and Bernard Maybeck receive special attention. Clarence Stein, Goodhue's chief draftsman for Tyrone, New Mexico, later designed the Canadian company towns of Kitimat and Temiskaming, not to mention Radburn, New Jersey, America's first New Town.[17] Their contemporaries in Sweden and Finland were Gustaf Wickman, Ralph Erskine, and Alvar Aalto. Further comparisons can be drawn between their work and the layout of towns or *ingenios* designed by Manuel Graña and Charles Thays for the sugar industry in Argentina, which Paterlini de Koch describes in detail in Chapter 7.

At the end of the book, a brief Bibliography has been compiled from the recommendations of each contributor. Because so little has been written about company towns and because the sources are not well known, students and other scholars seeking additional information about the towns cited may find it there.

Notes

1. Lewis Mumford derived some of his terminology, including "paleotechnic," from the writings of Patrick Geddes. Mumford uses the term, *Abbau*," from German, "to cut down, reduce, exhaust, demolish"; see *The Culture of Cities* (New York: Harcourt, Brace, and World, 1938), 150; W. W. Rostow, *The Stages of Economic Growth: A Non-Communist Manifesto* (Cambridge: Cambridge University Press, 1960), 36–40.

2. The *Oxford English Dictionary* suggests an American derivation for *company town*, 3:590; Victor S. Clark, *History of Manufacturers in the United States, 1607–1860*, vol. 1 (New York: McGraw-Hill, 1929), 445.

3. Mark Twain, *Sketches New and Old* (New York: Harper and Bros., 1899), p. 75.

4. Mark Girouard, *The English Town* (New Haven: Yale University Press, 1990), 248.

5. Two unusual company towns in which workers participated in profit sharing were the Familistère at Guise, France, and Leclaire, Illinois. See J.-B. Godin, *Solutions sociales* (Paris: A. Le Chevalier, 1871), and Leo Balmer, Stefan Erni, and Ursula von Gunten, "Cooperation between Capital and Labour," *Lotus International* 21 (September 1976: 59–71; John S. Garner, "Leclaire, Illinois: A Model Company Town, 1890–1934," *Journal of the Society of Architectural Historians* 30 (October 1971): 219–27.

6. Walter L. Creese, *The Search for Environment: The Garden City, Before and After*

(New Haven: Yale University Press, 1966), 13–60; see also James Hole, *The Homes of the Working Classes* (London: Longmans, Green, 1866); Budgett Meakin, *Model Factories and Villages: Ideal Conditions of Labor and Housing* (London: Fisher and Unwin, 1905); O. M. Becker, "The Square Deal in Works Management," *Engineering Magazine* 30 (December 1905): 536–53; Frederick W. Taylor, *Shop Management* (New York: McGraw-Hill, 1911).

7. For Victorian views of the industrial city, see Gertrude Himmelfarb, *The Idea of Poverty: England in the Early Industrial Age* (New York: Alfred A. Knopf, 1984), 504–21; Asa Briggs, *The Making of Modern England, 1783–1867* (New York: Harper and Row, 1959), 489–523; Friedrich Engels, *Die lage der arbeiten den Klasse in England* (Leipzig: O. Wigand, 1845); Charles Dickens, *Hard Times* (London: Bradbury and Evans, 1854); International Housing Congresses, 1st in Paris, 1889, 2d in Marseilles, 1892, 3d in Bordeaux, 1895, 4th in Brussels, 1897, 5th in Paris, 1900, 6th in Dusseldorf, 1902, 7th in Liege, 1905, 8th in London, 1908, 9th in Vienna, 1910.

8. Richard T. Ely, "Pullman: A Social Study," *Harper's Monthly*, February 1885, 452–66; Graham Romeyn Taylor, *Satellite Cities: A Study of Industrial Suburbs* (New York: D. Appleton, 1915); Edith Elmer Wood, *The Housing of the Unskilled Wage Earner* (New York: Macmillan, 1919); Lawrence Veiller, "Industrial Housing Developments in America," *Architectural Record* 43 (May 1918): 547–59; see also Thomas C. Cochran and William Miller, *The Age of Enterprise* (New York: Macmillan, 1942), 18–19; D. Creamer, "Legislation on Company Stores," *American Federationist* 43 (1936): 365–75; George Creel, "The Feudal Towns of Texas," *Harper's Weekly* 60 (1915): 77; O. S. Johnson, *The Industrial Store: Its History, Operations and Economic Significance* (Atlanta: University of Georgia Press, 1952).

9. Harry Hearder, *Europe in the Nineteenth Century: 1830–1880* (London: Longman, 1966), 119–31; David S. Landes, *The Unbound Prometheus* (Cambridge: Cambridge University Press, 1970), chaps. 2–3; Fernand Braudel, *Capitalism and Material Life: 1400–1800* (New York: Harper and Row, 1973), 381; Jacquelyn D. Hall et al., *Like a Family* (Chapel Hill: University of North Carolina Press, 1987) 114–80; *The Strike at Pullman: Statements of President Geo. M. Pullman . . . before the U.S. Strike Commission* (Washington: U.S. Government Printing Office, 1894), 36.

10. *Strike at Pullman*, 37; for an overview of Pullman see Stanley Buder, *Pullman: An Experiment in Industrial Order and Community Planning, 1880–1930* (New York: Oxford University Press, 1967); for an assessment of Pullman's architecture and planning see John S. Garner, "S. S. Beman and the Building of Pullman." in John S. Garner, ed., *The Midwest in American Architecture* (Urbana: University of Illinois Press, 1991), 231–49; Ida M. Tarbell, *New Ideals in Business* (New York: Macmillan, 1917), 146.

11. See Leslie Stephen, *The English Utilitarians* (New York: A. M. Kelley, 1968), and Mary Peter Mack, ed., *A Bentham Reader* (New York: Pegasus, 1969); Robert Owen, *A New View of Society, or, Essays on the Principle of the formation of human character . . .* (London: Cadell and Davies, 1813); Lucy Larcom, *A New England Girlhood* (Boston: Houghton, Mifflin, 1889), 170–85; William Scoresby, *American Factories and Their Female Operatives* (London: Longman, Browne, Gray, 1845), 25–27; John Coolidge, *Mill and Mansion: A Study of Architecture and Society in Lowell, Massachusetts, 1820–1865* (New York: Columbia University Press, 1942), 105.

12. Gerald Burke, *Towns in the Making* (New York: St. Martin's Press, 1971), 137.

13. [Massachusetts] *Bureau of Labor Statistics, Seventeenth Annual Report* (Boston: Wright and Potter, 1886), 186.

14. Edwin L. Shuey, *Factory People and Their Employers: How Their Relations Are Made Pleasant and Profitable* (New York: Lentilhon and Company, 1900), 136, 211.

15. Paul Lampl, *Cities and Planning in the Ancient Near East* (New York: Braziller,

1968), 30–31; E. A. Gutkind, *Urban Development in Central Europe,* vol. 1 of *International History of City Development*, (New York: Macmillan, 1964), 169–70; R. S. Fitton, *The Arkwrights* (Manchester: Manchester University Press, 1989), 187; Marcus T. Reynolds, *The Housing of the Poor in American Cities* (Baltimore: Guggenheimer, Weil, and Co., 1893), 23, 25, 27; Albert Benedict Wolfe, *The Lodging House Problem in Boston* (Boston: Houghton, Mifflin, 1906), 100; *Strike at Pullman*, 20–21.

16. I am indebted to Narciso Menocal for directing my attention to Nuevo Baztan, which is located about twenty kilometers southeast of Madrid. A. Lopez Duran, "Nuevo Baztan," *Arquitectura* 14 (1932): 169–75; see also George Kubler, *Art and Architecture in Spain and Portugal* (Hammondsworth: Penguin, 1959), 32–33; illustrations of Arc-et-Senans were published by C. N. Ledoux in his *L'Architecture considerée sous le rapport de l'art*, (Paris, 1804); Michel Parent, *Salines royales d'Arc et Senans* (Paris: Dermont, 1971), 1–10; Louis Blanc, *Histoire des Salines de Chaux et de Franche-Comté* (Bescançon: Imprimerie Moderne de l'Est, 1961), 3, 5–6.

17. Lewis Mumford, "A Modest Man's Enduring Contributions to Urban and Regional Planning," *AIA Journal* 65 (December 1976): 19.

I

COMPANY TOWNS
IN EUROPE AND
SCANDINAVIA

1

Merthyr Tydfil and Early Ironworks in South Wales

BRUCE THOMAS

By the sixteenth century iron making and shipbuilding had seriously depleted the wood supply in the two great southern English woodlands, the Weald near London and the Forest of Dean near the Welsh border. Henry VIII, concerned by his dependence on Continental and Scandinavian armaments, ordered a survey of potential British metalworking sites. Wales, with still-wooded forests and numerous rivers, was identified as a prime location for expanded iron production. The county of Glamorgan in South Wales, made up in part by steep valleys of the Brecon Beacon foothills, contained most of the potential Welsh sites.[1]

Although water and wood were the initial attractions, by the eighteenth century—after Abraham Darby successfully demonstrated that coal and coke could take the place of charcoal in the making of iron—it was clear that coal was South Wales's gold. West of the Forest of Dean, beyond the River Wye, the northern edge of the great South Wales coal basin pushed up to the surface in a vein more than a mile wide and two hundred feet deep. Soon a chain of iron furnaces and foundries running across the head of the valleys west of the River Usk traced the line of the outcropped band of coal. Their numbers grew rapidly: in 1788, eight blast furnaces were under fire in South Wales; by 1812 the number was ninety. Elsewhere in Britain, burgeoning technological and economic revolutions began to transform small medieval village centers of production into what would grow into modern industrial cities. In almost all instances urban growth resulted not from the creation of new towns or the conversion of agrarian market villages into new hives of industry but from an expansion of existing small centers of manufacturing. The phenomenon was particularly visible in the English Midlands and North, where both metalworking and the textile industry encouraged rapid urban expansion.[2]

Wales, however, was another story. New ironworks there took root in almost empty valleys. Even by eighteenth-century standards, the principality of Wales was markedly rural. The entire population was less than 400,000, about the size of Devon. Cardiff and Swansea each had fewer than 2,000 inhabitants. The largest town, Wrexham, had barely more than 4,000, one-tenth the population of Bristol. Glamorgan numbered less than 50,000 people, with most concentrated in the coastal plain in the south. In the Valleys (as highland South Wales is known) even the most populous areas contained only about ten households per 1,000 acres.[3] The flavor of Welsh highland life and the standard of living were still medieval. Narrow valleys focused inward on a decidedly local everyday life structured by traditional pastoral rituals and practices. Most land was owned by absentee landlords who clustered in the more hospitable lowlands, a petty aristocracy with little interest or skill in administering their land, part of what one historian has referred to as "a native hayseed squirearchy."[4] With the gentry showing only a minimal interest in their lands, highland farmers maintained a great deal of independence. Many farms had been worked by the same family for hundreds of years, usually renting for £3 or £4 per year on very long leases.[5]

At first iron making and coal extraction in the Valleys remained, as they had been for centuries, minute-scaled, one-man industries, little more than supplements to the rural pastoral economy. Yet by the mid-eighteenth century much of Wales was moving inexorably toward a modern economy, one based on industrial development fueled by capital investment, even if few recognized the indicating signs. If a man sank a coal pit on one corner of his farm, often his landlord did not charge him for the fuel: it simply was not worth the bother. But that—and everything else about the Valleys—would change.

Throughout an industrializing Britain a new and very different relationship—or perhaps shotgun wedding—was forged between people and place. Few industries so affected the environment as did iron making. The single forge in the clearing grew into a great ironworks filled with large, expensive furnaces and cavernous shed buildings housing a variety of fining operations such as rolling and hammering that formed usable iron shapes. Such modernized works became infernos, whose intense flames turned nighttime skies into glowing orange sunrises, seen from as far away as fifty miles. Ore, limestone, and coal, fuel for furnaces freed from the woods, were gouged from surrounding hills and meadows, leaving open wounds in the earth. Excreted waste from the manufacturing process—slag and cinders—covered any open ground, sometimes burying buildings, and often smoldering and glowing for decades. And, perhaps most significant, legions of workers were drawn to isolated narrow valleys to operate the modern works.

Across the head of the Valleys, at Nantyglo, Ebbw Vale, Rhymney, and Tredegar, protourban settlements emerged at new ironworks. The Welsh geographer Harold Carter has noted, "The nascent towns were fundamentally manufacturing or mining camps which can be compared without exaggeration with the early mining camps of the American West." Furthermore, Carter identifies even in the earliest Welsh industrial settlements a physical form common to the Valleys' towns. The shape of the land dictated a linear settlement pattern. Works stretched along the level floor of the valley, claiming as was their nature the best building land. On the hillsides, new rows of workers' cottages huddled just above the works on flattened terraces known as valley benches. At the crest of the valley, farms, many of which predated the new industry, spread over the plateaued hilltops.[6] It was an elemental physical landscape, that is, a built environment in which the very limited number of parts belied the complexity often thought to be inherent in urban form. Moreover, the Valleys' topography prohibited patterns of outward expansion often associated with urban growth, focusing the settlement's growth ever inward on itself. In such a crucible, contrast between and adjacency of the limited number of protourban elements intensified the experience of the built environment.

Nowhere was this phenomenon more evident than in Merthyr Tydfil, the largest of the Valleys' iron towns—and by the mid-nineteenth century the biggest city in Wales and one of the greatest iron-making centers in the world. Although located on the River Taff, only twenty-five miles north of the Bristol Channel and Glamorgan's relatively accessible coastal plain, Merthyr was almost completely isolated in the Brecon Beacon mountains. For centuries it existed as a pastoral village of no more than three dozen cottages and two ancient manor houses gathered about a decayed and crumbling church dedicated to its martyr. Change was slow, even by the glacial standards of a preindustrial world. The marks on the land of the few Welsh who lived there were minimal, and few outsiders dared traverse the rugged terrain. Yet, within only a few decades of the arrival of modern iron making in the late eighteenth century, visitors would flock to Merthyr to glimpse the sublime wonders of modern industry. Thomas Carlyle described Merthyr as "the squalidest, ugliest place on earth," marveling, "it is like a vision of hell, and will never leave me." A fictional curate created by Anthony Trollope fainted dead away on learning, to his horror, that he had been posted to Merthyr.[7] G. W. Manby found Merthyr's residents to be "sooty legions so disfigured by smoke, [that they] pictured more the looks of infernals than human beings," ascribing their fantastic appearance to "the ill effects of their dreadful vocations."[8] One of the most disturbing aspects of Merthyr was that it seemed so different from any other towns with which a visitor might be familiar. The *Cambrian Tourist* complained, "When you are upon [Merthyr], you are obliged to inquire where it is, and the way to it . . . the town itself is nowhere visible; it is without form or order."[9] But Merthyr was not without order; it was merely a form very different from that of towns not born of a heavy industry such as modern iron making.

Merthyr's transformation began with the leasing of large tracts of land by men who had no intention of either subleasing to tenants or farming themselves. Immediately, the new resident entrepreneurs changed the pattern of landholding from what was effectively, if not legally, large numbers of small owners to a very few large owners, a pattern of consolidation characteristic of the new industrialism. With control in the hands of men fired with the entrepreneurial zeal of the early Industrial Revolution rather than those of small tenant farmers, submerged in generations-old patterns, major change was almost assured.

The new Merthyr was fashioned out of four ironworks and their associated communities. In 1759 the Reverend Thomas Lewis of Llanishen, owner of several small iron forges in South Wales, obtained from the dowager Lady Windsor the reassignment of Thomas Morgan's 1747 "three-life time" lease for two thousand acres with mineral rights of the Dowlais hilltop east of Merthyr village for £31 per year. Morgan had used the land as a hunting ground, but Lewis had other plans. His subsequent building of the first larger furnace there is considered the beginning of the modern iron industry in South Wales. In 1763, John Guest of Brosely, Shropshire, and Isaac Wilkinson, one of Lewis's partners, signed a lease with the earl of Plymouth for his land along the river south of Merthyr. Two years later Anthony Bacon and William Brownrigg, having heard of Lewis's venture, leased from Messrs. Talbot and Richards of Cardiff a five-mile by eight-mile tract of land known as Cyfarthfa on the west bank of the Taff opposite Merthyr village. The three leases, together with the 1780s lease at Penydarren along the Morlais Brook between the old village and Dowlais, outlined an industrial triangle that filled the flattened bowl at the head of the Taff Valley, surrounding and eventually consuming preindustrial Merthyr Tydfil. Throughout Merthyr's heyday, each of the four leases remained autonomous. Each developed its own community that, although often similar in physical pattern to the others, was readily identified as Dowlais, Plymouth, Cyfarthfa, or Penydarren.

The first works were relatively small and of limited production. A 1763 plan of Lewis's so-called Merthir Furnace shows a grouping of buildings less than 150 feet across (Fig. 1.1). The largest building, labeled "cast house," measuring about thirty-five by eighty-five feet, was bigger than the typical cottage but no greater than Merthyr's two manor houses. The scale began to change significantly, however, near the turn of the century with the construction of a second Cyfarthfa works. A demand for ordnance for the American wars allowed Bacon to build a new, much larger works to produce cannon.

Cyfarthfa was soon one of the wonders of the early Industrial Revolution. A great iron overshot waterwheel, "Eolus" as it was called, measuring fifty feet in diameter and six feet across and weighing approximately one hundred tons (British), was reputed to be the largest of its kind in the world. With twenty-five-foot diameter secondary wheels on either side, it operated bellows at four bloomeries and four fineries. The wheel turned by water fed from hills across the river by a double aqueduct mounted on stone piers sixty to seventy feet high. Manby rhapsodized that the aqueduct, a combination of stone, wood, and iron, maintained an "apparent lightness of the whole" that "contrasted with the massy [sic] boundary of the river, has not only a singular, but [also] a very interesting and pleasing appearance."[10] Merthyr's ironworks were beginning to be noticed as new and noteworthy. More significantly, the works were beginning to generate new industrial webs connecting mills and furnaces with raw materials. Trams laced back and forth over—and even through—the hills, as webs of iron began to supersede older, more fragile stands of a pastoral network of footpaths and animal tracks.

One vexing impediment stood in the way of this headlong expansion: the pack animal and mountain road system of transport, the primitiveness of which had, for centuries, isolated the Valleys. H. P. Wynndham, a 1775 traveler in Glamorgan, tactfully explained, "The mountainous roads are, in parts, as good as the nature of

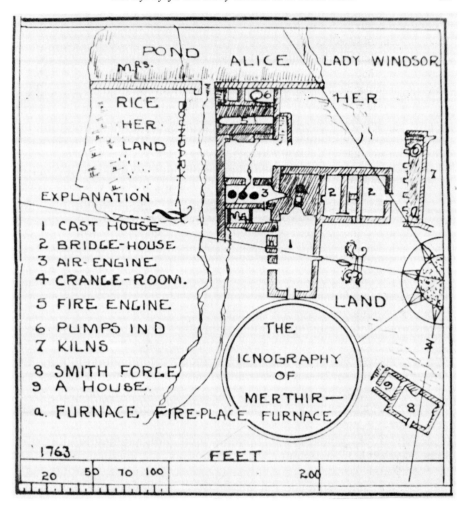

Figure 1.1 Plan of the "Merthir Furnace," 1763 (first modern furnace at Merthyr Tydfil, Wales). (John Lloyd, *The Early History of the Old South Wales Ironworks, 1760–1840* [London: Bedford Press, 1906].)

the country will admit."[11] Not only was transport slow and limited to small loads, but at an average cost of one shilling per ton per mile, it was also prohibitively expensive for the ironworks' large volumes and heavy loads.[12]

Throughout the latter half of the eighteenth century, Britain, and in particular the English Midlands, was awash in a mania of canal building. In 1790 the Merthyr iron masters, many of whom had become familiar with Midlands canal projects through their furnaces there, solved the transport problem in a single stroke by agreeing to build a canal from Merthyr down through the Taff Valley to Cardiff. The initial idea is said to have come from Penydarren's Samuel Homfrey, who was a friend of the resident engineer of the Staffordshire and Worcestershire Canal. A building act was passed authorizing six hundred shares of £100 each for capital. The six hundred shares went to seventy-seven initial subscribers, the largest of whom were the Crawshays, Bacon's successors at Cyfarthfa. The rest were divided among the other ironmasters, a few bankers, the marquess of Bute at Cardiff, landowners along the canal's proposed route, and the owners of a small ironworks near Cardiff.

Construction costs ran almost double the initial amount raised, but in 1794 the Glamorganshire Canal was completed at a cost of £103,660. Located on the west side of the River Taff, the canal dropped more than five hundred feet over a length of twenty-five miles, through fifty-one separate lock locations. If hauled continuously, a twenty-four-ton capacity barge might make the trip from Merthyr to Cardiff in twenty hours. The canal was an immediate and phenomenal success. In 1785 the combined iron production of Glamorgan and Monmouthshire had been sixty tons per week. With the canal in operation, in 1803 Penydarren alone—not even Merthyr's largest works—produced fifty tons per week.[13] More than any single building project, the Glamorganshire Canal opened Merthyr to large-scale industrial and urban development. Moreover, it was also the first project to alter the South Wales landscape in an extensive and systematic manner. Before modern industry came to the Valleys, life was, as it had been for centuries, insular and hard. Small communities, isolated by the shape of the land, worked and lived to the rhythm of the seasons and the sun. After the canal was put into operation, Merthyr's inhabitants still lived a hard life, but they were no longer quite so alone. A great artery now connected them to the prosperous and less isolated coast—and to the world beyond. To handle the swelling traffic of goods in and out of Merthyr, the canal operated around the clock with double shifts of lockkeepers. A line of torches in the night illuminated locks and towpaths, splitting a once-dark valley and connecting Merthyr to the outside world.

With the transport bottleneck broken, Merthyr began to assume its modern form. At each of the four leases, an independent community based on employment at the ironworks, a condition that might optimistically be described as familial, emerged. Entire families worked in the various undertakings of the larger family, that is, the iron company. The company provided not only work but also access to shelter and fuel, and occasionally medical care, sick funds, and even education. In this way each new industrial community evinced a social structure analogous to traditional rural manorial and estate patterns with which most of the workers were recently familiar.[14]

Dowlais, Plymouth, Cyfarthfa, and Penydarren had physical as well as social characteristics in common. Each was composed of the same basic elements: works, a workers' housing district, and the imposing residence of the ironmaster (Fig. 1.2).[15] Works, along the water's edge, dominated (Figs. 1.3, 1.4). Blast furnaces, in which intense fires separated metal from ore, were the largest structures. Mechanical power for bellows to produce blasts of air required to reach smelting temperature restricted the siting of seventeenth- and eighteenth-century furnaces to riversides. Eventually, however, incorporation of steam power in the nineteenth century allowed for slightly greater flexibility in the location of furnaces. Made of a combination of brick and stone, the blast furnace's four faces sloped slightly inward as they

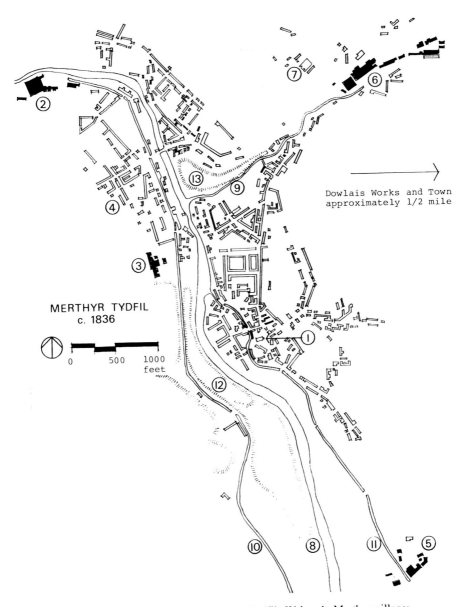

Figure 1.2 Plan of the ironworks of Merthyr Tydfil, Wales: 1. Merthyr village; 2. Cyfarthfa Works; 3. Ynysfach Works (Cyfarthfa); 4. Georgetown (Cyfarthfa housing); 5. Plymouth Works; 6. Penydarren Works; 7. Penydarren House; 8. River Taff; 9. Morlais Brook; 10. Glamorganshire Canal. (Drawn by Bruce Thomas, 1991.)

Figure 1.3 View of the Cyfarthfa Works, ca. 1810. (Woodcut from J. G. Wood, *Wood's Rivers of Wales*, 1813.)

rose to form a truncated pyramid, each structure almost a cube forty to fifty feet square on a side. The oven and flue in the middle of the pyramid might be ten to fifteen feet in diameter, with massive walls around to hold the heat, resembling, as a London *Morning Chronicle* reporter commented, "a huge soda-water bottle, encased up to the shoulders in a cube of compact masonry."

When possible—at Cyfarthfa and Penydarren, for example—banks of blast furnaces were built against sloping hillsides to facilitate charging from above and tapping below. About ten feet below the tops, a masonry platform, the "tunnel-head" as it was called, connected the bank of furnaces. Trams carried ore, coal, limestone, and cinders to the platform, where groups of men and women broke the material into smaller pieces and wheeled loads to four charging doors cut into the neck of each furnace. They fed the fire continuously, keeping the furnace full to a depth of forty feet, level with the height of the charging platform. Skilled workmen carefully managed the mix, weighing or measuring each load dumped into the furnace: ore yielded the iron itself, coal fueled the fire and supported the mass of the mix, and limestone and cinder acted as flux to separate metal from ore. All the ingredients combined in a vitrified mass through which heavier iron descended to collect at the bottom of the furnace.[16]

Long flights of stone stairs connected the charging platform with the foot of the bank. At the base of each furnace three pipes, each approximately three feet in diameter, funneled blasts from the bellows into the fire at a height of four feet above the ground. Two large openings spewed flames as slag drained continuously in channels of white-hot lava. The furnace was tapped by inserting an iron bar through an opening in the dam plate at the hearth door. A few blows from a sledge hammer

Figure 1.4 View of the Penydarren Works, Merthyr Tydfil, Wales. (Woodcut from J. G. Wood, *Wood's Rivers of Wales*, 1813.)

forced the bar through a crust of vitrified sand, opening a hole for a stream of liquid iron, a "runner" as it was known. The white and yellow runner, encased in a violet aurora, flowed into long, narrow sand molds. The molds were said to resemble a sow and her litter, and the name *pig iron* was applied to the blast furnace's product.

In some instances, runners flowed directly into refineries that removed more impurities from the metal. Often grouped in numbers in a single long gabled shed, refineries were square open pan furnaces set inside masonry corner buttresses supporting thirty-foot-high chimneys. After the iron was reheated in the refinery by coal fire and air blasts for a few hours, liquid metal was again run off. The heavier iron filled the bottom of the molds, leaving a top crust of cinder and impurities. Water thrown on the hot metal further removed superfluous carbon and oxygen in great luminous clouds of steam. Once the refinery's pigs cooled, laborers broke away the slag and cinders and carted away and loaded the waste onto trams. Wielding huge two-handed sledge hammers, pairs of men then broke the remaining cast iron into smaller pieces in preparation for converting it to wrought iron.

In most cases wrought iron was made in puddling furnaces grouped in vast ranges of sheds "indifferently called," as the *Morning Chronicle*'s man observed, "mills or forges, and consisting simply of roofs perforated by a great number of chimneys . . . supported on all sides by pillars of masonry." A typical puddling furnace was an oven made of brick, about four feet wide by eight feet long, supporting an overhead chimney. Coal or coke fires heated the furnace trough as air blasts were blown over the melting pig iron. Using a long rod, the furnace operator, or "puddler," stirred the molten iron to promote a decarburizing action and remove impurities introduced by the coal. The puddling process required hours of stirring for each mass of wrought iron; like blast furnaces, puddling furnaces seldom cooled, being manned by three shifts around the clock. When the puddled iron reached a proper consistency, it was divided into "puddler's balls" ready for final working.

In gabled sheds, alongside puddling furnaces, hammers and rollers pounded iron balls into usable shapes. Laborers, known as "shinglers," grasped the hundred-pound balls of iron in huge pincers, lifting them onto anvils where water- or steam-powered hammers weighing as much as six thousand pounds beat the iron into compressed form (Figs. 1.5 and 1.6). The *Morning Chronicle* reporter found it particularly intriguing "to see how the true metal alone can endure this enormous pressure [as] at each successive compression the dross gushes out from its pores in small streams of a bright yellow, like . . . buttermilk perspiring through butter under the hands of the dairymaid." In some locations the noise was so great that the hammer was replaced by a less efficient but quieter "squeezer," an enormous iron lever hinged to an anvil, in which the iron ball was gradually compressed by the action of the lever. Next, the rough bars that emerged from hammers or squeezers were passed many times through rollers, drawing them into rails or rods. Great circular saws then cut the iron, "with a noise not to be described," into required lengths. After rough edges were filed away, the product was ready for transport.[17]

Figure 1.5 Interior view of a Cyfarthfa cast house, with castings in foreground, furnaces at left. The large spans are carried by cast and wrought-iron columns and trusses as well as heavy timber columns and beams. (Painting by Penry Williams, 1825. Cyfarthfa Castle Museum, Merthyr Tydfil, Wales.)

With its deafening blasts, snapping, crackling, and hissing escaping gases, vivid furnace flames, glowing ribbons of molten metal, and thunderous hammering, iron making was the most striking and sublime of industries (Fig. 1.7). It also shaped some of the most dense and frightening built environments an industrializing world had yet seen.

As Merthyr's iron companies prospered, works sites became hives of industry. The blast furnace's size was optimal: increases in production necessitated more structures rather than larger ones. Puddling furnaces were inexpensive to build and their number increased rapidly at every works. Moreover, technological improvements in rolling and hammering filled the shed buildings with more and larger equipment. The incorporation of steam power in the early nineteenth century filled works with multistoried engine houses in which the great globes of governors echoed circular openings typically cut into gabled building ends at Merthyr.

Even though Dowlais and Cyfarthfa opened new separate works complexes, more and more activity was pressed into a limited area. Piles of raw materials and finished product lay everywhere. Tram lines laced through and under everything. Recent excavation at Dowlais has revealed layer built atop layer, an industrial equivalent of the tells of ancient Jericho.[18]

One of the most striking aspects of the new industrial landscape was the prox-

Figure 1.6 Cyfarthfa Ironworks, "shingling," a process of extracting slag from iron prior to rolling. (Watercolor by Julius Caesar Ibbetson, 1795. Cyfarthfa Castle Museum, Merthyr Tydfil, Wales.)

Figure 1.7 Dowlais Ironworks, Dowlais, Wales. (Watercolor by George Childs, 1840. Welsh Industrial and Maritime Museum.)

imity of works to houses. Two visiting Londoners noted in amazement that "the adjoining habitantings [sic] of the different persons connected with [the works] appeared as if their entire fronts were illuminated from the intense reflection of the fires."[19] Benjamin Heath Malkin, a visitor in 1803, observed with alarm that the house in which he stayed was "surrounded with fire, flame, smoke, and ashes."[20] The iron masters themselves enjoyed the location of their homes, "as it should [be]," it was romantically claimed, "[where] the glaring light of the furnaces, and the thud of hammers were, to a master who had brought them into existence, a welcome sight and sound."[21]

In effect, with a predominantly Welsh work force living there, housing districts at the Merthyr leases were industrialized, protourban forms of familiar Valleys' villages, albeit ones suddenly adjacent to flaming, banging works. The first industrial workers' houses at Merthyr were not dissimilar to the scattered houses of the preindustrial village. In size, layout, and materials they were often indistinguishable from preindustrial dwellings. As they had for centuries, rubble-stone walls predominated. Even a few thatched roofs—surely somewhat of a risk with flames and cinder and hot ash all about—remained. Just as the new blast furnaces that rose in the works were not significantly different from their rural predecessors, so the scale and form of a new worker's house were not so different from a traditional Valleys' cottage. Only when houses began to be grouped in large numbers, when the scale of development drastically increased as it had at the works, would the landscape of houses differ significantly from its pastoral predecessor.

That time soon came. Expanding works devoured favored locations in the glare of the furnaces, and stables and spare rooms in farmers' cottages could no longer accommodate the growing number of workers and their families. Masters and men alike needed new homes. But few speculators were eager to build houses. All the ironmasters' capital—or as much as they cared to commit—was in the works. Moreover, the mineral and commercial potential of land in and around an emerging industrial center was evident. No one wanted to forego possible riches for the fixed return of housing. Consequently, houses were haphazardly thrown up, "built in scattered confusion without any order or plan," as Malkin observed.[22] Yet, modest and randomly situated as they were, the workers' cottages were themselves a new form of housing.[23] Merthyr's growing population could not live for long in pastoral cottages and soon occupied housing set in an evolving urban context.

As each lease's community grew, its landscape of houses transformed itself from scattered cottages to urban rows. From the middle of the eighteenth century to 1800 Merthyr's population increased from a few hundred to more than seven thousand, and then from 1800 to 1851 to almost fifty thousand. At first, new workers and their families repeated an old pattern and lodged in farmhouses or wherever they could, but in an increasingly urbanized setting rather than in a pastoral world. To house the influx of workers, additions specifically built to accommodate new arrivals sprouted on the ends of farmhouses. Soon one-room cottages gave way to two-story terraced houses. By the middle of the nineteenth century, one observer noted, "The first impression of a stranger who visits Merthyr is, that it is a town of workmen's houses."[24]

In most instances the new houses themselves were not bad. Almost all were built of stone, most with walls of local rubble (Fig. 1.8). All houses, whether lived in by English immigrant ironworkers or native Welsh or financed by English capital (as some were), were put up by local builders. Construction techniques and materials, except for roofing slates from North Wales brought up the canal, were those of the Valleys. Wood was far too scarce and valuable as fuel or for mine bracing to be used for houses. Not until a tax on bricks was repealed in 1850 did brick begin to replace rubble stone for building.[25] Walls were invariably whitewashed, a traditional local practice. T. E. Clarke observed, "The custom of whitewashing cottages, villages, and farms, and extending even to stables, barns, and walls of yards and gardens has prevailed here from very remote ages." (He grumpily complained that "the glare of the whitewash on the walls and cottages too often offends the eye.")[26] In some cases walls were coated with cement to keep out the wind and rain, a precaution that also caused windows to be sealed with paint.[27]

Some of the new two-story cottages were as little as eight feet by ten feet in plan. But in most cases a larger two-up, two-down room layout was favored. The ground floor contained a door and window, or two windows flanking the door, with one or two windows above on the second story. One ground floor room usually served as the principal room where cooking, eating, and gathering took place. In accordance with the relative prosperity of the iron industry, some workers' houses were filled with furniture.

Because iron making was a dirty job, many laborers bathed daily, a remarkable

Figure 1.8 A row of houses on Pond Street, Dowlais, ca. 1840, Wales. (Photograph, 1977, National Museum of Wales, Cardiff.)

frequency in the nineteenth century. In most cases their wives kept even the meanest cottages clean and tidy. Windowsills and thresholds were regularly whitewashed in the daily battle against soot and ash. Although the industry drew many single men to Merthyr, and public houses and gin palaces were numerous and well attended, for many workers home life centered on an evening meal and the hearth. Visitors remarked on the Merthyr workmen's practice of gathering in each other's homes to drink beer. Perhaps surprisingly, books were a common addition to many homes. The *Morning Chronicle* reporter noted, "I must again mention the booksellers, because I consider them in proportion more numerous than the other trades . . . a circumstance significant of the tendency to home and fireside amusements, which deserve notice and encouragement in a place where, by far, the bulk of the population is made up of the working classes."[28]

When a house was lived in by only one family, it was common for the parents to take the other ground floor room as their bedroom and the children to occupy the upper floor. Expansion usually took the form of adding a third room, often a kitchen, at the back of the lower floor.[29] Very few back-to-back houses were built, unlike in industrial towns elsewhere in Britain.

This rather comfortable picture of domesticity was, however, not often the rule. By midcentury one investigator found one-up, one-down houses with three beds to a room, occupied by five or six people per room. At Penydarren, a newspaper reporter found a not atypical one-up, one-down "inhabited by two families and a lodger. . . . In the upper room were three straw beds on the floor. The men and their wives severally occupied two of them and the children the third."[30]

Invariably the new terraces' inhabitants, most of whom had only recently left work on the farm for the promise of industry, lived in the rows as they had in the countryside. Even at the Triangle at Plymouth, a progressive model development with rows enclosing a three-sided court, Lowe notes: "[Houses] had been built in a way that matched the habits of a population only a step removed from rural life. Each house had a garden where refuse might be burned or buried; at least three had privies there. No doubt the other inhabitants used the hillside behind their homes just as their rural antecedents had used the field hedgerows."[31]

Near the middle of the nineteenth century, when cholera, typhoid, and enormously high child mortality rates made clear some of the shortcomings of city life, many of the problems were rightly attributed to living habits and patterns that, although acceptable in the countryside, proved disastrous when practiced in the city.

Merthyr's industry and environment might fairly be described as mixed blessings. The ironworks not only provided ostensibly regular employment but also offered relatively high wages. Moreover, Merthyr was not without the urban vitality that proved to be so seductive to an isolated and impoverished rural population. On Saturday evenings well-dressed citizens might be seen promenading along Merthyr's sooty High Street past shops admittedly few in number but filled to overflowing with goods. Yet the nature of the work and conditions in communities grown around the ironworks often offset apparent advantages.

A laborer's evening meals frequently included meat and beer. But, as even the most rigid moralists agreed, physically demanding work such as iron making necessitated the expense of good-quality food and quantites of drink. Workers exposed daily to harsh highland weather as well as to fire, smoke, and gases in the works also required the heaviest clothes for protection, and even those fabrics soon wore through and had to be replaced. A Penydarren "coke-girl" worked eleven hours per day stacking coal, earning 5s. per week. Remarking on the high cost of clothes required for her outside work, she admitted, "without the assistance of my father and mother I could not live."[32] (Because of the strength required for most jobs, few women were employed in the works, but some found places.) Walking or standing on ground strewn with hot cinder and ash burned the soles off shoes. One old woman working at ore calcinating kilns above a blast furnace bank had to replace her shoes every five weeks. In 1850, when Merthyr wages averaged 15s. per week, shoes cost 8s. per pair. Other laborers wore thick wooden soles in an attempt to make their shoes last.

In comparison to the countryside, and even to other cities, house rent was high, particularly, as the *Morning Chronicle* noted, "considering the scanty accommodations afforded."[33] The poor paid most dearly for housing; to protect themselves against unpaid rents, landlords commonly charged higher rates to those who seemed most likely to be short occasionally. A sick young man and his wife lived near Cyfarthfa in a 6 × 9-foot, unplastered, unceilinged shack for which they paid 2s.6d. per week.[34]

Like most heavy industries, iron making fluctuated notoriously. In good times a

Merthyr puddler might earn as much as 50s. each week and a roller 75s. But as the industry began to decline, wages plummeted. Consider the plight of a Penydarren secondhand puddler earning 15s. per week in 1850. After paying 8s. monthly for rent, 6s.6d. for coal, 4d. to the sick fund, and 4d. for repair of his furnace, he was left with less than 11s. per week to feed and clothe a family of six. (In Merthyr, bacon cost 6–10d. per pound, cheese 3–7d. per pound, potatoes 6d. for 8 pounds, butter 10d. per pound, sugar 6d. per pound, coffee 1s.6d. per pound, and tea 4s.6d. per pound.)[35]

As terraces multiplied at each lease, housing districts began to assume a physical and visual presence to contrast the larger-scaled, more spectacular works. This was most evident at Cyfarthfa where the huge amount of space made possible distinct and separate works and housing areas, and at Dowlais where the Abergavenny Road split the lease in two. At Dowlais a "Dowlais Town" and "Dowlais Works" faced each other across the High Street. Below, the works, glowing and smoking, stretched parallel to the road; above, dark rows of stone houses climbed the slope up to the face of Norlais Hill.

The monotony of the house rows was rarely broken. Stores were usually just the lower floor of a house in the row opened to the street. Chapels echoed house forms and, although larger than the typical cottage, fit neatly into street rows. Chapels were a particularly significant building type in Wales. One historian has even speculated that, in the harsh light of industrializing Wales, chapels might shine as the national architecture.[36] The chapel's only rival as a center of cultural and social life for the Welsh-speaking population was the public house. In fact, many Dissenting congregations began in saloons. Pubs were also similar in form to houses—or simply were houses—and in almost all cases fit unobtrusively into the rows.

Over time, public houses and chapels were differentiated architecturally. Unlike chapels, pubs found it unnecessary to proselytize, and embellished building fronts were not needed to advertise their powers of salvation. Conversely, when competition between chapel sects intensified, the chapel buildings themselves were enlisted for battle. From about 1830 the side-wall entry fell from favor, and the gable end became the entry wall, often turned to face the street. Moreover, the new larger chapels also displayed a greater tendency to embellish, with facade arrangements, materials, and detail derived from neither liturgical sources nor vernacular tradition but from an outside world of architectural fashion.

Neither works nor laborers' houses exhibited architectural pretensions, either in individual buildings or in the grouping of structures. That was not the case, however, with the third element common to each of Merthyr's iron communities. The big house of the ironmaster was intended literally and figuratively to elevate its owner above his workers. As early as 1790 Merthyr's ironmasters began to build their escapes, fantasies designed to transport their inhabitants to a world of the rural landed English aristocracy that would prove so irresistible to generations of industrialists.[37]

When Francis Homfray and his sons acquired the lease at Penydarren in 1786, one of their first projects was to construct a stately house and grounds on the slope above the works. The motives for building Penydarren Place (as it was called) were probably complex. As latecomers—the Penydarren Works started up twenty years after Dowlais, Plymouth, and Cyfarthfa—and with experience at Cyfarthfa behind them, the Homfrays apparently found little charm in the glow of the furnace and the thud of the trip-hammer that so comforted the founders of the industry. Moreover, building Penydarren Place not only removed the Homfrays from the harsh environment of the works but also elevated them in prestige to a level nearer that of the master at Cyfarthfa. The Homfrays' house itself was straightforward enough, although its size alone was quite a departure from any local residence except the grandest old manor, the Court House. Penydarren Place was a two-story, five-bay block with flanking setback wings. An Ionic porch and plain parapet with simple cornice provided touches of high-style ornament.[38] But the most striking and escapist feature was the grounds. J. G. Woods's often-quoted contemporary description tells of a house and grounds "sufficiently removed from the town by the extent of the pleasure grounds, and containing all the conveniences and luxuries requisite for a family of wealth and importance."[39] Malkin commented, "With fine and well-planted gardens, green-houses, hothouse, and all the accommodations befitting the residence of a wealthy family . . . the splendours of Merthyr Tydvil [*sic*] begin and end with this mansion."[40]

In 1817, John Guest built Dowlais House, a large stone box in the Georgian architectural fashion of the day, set in heavily landscaped grounds at the top of the High Street. The house was shielded by planting, and the works were some distance away, but Lady Charlotte Guest, for whom the house was built, described her new home as "quite unlike all I had ever before seen or even imagined." Her mother was less tactful, calling Dowlais House "the Cinder-hole."[41]

In 1824, William Crawshay II, to his father's disgust, outdid everyone. He built a medieval fantasy, a mock-Gothic castle designed by Robert Lugar, an architect known for his picturesque houses and romantic sham castles. Cyfarthfa Castle's seventy-two rooms, with 365 windows (the number was regarded as particularly inauspicious by locals) cost £30,000, prompting William I to write angrily to his son: "Ambition has directed you to build a great and expensive house, but I advise you to do no such thing. Is it wise at any time to build on so large a scale? No man can say what it will cost to finish, to furnish, to maintain."[42] William I's concerns were financial, but they might just as readily have been social. When the modern iron industry began to alter Merthyr's landscape, everyone shared a common environment. Expanding works and ever more crowded rows of workers' cottages were necessary if entrepreneurs or common laborers were to realize the industrial world's new possibilities.

The big houses broke that pattern. They not only introduced architectural pretense to a pragmatically constructed environment but also began to splinter what might be considered, in outward appearance at least, an egalitarian social pattern. The heat of furnaces and the thud of hammers singed and deafened ironmasters and workers alike. But the big houses—significantly, built not by founders but by succeeding generations—were more symbolic than practical. They emphasized the differences between masters and men and stood as tangible examples of "how to live." The big house suggested a hierarchical order: here was another type of "mill," one in which masters and men could be hammered into their proper social forms.

Manor houses and castles in medieval society held social and symbolic significance born not only of their size and form but also of the place of their owners in the order of things. The big houses formed part of a new industrial landscape composed not only of utilitarian buildings but also of social and cultural symbols. It is not surprising, then, that when labor unrest flared into open conflict in the Rising of 1831, troops called in to crush the insurrection garrisoned at Penydarren Place. Nor is it unexpected that the crowd assembled and grew angry among rows of cottages and then marched to Cyfarthfa to shout their demands to an ironmaster looking down on them from the balcony of his fantasy castle.

In addition to works, housing terraces, and masters' mansions, the very by-products of the iron industry reshaped the landscape. With increased production, piles of raw materials began to surround the works. Finished products filled not only storage yards but roads. Malkin noted, "Bars and pigs of iron are continually thrown to the hugely accumulating heaps that threaten to choke every avenue of access."[43] Heaps of bars and pigs, or piles of coal, at least were signs of productivity. In contrast, the ever-growing mounds of waste, tips of slag, or ash or cinders, were more ominous evidence of a landscape exploited, signs of a discarded environment whose resources were exhausted.

Tips were the new mountains of Merthyr; indeed, some called the town "a Paradise of Cinders." Year by year they filled every available space and grew higher. Sixty-foot tips were common.[44] To the east the great "White Tip" at Dowlais towered above Merthyr. To the north and west slag heaps dwarfed houses at Cyfarthfa. The *Merthyr Guardian* complained that the Penydarren cinder tips, estimated to be three hundred feet high, "are situated almost in the centre of town . . . and [are] certainly a very great disfigurement to the town—like some tall cliff that lifts its awful form."[45] Disturbingly, the new mountains were not merely inert piles of refuse but, like the works, alive. Pillars of smoke rose above the tips of cinder, and ash glowed red through the night, often for decades as fresh ash was continuously dumped. Describing such a sight, T. E. Clarke wrote: "Railway embankments, compared with these tips or heaps, are mere pigmies; the great heat of the cinders causes them to smoulder for many years. In the evening they may be seen studded with beautiful flames of various hues, caused by the burning of the sulphur which is emitted from the minerals."[46] Tips quite literally reshaped Merthyr's topography. Farmhouses were buried and then decades later "discovered" as cooled tips were excavated to put up new house rows. Merthyr's inhabitants, completely dependent on the fortunes of the industry, could do little but stand by and be slowly squeezed and buried.

A small dispute over the Reverend Mr. Maber's glebe field illustrated the situation. Penydarren, whose works were just up the road, received permission from the rector to tip on his glebe field and covered it with heaps of cinders. But Plymouth claimed to hold a prior agreement leasing the field to them. They consequently regarded the freshly dumped cinders as their property and began to haul them away to use at their furnaces. In Penydarren's view this was no less than outright theft. To put a stop to Plymouth's thievery, Penydarren proceeded to cover the cinder tips with a form of refuse that Plymouth found less desirable. While the two ironworks fought their petty battle, as John Lloyd wrote, "What has become of the Rector's glebe land, and whither it is recognisable . . . is another matter."[47]

Tips changed the conformation not only of the land but also of the water. Persistent dumping on the banks of the Taff and Morlais washed waste to the bottom of both, causing the riverbed to rise as much as twenty feet above its natural level and to overflow. Even more disturbing, the water table of the entire valley floor rose, resulting in such disquieting effects as water gushing from graves, overturning headstones and pouring the contents into the roadways.[48]

Once cooled and stabilized, however, tips were not without their value. Newly recovered land ("Newfoundland" as it was called) for houses was but one use. During the Rising of 1831 the insurrectionists took up a position atop the Penydarren tip, whose height gave commanding access to the entire rear of the Castle Inn, where the troops held forth.[49] Others merely considered the tips favorable vantages from which to view the town. Clarke observed that "those [tips] at the junction of the Taff and Morlais, command a fine view of the town and the vale."[50] The *Guardian* noted, "It was from the summit of these tips that strangers generally took a view of our iron works, and they were well adapted for the purpose." It was even suggested that a fifty-foot-high tower be built atop the Penydarren tip "as regards curiosity," and that for convenience a tunnel be cut through it.[51]

Transient single men in particular were drawn to Merthyr's ironworks; by mid-century it was estimated that approximately ten thousand "strangers" (to use the contemporary term) annually made their way to the works.[52] Many found themselves in an area called "China." Originally known as Pont-y-Storehouse, China was a low-lying area on the river north of the village, opposite Cyfarthfa. The area had begun as a nondescript group of houses for the first Cyfarthfa works. But gradually Pont-y-Storehouse was separated from both village and works as Penydarren's and Cyfarthfa's tips rose around it, and the focus of Cyfarthfa shifted to the south with the building of the second works. China's name indicated not only its increasingly remote location but also its distance from propriety, social convention, and legality. Notorious for its thieves and prostitutes, China, which was also known as the "Celestial Empire," had its own unofficial royal family, a king and queen of crime and vice who reigned with a certain degree of sovereignty. The *Merthyr Guardian's* regular column headed "CHINA AGAIN" recounted harrowing stories of men who descended into the depths of the Empire in search of adventure and were often drugged and robbed.

China suffered not only from physical isolation and lawlessness but from the fact that it did not "belong" to any of the ironworks' communities. Carter and Wheatley cite figures illustrating China's predicament: the percentage of unskilled laborers was almost three times the mean for Merthyr; the percentage of Irish, always the lowest on the social and economic scale, was almost four times the average elsewhere; the percentage of Merthyr-born was less than average; and the percentage of households with lodgers was higher. Household density was as great as in any other location in the valley. But perhaps most significantly, one-third fewer of China's residents were employed in iron manufacturing than was the Merthyr average.[53] With few jobs other than those provided by the iron industry available, the Celestial Empire's citizens were left with illegal activities as principal sources of income. China's situation illustrates the importance of "belonging" in Merthyr's elemental industrial environment. As Ieuan Gwynnedd Jones points out, the four

Merthyr works communities were "based not merely on individual, contractual relationships but operated also at the profounder social level of the family . . . whole families were employed in the works or in associated undertakings and were therefore subjected as families to the same social disciplines."[54] That structure was nonexistent in China.

In contrast, the built environment at each works community emphasized familial organization. As each works became more established and its accompanying community grew, the contrasting pattern of works and "town" became apparent. There was, at this stage, an inherent order in the urban—or perhaps protourban—development at each lease. Admittedly, it was a harsh, paternalistic order lacking in familiar urban elements found in towns and cities not formed by heavy industry. But within that order a China was unlikely. Only when the separate protourban nuclei expanded farther, when their tips piled over into the village or the next lease, when the tight paternal structure began to be diluted by community size, when "suburban" fringes of building began to form interstitial areas caught between already established communities, could a place like China emerge.

It is no surprise that the expansion of industry in a limited area might produce a worsening physical environment, for it has happened often enough elsewhere. But the notion that the growth of separate nodes of development into a more cohesive urban community could also produce a worsening urban landscape is not expected. Paradoxically, as Merthyr became more "civilized"—in the literal meaning of the term—as it grew from a collection of frontier manufacturing settlements into something more like a "real" town, both social and physical conditions worsened. Municipal reforms stemming from urban insurrections throughout Britain in the early 1830s helped Merthyr to emerge from its early industrial form into a more independent, more varied modern city. Even lacking a municipal council to initiate programs—the ironmasters successfully fought off incorporation until midcentury—Merthyr's landscape began to be modified by the addition of new institutions housed in identifiable new buildings. The once visually distinct and elemental three-part landscape of works, laborers' cottages, and masters' mansions became alloyed.

Only four years after the Rising of 1831, when open class warfare bloodied Merthyr's streets, a new market hall was proclaimed the product of "high and honourable feelings, the best qualities of hand and heart, in men of all parties." The *Guardian* cheered, "We shall rejoice to see the day when such qualities are united for the laudable purpose of making Merthyr what it ought to be—as distinguished for the architectural beauty of its town, as it is for the intelligence, the wealth, and the respectability of its inhabitants."[55]

The new market hall, a Dowlais Mechanic's Institute (paid for by workers' subscriptions), and a new shop district in old Merthyr village were just a beginning. A Dowlais market hall followed six years later, then a Dowlais reading room and library. Two years later a temperance hotel in the mistreated village glebe land was converted into a library, where, the *Guardian* reported, "It was truly delightful to see professional gentlemen, tradesmen, and working people mingling together freely and pleasantly."[56]

Each day, or so it appeared, the cry for more new institutions increased. The

Guardian observed that the Post Office "wants enlarging, in order to keep pace with the demands of a place so large." In the same issue it was noted, "Few places afford so many facilities for the cheap construction and support of baths and wash houses, as the vicinity of our iron works."[57] Another proposal suggested "that a more efficient method of cleansing the streets from the accumulation of unwholesome dirt, be brought into operation." Even the luxury of street lighting was considered for "the important and rapidly advancing town of Merthyr." An opponent grumbled, "The furnaces of Cyfarthfa and Penydarran afford light enough."[58]

By the late 1840s the change in Merthyr's landscape was noticeable. Merthyr was a more varied and physically sophisticated town than it had been only a few decades earlier. The compartmentalized built environment of the iron communities was now diluted and punctuated by new buildings and by the commercial emergence of the revitalized old village. And yet, even as physical and social advances were effected and as the desire for reform continued to blossom, Merthyr collapsed. The railroad boom, the iron industry's salvation in the late 1830s, turned to bust. Suddenly the local ironstone was all but played out and the cost of importing large quantities seemed prohibitive. New port facilities at Cardiff and Newport made exporting coal more profitable than using it to fuel Valleys furnaces. Cholera returned in 1849, striking one in every twelve, with the rate much higher in the most crowded housing districts. For the life of its modern existence Merthyr had bent its landscape to the requirements of its only industry, depending on the efforts of its ironmasters, private speculators, and the sensibilities of individual citizens for the ordering of its environment. The insufficiency of those efforts was driven home with the nails in each new coffin in the workers' cottages, where four of five children failed to survive their first years of life.

In 1856, the Bessemer converter revolutionized steel production in much the same way Darby's and others' inventions had changed the iron industry a century earlier. In 1861, a new open-hearth process of steel making that required expensive new techniques of production was perfected at Swansea. Merthyr's ironmasters had a great sum invested in works filled with outdated furnaces, and most made the transition to steel production poorly, if at all. To top it off, near midcentury the original three-life leases all expired, and new leases were much less favorable to the ironmasters. Iron making, the industry that urbanized the largely empty Valleys in less than a century, went elsewhere in Wales and eventually disappeared almost completely from the principality. A grand duke of Russia visited Merthyr in 1847 and, like tourists before him, witnessed an amazing industrial urban landscape. But he saw a fading spectacle, one that soon would no longer be a wonder of the world but merely another grim, gritty industrial town.

The urban environment of industry underwent rapid changes. Throughout both initial and subsequent phases of the Industrial Revolution the fortunes of the dominant industry simply overwhelmed other structural determinants in towns such as Merthyr. As the ironworks closed one by one in the second half of the nineteenth century, their remains were left to crumble. Empty stretches, once farmland built over with blast furnaces, went back to seed. And over the course of another one hundred years even those ruins vanished. No buildings remain from Merthyr's mighty past except a few rows of workers' cottages and one pump house at Cyfarthfa. The dark streets of houses, the most humble aspect of Merthyr's elemental landscape, lasted longer than the spectacular works that once lit up the night sky. The descendents of the men and women whose sweat built a modern iron industry lived on, long after the entrepreneurs and their big houses disappeared.

Many architectural and urban historians take it as an article of faith that the man-made landscape is an integral part of society, that it is more than merely a stage on which lives are played out but is itself a crucial part of the drama. In an industrial setting, where the physical reality of place is often radically altered and reshaped, the integral nature of the physical environment and the drama of everyday life is perhaps most readily apparent. In Merthyr, where the modern iron industry wrought a most striking and terrible environment and where social and physical landscapes were so clearly compartmentalized, the relationship between physical and social structure was cast in a very clear light.

At Merthyr the built environment was *not* the primary issue to those who created and inhabited it. For the observer of the landscape it would be tempting to believe that in the Rising of 1831 insurrectionists marched through the town decrying mean housing, or cramped streets, or the general degradation of the environment. But, of course, they did no such thing. The insurrectionists' most important concerns were more personal and immediate: the repeal of wage cuts, the abolition of debtors' court that seized their meager property or imprisoned them, and wages to buy enough bread to keep a family alive. At Merthyr, and in scores of industrial towns, everything was secondary in importance to the requirements of the dominant industry. Even after cholera returned to pay another deadly visit to Merthyr's most miserable streets, the physical environment was not singled out as a major problem. An 1848 hearing concerning a proposed board of health that would regulate building had to be held in the marketplace because "there was no room large enough in the town to hold the persons who wished to be heard against the adoption." The ironmasters' hands must be seen in this, of course, but there was also legitimate popular opposition based on the grounds that Merthyr's most pressing problems were less those of an unsanitary and dangerous environment than inequitable terms of employment and lack of food.[59] All around an extraordinary physical environment loomed, but it was not a direct concern of hungry men.

Considering the degradation of the human condition and the destruction of the natural landscape inflicted by industrial development, it is easy to overromanticize the preindustrial world. In reality, the eighteenth-century countryside was not Arcadia but a hard and often lethal habitat. It was hoped and thought that industry would improve and civilize Nature. Even though they might prove to have disastrous consequences, industrialization and accompanying urbanization were regarded by agricultural laborers as a refuge. A harsh, degraded landscape was the price of better, more regular (or so it seemed) jobs than could be had in the countryside. Thousands abandoned the marginal economic life of pastoral farming for the relative prosperity of manufacturing. In the process, as the midnineteenth century investigator T. W. Rammell noted, "A rural spot of considerable beauty, and with more than the average natural facilities for drainage and water-supply, has become transformed into a crowded and filthy manufacturing town."[60] *The Times* of London concurred: "[Merthyr] itself is a miserably, ill-built, dirty place." But, it was added, "the population seem too busy to mind what their streets or houses are . . . it is a place where no one would live for choice, except to make money."[61]

At Merthyr a more rounded social and physical environment that began to appear near midcentury was of little help to men and women engaged in a struggle that most of us can only dimly imagine. Those of us who are accustomed to a more well-modulated and varied urban environment might perceive the nineteenth-century Valleys' elemental landscape of iron to be unusually harsh and ill formed. But in the context of those who experienced it, the landscape was a means to an end: for Merthyr's ironmasters a way in which to manipulate the social and physical order to gain enormous wealth; for common workingmen and their families a hard road but one that all hoped would lead to a better life.

Notes

1. Gareth Elwyn Jones, *Modern Wales: A Concise History c. 1485–1979* (Cambridge, 1984), 14.

2. C. W. Chalklin, *The Provincial Towns of Georgian England: A Study of the Building Process, 1740–1820* (London, 1974), 45.

3. Roy Porter, *English Society in the Eighteenth Century* (Harmondsworth, 1982), 50; Arthur H. John, "Glamorgan, 1700–1750," in *Glamorgan County History*, ed. Arthur H. John and Glanmor Williams, vol. 5, *Industrial Glamorgan from 1700 to 1970* (Cardiff, 1980), p. 4.

4. Porter, *English Society in the Eighteenth Century*, 50.

5. Charles Wilkins, *The History of Merthyr Tydfil* (Merthyr Tydfil, 1908), 146.

6. Harold Carter, *The Towns of Wales*, (Cardiff, 1965), 309–10.

7. As quoted in F. Vaughn, "Some Aspects of Life in Merthyr Tydfil in the Nineteenth Century," *Merthyr Historian*, vol. 3 (Merthyr Tydfil, South Wales, 1980), 92.

8. G. W. Manby, *An Historic and Picturesque Guide from Clifton, through the Counties of Monmouth, Glamorgan, and Brecknock* (Bristol, 1802), 189–190.

9. *The Cambrian Tourist* (London, 1830), 42–43.

10. Manby, *Historic and Picturesque Guide*, 190–191.

11. As quoted in Harold Pollins, "The Development of Transport, 1750–1914," in *Glamorgan County History*, ed. John and Williams. 5:421.

12. R. O. Roberts, "Industrial Expansion in South Wales," in *Wales in the Eighteenth Century*, ed. Donald Moore (Swansea), 113.

13. Wilkins, *History of Merthyr Tydfil*, 247.

14. Ieuan Gwynnedd Jones, "Politics in Merthyr Tydfil," in *Glamorgan Historian*, ed. Stewart Williams, (Cowbridge, South Wales, 1974), 10:53.

15. Harold Carter and Sandra Wheatley, *Merthyr Tydfil in 1851: A Study of the Spatial Structure of a Welsh Industrial Town* (Cardiff, 1982), 9.

16. Anon., "Labour and the Poor: The Mining and Manufacturing Districts of South Wales," [London] *Morning Chronicle*, 18 Mar. 1850, 5.

17. Ibid., 6.

18. *Western Mail*, 19 July 1982, 8.

19. Tegwyn Jones, ed., "A Walk through Glamorgan," in Williams, ed., *Glamorgan Historian*, 11:114.

20. Benjamin Heath Malkin, *The Scenery, Antiquities, and Biography of South Wales from Materials Collected during Two Excursions in the Year 1803* (London, 1804), 178.

21. John Lloyd, *The Early History of Old South Wales Iron Works (1760 to 1840)* (London, 1906), 64.

22. Malkin, *Scenery, Antiquities*, 177.

23. Jeremy Lowe, *Welsh Industrial Workers Housing 1775–1875*, (Cardiff, 1977), 8.

24. *Morning Chronicle*, 4 March 1850, 6.

25. Lowe, *Welsh Industrial Workers' Housing*, 4.

26. T. E. Clarke, *A Guide to Merthyr Tydfil* (London, 1848), 16.

27. W. J. Williams, "Life in Nineteenth Century Cefn Coed" (extracts from the manuscript work of W. J. Williams, M.A., director of Education, Cardiff), (Cardiff: Cefn Coed and Vaynor Local History Society 1960), 2–3.

28. *Morning Chronicle*, 18 March 1850, 5.

29. Williams, "Life in Nineteenth Century Cefn Coed," 3.

30. Jules Ginswick, ed., *Labour and the Poor in England and Wales 1849–1851: The Letters to the Morning Chronicle from the Correspondents in the Manufacturing and Mining Districts, the Towns of Liverpool and Birmingham and the Rural Districts*, vol. 3 *The Mining and Manufacturing Districts of South Wales and North Wales* (London, 1983), 66.

31. Jeremy Lowe, "The Triangle, Pentrebach, Merthyr Tydfil," *Industrial Archaeology* 15, no. 2 (Summer 1980):146–56.

32. *Morning Chronicle*, 21 March 1850, 5.

33. Ibid., 8 Apr. 1850, 5.

34. Ibid., 29 Apr. 1850, 5.

35. Ibid., 8 Apr. 1850, 5.

36. Anthony Jones, *Welsh Chapels* (Cardiff, 1984), 2.

37. See Martin J. Wiener, *English Culture and the Decline of the Industrial Spirit, 1850–1980* (Cambridge, 1981).

38. John B. Hilling, "The Buildings of Merthyr Tydfil," in Williams, ed., *Glamorgan Historian*, 8:173.

39. J. G. Woods, *Rivers of Wales* (London, 1813), cited in Margaret Stewart Taylor, "The Big Houses of Merthyr Tydfil," in *Merthyr Historian*, 1:117.

40. Malkin, *Scenery, Antiquities*, 177.

41. Anon., "A Run on the Rails and a Few Days amongst the Furnaces of South Wales," *Bristol Times*, 21 Feb. 1851, 6, as quoted in Carter and Wheatley, *Merthyr Tydfil in 1851*, 12.

42. Taylor, "Big Houses of Merthyr," 118.

43. Malkin, *Scenery, Antiquities*, 178.

44. Anon., sketch map, 1833, Glamorgan County Records Office, Cardiff, document no. 39.

45. *Merthyr Guardian*, 3 Feb. 1844, 3.

46. Clarke, *Guide to Merthyr Tydfil*, 14.

47. Lloyd, *Early History of South Wales*, 80.

48. Clarke, *Guide to Merthyr Tydfil*, 47; Charles Herbert James, *What I Remember about Myself and Old Merthyr* (Cardiff, 1892), 11.

49. Gwyn A. Williams, *The Merthyr Rising* (London, 1978), 138.

50. Clarke, *Guide to Merthyr Tydfil*, 15.

51. *Merthyr Guardian*, 3 Feb. 1844, 3.

52. T. W. Rammell, *Report to the General Board of Health on the Town of Merthyr Tydfil* (London, 1850), 13.

53. Carter and Wheatley, *Merthyr Tydfil in 1851*, 31–35.

54. Jones, "Politics in Merthyr Tydfil," 53.

55. *Merthyr Guardian*, 28 Mar. 1835, 3.

56. Ibid., 5 Dec. 1846, 3.

57. Ibid., 14 Aug. 1847, 3.

58. Ibid., 6 Jan. 1838, 3; 20 June 1836, 3; 26 Jan. 1839, 3.

59. Moelwyn Williams, *The South Wales Landscape* (London, 1975), 221.

60. Rammell, *Report to the General Board of Health*, 24.

61. *Merthyr Guardian*, 23 Dec. 1843, citing *The Times of London*, 3.

2

Noisiel-sur-Marne and the Ville Industrielle in France

JOHN S. GARNER

When Tony Garnier arrived in Paris from Lyon in 1889 to complete his studies in architecture, he would have been attracted to the great Exposition then occupying the Champs de Mars and spilling over to the grounds of Les Invalides. From the upper platform of Eiffel's tower, which had been criticized for being "a work more American in character than European"[1] because of its exposed structure of wrought iron, Garnier could have surveyed the vast array of exhibits and pavilions that stretched below. Much of the foreground south of the tower was occupied by the gargantuan Galerie des Machines, a building that sheltered sixty-three thousand square meters of exhibition space and contained everything from steam locomotives to a single-cylinder internal combustion engine. Because the exposition marked the centennial of the French Revolution, special emphasis was placed on social advancement and a part of the exposition was given over to a section entitled "social economy." In stark contrast to the monumental buildings of iron that occupied the midway were a cluster of small frame and masonry houses that lay in the distance. Although hastily constructed on the parade ground north of Les Invalides, this portion of the *section sociale économie* could be seen from the tower. The seven houses placed there were examples of company-owned dwellings rented to workers of mining and industry. A house based on a model of those erected by the Anzine Copper Company near Valenciennes in the Alsace received a gold medal because of the improved living standards it offered a miner and his family; the silver medal went to a brick double-family house of the Menier Chocolate Company of Noisiel, a model industrial village located twenty-five kilometers east of Paris; and a frame double-family house exhibited only in drawings and photographs by the Ludlow Manufacturing Company of Ludlow, Massachusetts, took the bronze. Apart from the houses, the layouts of the fifty-one mining and manufacturing enterprises participating in the exhibit were depicted in plans, photographs, and illustrated souvenirs together with their products. Menier, for example, built a triumphal arch of fifty thousand kilograms of their yellow-wrapped chocolate bars. When the estimated 32 million visitors to the exposition departed, they carried away more than souvenirs and a craving for chocolate; they left with a greater awareness of industrialization and its pervasiveness in Western society. Tony Garnier (1869–1948) would eventually complete his studies at the École des Beaux-Arts and then go on to win the coveted Prix de Rome in 1899. A pension attached to the prize gave him the opportunity to design *Une Cité Industrielle*, which he completed in sketches in 1904, published later as a folio volume (1917). The stir of attention brought about by the publication, which illustrates a modern industrial city with model housing and other buildings to improve the lives of industrial workers, and the influence it exerted on a younger generation of architects, including Le Corbusier, established Garnier's reputation as an urban visionary and reformer.[2]

It is unlikely that Garnier met the person responsible for the housing exhibit at the exposition, Emile Muller (1823–1889), who died later that year. But at some point in his studies, he must have been made aware of Muller's work on behalf of the working classes, the society he founded to improve their living conditions (l'Association des industriels de France), and his publications that illustrated model housing in industrial layouts. Muller had sought a rapprochement between government and industry with recognition and incentives for those industrialists who provided improved living environments for their employees. The popular uprising of 1848 that brought Louis Napoleon to power resulted in various reform initiatives. Prizes were awarded to build better houses and housing estates for the laboring classes, *les cités ouvrières*. An opportunity to demonstrate model housing at the Paris Exposition of 1855, in response to the example of the London Exposition of 1851, where a model tenement had been exhibited under the patronage of Prince Albert, was lost. In 1867, however, Muller succeeded in gaining permission for an exhibit. Then, and again in 1878, workers' houses were erected on the exposition grounds and cash prizes awarded. Not until 1889 were the first medals awarded; from that date forward workers' housing received greater attention internationally.[3]

Muller was a graduate of the École Centrale des Arts et Manufactures. His diploma in civil engineering earned him a position with a railway company, and it was the living conditions he encountered among the railroad laborers that persuaded him of the need for low-cost rental housing. In 1846 he left the railroad and returned to his native Mulhouse, where a local industrialist, Jean Dollfus, hired him to design some houses for a ribbon factory in nearby Dornach, Germany. The factory had been founded in 1756 by Johannes Dollfus and the enterprise later renamed Dollfus-Mieg and Company. A larger textile mill erected in Mulhouse in 1797 became the city's principal employer (Fig. 2.1). Mulhouse was an old city, and the textile mills, of which there were several, lay outside the original quarter. For the most part, the housing of the textile workers was poorly conceived and insufficient in number. Even the newer apartment blocks or *casernes* that housed upward of

Figure 2.1 View of the textile factory of Dollfus, Mieg & Co., Mulhouse, France, ca. 1836. (Département des Cartes et plans, Va 68 t.3, Bibliothèque Nationale.)

twenty families were found to be undesirable. Two visitors to Mulhouse, Auguste Penot and René Villermé, reported on the conditions they encountered. Penot took exception to the *casernes*, so named because of their spartan military appearance, finding that families forced to live in cramped quarters and within close proximity suffered greater social deprivation. Overcrowding and lack of privacy were worsened by the practice of taking in single lodgers to assist with rents. Penot observed in 1836: "We discover at Mulhouse, and in other parts of the upper Rhine, large vulgar buildings that we have designated under the name casernes. . . . But that is the least consideration, because gathered together in the same house, a large number of unrelated families are rarely accorded a moment's peace and thus given to grave disorders."[4]

An exception to the *casernes* were the cottages, *les petites maisons*, also to be found in Mulhouse, several of which had been constructed for the textile mills of Dollfus-Meig and Company. Villermé, a physician and reformer and a contemporary of Edwin Chadwick, was among the first to call attention to the incidence of disease and mortality in poor and congested neighborhoods of substandard housing. On a visit to Mulhouse in 1847, he witnessed the construction of houses for thirty-six families, in which each apartment contained two rooms, a small kitchen, an attic and basement, and a small garden where the family could raise vegetables to supplement their diet. He recognized that small semidetached cottages for two to four families could be built more reasonably outside large cities. Apartment blocks for both single workers and families were a necessity for reasons of economy in cities like Paris or Brussels, and Villermé called attention to the Belgian government's housing legislation of 1849 that provided incentives for the construction of *cités ouvrières* and served as a model for the French housing act of 1852. Nonetheless, he remained convinced that the answer did not lie in the construction of large apartment blocks (*grand ensembles*) but rather housing estates composed *exclusivement de petites maisons non contigues*.[5]

In 1852 Muller designed for Dollfus a new housing quarter in Mulhouse composed of row houses and four-family houses or quadraplexes (Fig. 2.2). The quarter was laid out in long rectangular blocks of identical houses, each built of brick with a stucco veneer. What distinguished this development was not the architecture but the layout and the terms by which a worker and his family could acquire a home of their own. It was also the first location outside Paris where government funds from the housing act were used to assist a private project. A subvention of 300,000 francs was provided in 1853 from 2.1 million francs allocated to various housing societies by Louis Napoleon (by then, Emperor Napoleon III). To this sum a matching amount was subscribed by twelve shareholders, administered by Dollfus under the Société Mulhousienne des Cités ouvrières. The government funding paid for streets, sidewalks, water mains, fountains, trees, a public bath, bakery, and restaurant. The matching subscription was used for constructing the first houses. By 1866, Dollfus had erected 676 houses and by 1900, 1,243, representing an investment of 4,351,128 francs. A family's monthly rent of 25 francs was applied to the cost of the unit within the quadraplex, and after payments over a period of thirteen years and five months, the family acquired title to the apartment at cost plus interest. When in 1864 the French minister of public education asked the wife of a worker where her husband went for his "soirées," she replied that he remained at home "with us since we have our house."[6]

By providing better housing together with the amenities of a bakery shop and community bath, Dollfus assisted his employees in obtaining a better standard of living and the opportunity of aspiring to bourgeois standards insofar as domestic arrangements were concerned. Nor was Mulhouse an isolated example. Bourcart's industrial village at Guebwiller (1854) and Japy's village at Beaucourt (after 1862) followed the model established by Dollfus and Muller. Another industrialist, J.-A. Scrive, of the textile company Scrive Frères et J. Danset, made similar overtures to his workers. Founded in Lille in 1839, the company relocated in 1846 to Marquette, a planned town in the north of France, where the baneful influences of the larger industrial city could be avoided. The *cité ouvrière* at Mulhouse was not a company town. Employees had a choice of whether to purchase a dwelling in the new quarter or to live elsewhere in the city. At Marquette, however, there was no alternative. Virtually every aspect of the worker's life fell under the scrutiny and management of the company.

Of 350 workers employed by Scrive, nearly 200 occupied the quadraplex houses in Marquette that rented for a modest 60 centimes a week. Others lived in dormitories. Housing had always been a concern of the poor and laboring classes, whose scant earnings rarely secured the necessities of food and shelter. At Marquette, however, the cost of shelter was the workers' least concern. The availability of cheap accommodations at a fraction of a family's earnings left money for other uses. Men could earn 9–25 francs a week as mechanics and weavers, women weavers 7–12 francs, and children who spun the wool 4–9 francs. Single workers living in the

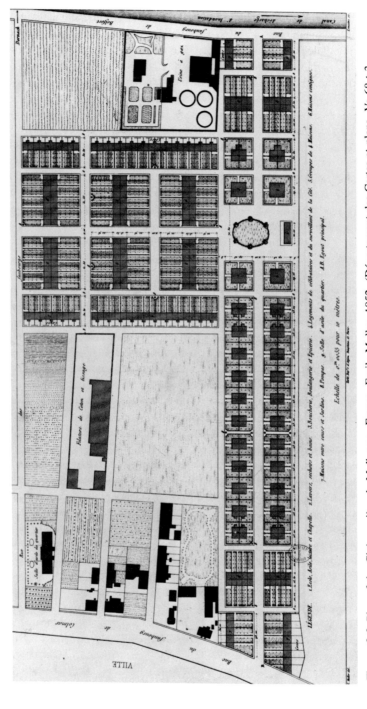

Figure 2.2 Plan of the Cité ouvrière de Mulhouse, France, Emile Muller, 1852. (Département des Cartes et plans, Va 68 t.3, Bibliothèque Nationale.)

company's dormitories could rent an iron bed for 5 centimes a night or 35 centimes a week. Food could also be obtained in the dorms at a rate of 4 fr.55 c. a week. That purchased a half liter of milk in the morning; a half liter of soup, meat, vegetables, and eggs at lunch; and milk, bread, butter, and beer in the evening. Plots for vegetable gardens were made available to families who wished to till them, and the company provided a *cuisinier* to help with suggestions about what to cultivate.

The model layout of Marquette was commissioned of the architect C. Tierce, who may have designed the buildings as well. Its residential blocks were similar to those of the *cité ouvrière* at Mulhouse with four-family houses placed along straight streets in a continuous line or *cordon* (Fig. 2.3). At center was the Catholic chapel. On either side lay the linen factories and administration building (Fig. 2.4). In a small park within the residential quarter were a refectory and baths that contained an *estaminet-tabagie*, a kind of coffeehouse and smoking parlor to offer an alternative to the *pernicieuses habitudes du cabaret*. In addition to beverages, billiard tables offered entertainment on the ground floor, while a music hall was located above. Across from the administration building was the chapel, and there was also a school where children of both sexes would receive an hour's instruction each day from an employee of the company.[7]

The differences between the employees' earnings and allowances could be saved. In 1849 Scrive founded a *caisse de secours* (savings bank), which provided a modest return on the workers' earnings but guaranteed a modest pension during periods of illness and after retirement. Doctor and pharmacy fees were free of charge. However, the company offered no sick leave to workers who were incapacitated because of alcohol, venereal disease, or fighting. Under other statutes of the company, fines were levied for tardiness to work and failure to clean looms as required each Saturday. For their service and fealty, workers would receive, from the bank, a retirement pension of between 150 and 300 francs a year after thirty years' employment, with the opportunity of remaining with their families in company housing. As modest as that sum may seem, it was a remarkable gesture for the period before 1850. On other occasions, the company sponsored organized recreation. Beginning the first Sunday of each July, a three-day holiday interrupted the work routine. Adults and children participated in sack and hoop races and in such traditional games as *jeux de boule*. Winners received prizes of 5–40 francs. Such organized events would become commonplace in model company towns of the later nineteenth century both in the countries of Europe and in North America. What may have been missing, however, were the human emotions resulting from spontaneity and voluntary choice, not only in regard to participating in games—given the employees' scant opportunities for leisure—but also as participants in a society that was closed and subordinate to the company in every regard. Rules and restrictions of various kinds imposed a mechanical discipline and social order (*l'habitude de l'ordre*) and "a system of complete protection."[8]

It is within this milieu of experiments in the layout and management of industrial villages that Menier built his factory at Noisiel on the Marne. Noisiel-sur-Marne epitomized the *ville industrielle* in that it combined the planning and paternal aspects of those other experiments with an unusual commitment to architecture. Jean-Antoine-Brutus Menier (1795–1853), patriarch of the House of Menier, pi-

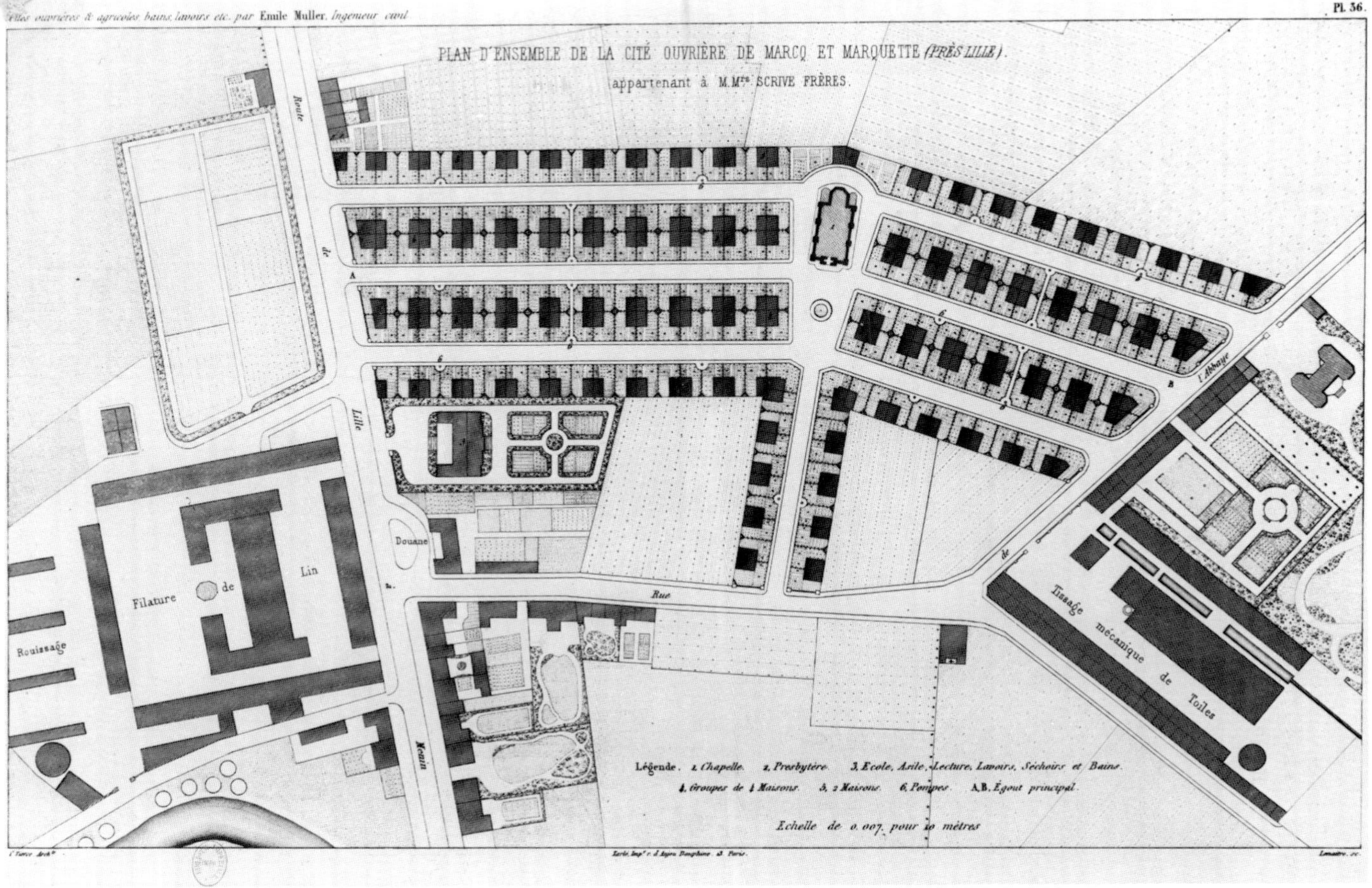

Figure 2.3 Plan of the Cité ouvrière de Marquette, France, C. Tierce, 1846. (E. Muller, *Habitations ouvrières et agricoles, cités, Bains et Lavoirs*, 1855–1856, pl. 36, Bibliothèque Nationale.)

VUE DE L'ÉTABLISSEMENT DE MARQUETTE.

Figure 2.4 View of the textile factories of M. M. Scrive Frères, Marquette, France, 1846. (*Notes sur la situation des ouvriers de l'établissement de tissage mecanique*, 1851, Bibliothèque Nationale.)

oneered in the manufacture of chocolate, transforming it from an expensive aphrodisiac to a popular confectionery item. The packaging of chocolate into tablets and bars can be attributed to him. After a brief period of training as a pharmacist's assistant in Napoleon's army, Menier was cashiered after Waterloo and returned to Paris to pursue his trade. As early as 1819 he founded a small drug business in the Marais district. However, in 1825 he expanded his enterprise through the purchase of a tract of land on the south bank of the Marne River east of Paris and half a kilometer east of the existing hamlet of Noisiel (Figs. 2.5 and 2.6). His new site was chosen because of the river and water power needed for his business.[9]

Chocolate had been introduced to Europe by Spanish conquistadors who brought it back from America. Derived from the fruit of the cacao, a tropical plant indigenous to Central America, it became an irresistible treat when mixed with sugar, vanilla, butter, and milk. Although sampled throughout the seventeenth and eighteenth centuries and favored by kings and queens (it was said to have been one of Anne of Austria's two passions, the other being Louis XIII), it remained an expensive import and was difficult to prepare until machines were devised to break the cacao beans and grind them into a farine or powder. Thus it remained a luxury item distributed by pharmacists who recommended chocolate as an antispasmodic and purgatory. During the nineteenth century, however, the manufacture of chocolate grew into an important alimentary industry in France, which had first perfected chocolate and imported, by far, the greatest quantities of cacao, averaging 720 tons a year in the period 1825–1834 and increasing to 43,000 tons by 1920, after which imports leveled off. By 1853, the French were already consuming 6 million kilograms of chocolate, and that amount would double by 1866. Although never inexpensive, a 2-franc Menier bar of tablets was by then within reach of the greater populace.[10]

The July Monarchy of Louis Philippe attempted to revive the industrialization of France that had been stunted by the collapse of the ancien régime and set back further by the Napoleonic Wars. Railroads, textiles, and iron smelting, supported by more liberal banking practices, numbered among the leading industries. The Society for the Encouragement of Industry attempted to promote these industries and others through exhibits and competitions to recognize achievement and productivity. In 1832, the society awarded Menier a gold medal for his method of fabricating chocolate, the first of a series of awards both at home and abroad that the manufacturer would receive for his product. By 1854, Menier's annual production of chocolate amounted to 688,000 kilograms; by 1869 it had increased to 3,846,648, and by 1879 to 15,000,000 kilograms, worth 60 million francs. Menier was the largest manufacturer of chocolate in France and undoubtedly the largest in the world at the time. During the 1870s alone, Menier chocolate won gold medals at the Vienna Exposition, Philadelphia Exhibition, and Paris Exposition. The elder Menier and each of his sons would also be cited for their individual contributions to industry, and each would receive the cross of the Legion of Honor in further recognition of his accomplishments.[11]

It was the application of machinery and especially the *broyeuse*, or mill with

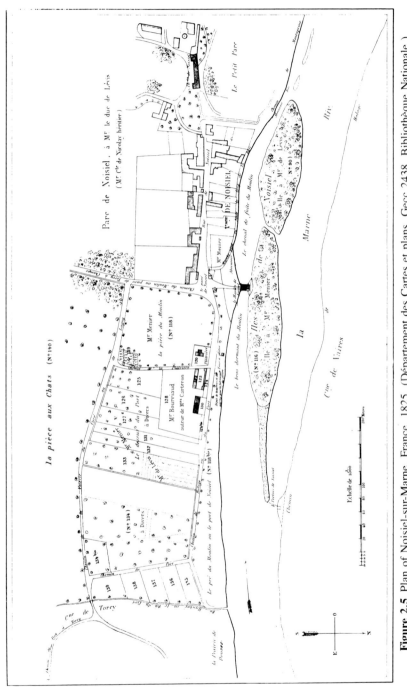

Figure 2.5 Plan of Noisiel-sur-Marne, France, 1825. (Département des Cartes et plans, Gecc 2438, Bibliothèque Nationale.)

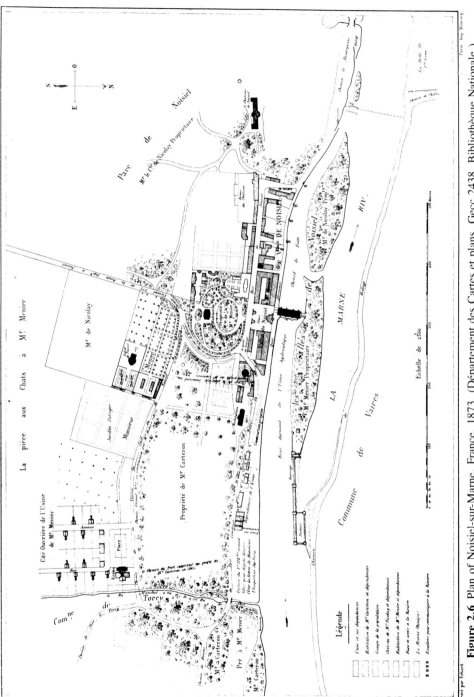

Figure 2.6 Plan of Noisiel-sur-Marne, France, 1873. (Département des Cartes et plans, Gecc 2438, Bibliothèque Nationale.)

granite tumblers to break the cacao beans, that set Menier in search of the power site he acquired at Noisiel.[12] An old mill that had existed since the time of Louis VII and was originally attached to the abbey of Gournay underwent a series of improvements, culminating in the famous turbine building of 1872 that still survives, although without its machinery. Because the turbine building was at the heart of the factories, providing the motive power, a description of its history and operation should preface the layout and design of the industrial village. Moreover, it has been a subject of interest to architectural historians, although never fully described. Marie Virginie Menier, wife of the company's founder, published a poem in tribute to the original mill in 1853. It begins: "For a thousand years it has braved the winds and storms, and remained steadfast despite the passage of time. But decrepitude and deep cracks would eventually take their toll"; thus "a hand of iron now marks its form."[12] And although the mill had been patched and repaired and must once have been picturesque, it could not keep pace with the demands of the growing enterprise and would eventually be replaced by the present structure (Fig. 2.7). The importance of the 1872 turbine building is both symbolic and technical. Sigfried Giedion, the Swiss architectural historian, placed the building in the vanguard of modern world structures because of its iron skeletal frame.[13]

Jules Saulnier (1817–1881) was the architect commissioned to design the new turbine building or *bâtiment sur l'eau* in 1869. The Franco-Prussian War, collapse of the Second Empire, and ensuing economic disruption postponed completion of the structure until 1872. Because of the nature of the building, it required an

Figure 2.7 Birdseye view of the factories of the Menier Chocolate Company, Noisiel-sur-Marne, France, 1876, with turbine building at left, château and workers' village at upper right. (Département des Cartes et plans, Va 77, t. 19, Bibliothèque Nationale.)

extraordinary structural design, permitting it to span a portion of the Marne, tap the river's power, and operate a complex of machinery. The building's foundation was masonry. Its granite piers sat firmly in the bed of a channel formed by a small isle in the center of the Marne and the river's southern embankment. The northern channel was dammed to accelerate the waters on the left bank, which flowed over a low contour dam placed between the building's piers and over which water poured into turbines set between the piers. The southernmost pier of the turbine building engaged the south embankment to admit access from other buildings within the industrial layout. The superstructure was a combination of metal and masonry. Wrought-iron tees formed a lattice truss, *un pont en trellis de fer*, the interstices of which were filled with brick to stiffen the walls and to make the truss rigid. To span the river and to house the heavy turbines and other machinery required an unusual structure, one that proved to be unique.[14]

Unlike his younger brother Charles, Jules Saulnier was not a graduate of the École des Beaux-Arts. However, he may have attended lectures at the École Centrale des Arts et Manufactures and perhaps at the École Spéciale d'Architecture. Neither was as prestigious as the École des Beaux-Arts, but both were more progressive insofar as design and technology were concerned. Saulnier knew Emile Muller, a graduate and later professor at the *École Centrale*, who also held appointment to the *École Spéciale*. Muller, in addition to being an engineer, architect, reformer, and educator, was the proprietor of a terra cotta works at Ivry. He manufactured the enamel-faced bricks and tiles used in the construction of Saulnier's turbine building. Whether Saulnier was a student of Muller's is not known, and it must be assumed that Saulnier received most of his architectural training through apprenticeship. It was through his association with an architect named Bonneau, whom Saulnier credits as his master, that the commission from the Menier family resulted. Bonneau had designed the Menier chateau at Noisiel-sur-Marne in 1854, and Saulnier may have been in Bonneau's employ at that time. Saulnier's first independent commission by the family was the Menier factory at St. Denis of 1862 on the northern outskirts of Paris. There he designed a wrought-iron frame building covered in tiles by Muller. The building was critiqued by Anatole de Baudot, a disciple of Eugene Viollet-le-Duc, in *Gazette des Architectes et du Bâtiment*. Its appearance and the simple, rational way in which the materials were combined impressed de Baudot, who decried the banal appearance of most factories but referred to Saulnier's work as "ingenious" and "an original motif." At the time, Viollet-le-Duc's rationalist ideas about the use of new materials in architecture were being compiled for his *Entretiens sur l'architecture* (1863). In that work, he illustrated the combination of cast- and wrought-iron structural components with traditional masonry. Earlier, however, Viollet-le-Duc lectured at various schools of design in and around Paris and may well have captured the attention of Saulnier. That Saulnier acquired his education through practice may account for his willingness to accept a less conventional approach to building design.[15]

Returning to the factories at Noisiel, and especially the turbine building, Saulnier applied techniques that he may have experimented with at St. Denis. He employed a structural system known as *pans de fer*, or plates of iron. This system emulated medieval heavy timber construction inasmuch as it provided a skeletal framework of posts, sills, plates, braces, and headers. But unlike heavy timber framing, the iron members were proportionally smaller in dimension to the spans they supported. Elevated railroad platforms of the early 1870s, especially those on the outskirts of Paris, employed such a system. Columns or piers would carry the platform above a street or viaduct (Fig. 2.8). The floor of the platform was composed of wide-flange I-beams or plates that spanned overhead between the columns and smaller iron joists that bridged between the plates. The wall above the plates (offering an enclosure for waiting passengers) was a combination of iron and masonry, the iron forming the framework and the masonry providing the infill. Above the plates, iron posts and intermediate studs were formed in the shape of double Ts, built-up sections, the reveals or webs of which received an infill of brick stiffened by iron headers and capped with a plate like the one below. At openings in the wall, where passengers would board trains, diagonal iron braces spanned top to bottom, that is, from plate to plate. Although Saulnier would introduce a latticework diagonal framing into his design, composite walls of iron and masonry were not unknown at the time.[16]

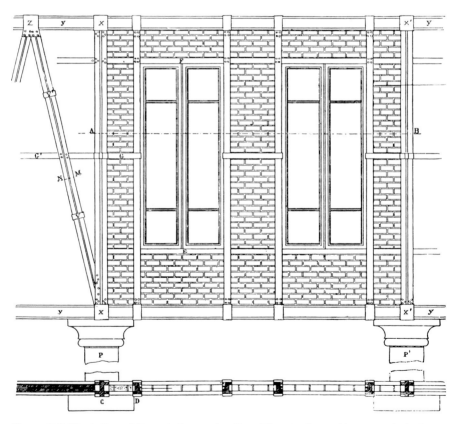

Figure 2.8 Illustration of *Pans de fer* construction. (*Gazette des architectes et du bati-ment*, 1, no. 8 [1872]), p. 93, Bibliothèque Nationale.)

Much has been made of the novel structural system used in the turbine building. It has even been suggested that William Le Baron Jenney, "father of the American skyscraper," may have been influenced by the techniques employed by Saulnier. Jenney was a student at the École Centrale (1854–1856), and he may well have known Muller and Armand Moisant, the contractor for the turbine building who graduated shortly before Jenney. But the structural framing employed by Jenney in such later works as the Home Insurance Building (1883–1885) had nothing in common with the *pans de fer* system. On the other hand, had Jenney used diagonal bracing in his skyscrapers, especially in the corner bays, his framing would have been sturdier and his buildings much more sound. Jenney's great contribution was in designing a fireproof framing system, which was not of concern to Saulnier, who exposed the metal framing members of his turbine building.[17]

Saulnier's design was for a four-story building of approximately 20 × 60 meters in plan. Four large wrought-iron girders, placed on the long axis of the building, two under the outer walls and two under the interior columns, spanned the four granite masonry piers between which the river flowed. The girders were built-up box section plates riveted together, the webs of which were greater than a meter in depth (Fig. 2.9). These carried much of the weight of the first three floors of the building and provided the underpinning for the outside wall trusses (the overall weight of the building was estimated to be seven hundred tons). The floor framing was carried by box section beams that were similar in design to the girders although smaller in section. These beams were set on a cross-axis to the building and attached to the columns by gussets in the form of bridles that were slipped over the beam and bolted into the top of the column. Along the outer walls, the framing of each floor was supported by knee braces extending from floor to ceiling and by the vertical framing members within the wall. No columns interrupted the space of the third or fourth floors. The framing of the fourth floor was a roof truss, the lower chord of which formed an elliptical support extending from floor to ceiling. Two wrought-iron suspenders within each bay and from the upper part of the truss assisted in supporting the floor below and allowing the clear span of the third-floor level. The flooring materials, similar to those employed in other mill buildings, were brick set in segmental arches to form shallow vaults between iron joists with a plaster fill and wooden decking above. Squares of oak cork provided a resilient surface. The exterior appearance of the building was enhanced by the brick and tile furnished by Muller, embossed with the design of cacao plants. Intended as a centerpiece for the industrial complex, the elevations of the building were quite striking (Fig. 2.10). The end elevation facing the courtyard contained a clock within a scalloped parapet, and the roofline was decorated by iron crestings and finials. Spandrels of yellow tiles with green cacao leaves and rose-colored flowers were overlaid with the black vertical and diagonal ironwork of the outer flanges of the wall framing, contrasting with the other buildings located nearby, which were low and constructed in brown brick.[18]

The foundation of the turbine building contained water wheels that transferred the hydraulic power through a system of axles and gears used to drive the grinding machines on the upper floors. Unfortunately, the water wheels were removed when the plant's power was later converted to electric generators, and only drawings of

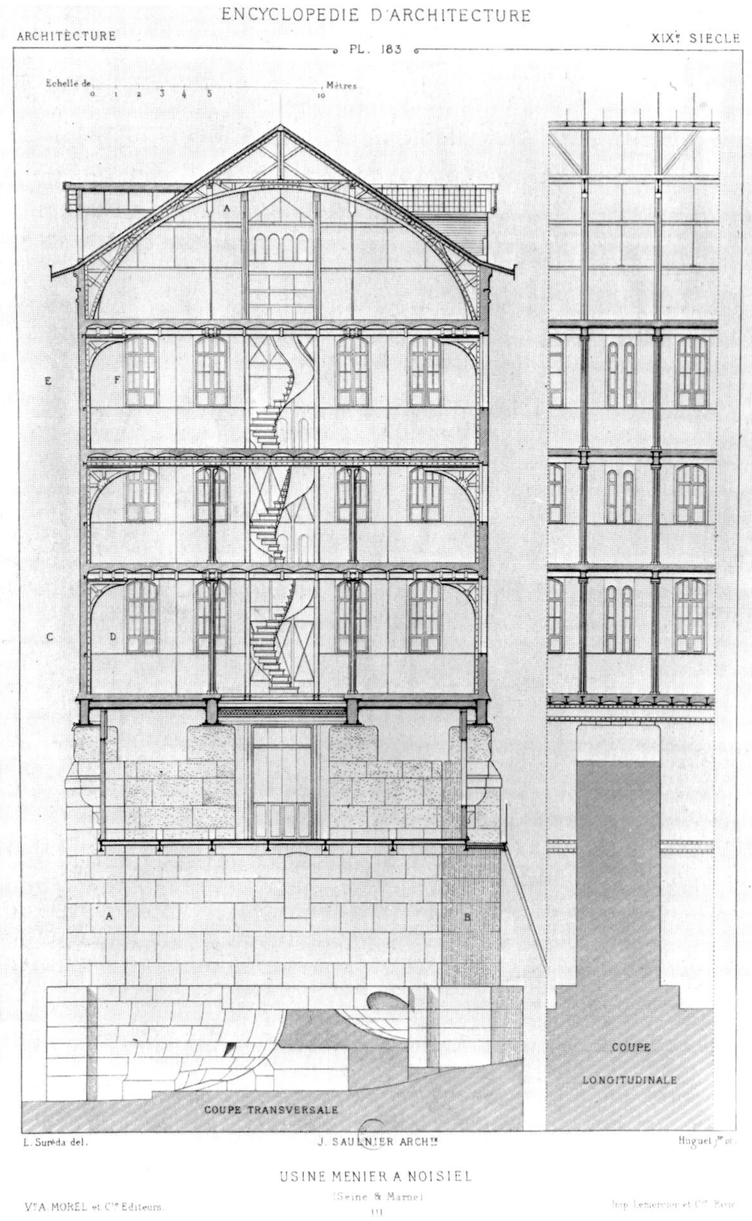

Figure 2.9 Section drawing of turbine building, Noisiel-sur-Marne, France, Jules Saulnier, 1871–1872. (*Encyclopedie d'architecture*, vol. 3, 1874, pl. 183, Bibliothèque Nationale.)

del.   J. SAULNIER . ARCH .ᵀᴱ   Ch. Huguet jⁿᵉ sc.

USINE MENIER , A NOISIEL

Figure 2.10 Elevation drawing of turbine building, Noisiel-sur-Marne, France, Jules Saulnier, 1871–1872. (*Encyclopedie d'architecture*, vol. 3, 1874, pl. 173, Bibliothèque Nationale.)

them survive. Each of the three bays between the piers contained a wheel. One had been acquired in 1855 after the second renovation of the original mill. It was reused in the central bay of the new building and operated in traditional fashion as an undershot wheel on a horizontal axle. The two outer wheels were purchased in 1872 and 1874 and were of a new design. They were turbines manufactured by M. M. Seraphin Frères and created by an engineer named Louis-Dominique Girard. Placed on a vertical axis, they operated on the principle of a siphon with water running through the center of the wheel or turbine, the weight and force of which would cause it to turn. Because of a modest waterfall of only two meters created by the dam, these turbines were considered to be more efficient. Despite the power generated by the water wheels, the company augmented its plant with two steam engines situated immediately southeast of the turbine building (Fig. 2.11). They operated the machinery when the river was down or frozen over.[19]

The purpose of the turbine building was to grind cacao and mix it with sugar. Raw materials arrived by wagon in the courtyard of the plant. Before they passed into the turbine building, however, they were processed in the buildings on the east side of the courtyard. Cacao beans were washed and roasted and the sugar of sugarbeets was refined before being delivered to the turbine building. Once prepared, they entered the turbine building from beneath the courtyard at the south end. Machines located on the first floor peeled the husks of the beans, which then ascended by conveyors to the second floor for grinding. Machines on the two upper floors mixed the two ingredients, which were then returned to ground level. In the buildings on the west side of the courtyard, vanilla, milk, and butter were added, and the batch was then cooked, pressed into tablets, refrigerated, packaged, and returned to the courtyard for shipping.[20]

Saulnier had been placed in charge of designing the entire factory layout, beginning in 1864, and his success in that endeavor entitled him to design an expanding village for the workers. Between 1825 and 1860 the work force employed by Menier was quite small, and it can be assumed that some housing could be found in the neighboring hamlet. But with the rebuilding of the industrial site and its expansion during the 1860s and 1870s, new lodgings for a growing work force were needed. Because there was no affordable transit at that time and because Saint Mande and other villages near the Porte de Vincennes on the eastern outskirts of Paris were too far away to reach on foot, the employees had to live near their place of work in accommodations provided near the factory on property owned by the company. The existing hamlet comprised one street of buildings immediately west of the factory on the rue de Noisiel, a chateau, and some farm buildings. Virtually all land to the south and west had been designated the Parc de Noisiel and remained in the ownership of the comte de Nicolay, who inherited the property from the duc de Levis in the early nineteenth century. Directly south of the factory lay the chateau and grounds of Menier. The chateau designed by Bonneau was modest in size and Neo-Grec in style. Of greater interest was the "picturesque" or English garden in which it was set. But adjoining Menier on the east was the property of a Monsieur Carteron, whose extensive holdings hemmed in the industrial site until well into the 1870s. To the south and southwest of Menier's château and garden, a large tract of

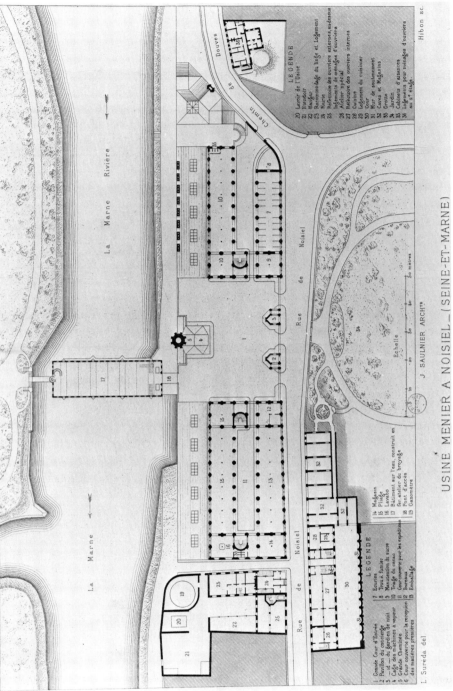

Figure 2.11 Plan of Menier Chocolate Company factories, Noisiel-sur-Marne, France, Jules Saulnier, 1864–1874. (*Encyclopédie d'architecture*, vol. 3, 1874, pl. 228, Bibliothèque Nationale.)

USINE MENIER A NOISIEL—(SEINE-ET-MARNE)

L Sureda del   Hibon sc.

J SAULNIER ARCH^{TE}

LÉGENDE

1 Grande Cour d'Entrée
2 Pavillon du concierge
3 Pont et cour du petit mail
4 Café des machines à vapeur
5 Grande Cheminée
6 Cour couverte pour la réception des matières premières
7 Écurues
8 Trou à fumier
9 Manutention du sucre
10 Triage du cacao
11 Cour couverte pour les expéditions
12 Bureaux
13 Emballage
14 Magasin
15 Filage
16 Lavoir
17 Bâtiment sur l'eau, construit en fer pour atelier du broyage
18 Pont d'accès
19 Gazomètre

LÉGENDE

20 Lavoir de l'Usine
21 Étendoir
22 Hôtel
23 Raccommodage du linge et logement
24 Marie
25 Réfectoire des ouvriers externes, au-dessus logements de ménages d'ouvriers
26 Atelier spécial
27 Réfectoire des ouvriers internes
28 Cuisine
29 Logement du cuisinier
30 Cour
31 Mur de soutènement
32 Caves et Magasins
33 Grotte
34 Jardin
35 Cabinets d'aisances
36 logements pour ménages d'ouvriers au 2e étage.

Échelle

5 10 20 30 40 50 mètres

La Marne Rivière

La Marne

Rue de Noisiel

Chemin de

Douves

farmland and forest had been acquired by the company. Approximately 1,500 hectares (3,705 acres), half of which was cultivated, lay situated on the rolling hills between the Marne River and the line of the Railroad of the East, several kilometers to the south. During the 1880s, Menier would construct a spur to serve his factory. At the edge of this tract, near his factory, although separated by Carteron's property, Menier built his *cité ouvrière de l'usine*.[21]

The plan of the housing estate was not unlike those earlier examples at Mulhouse and Marquette. And additional examples could be found in *les cités ouvrières* at Le Creusot for the steelworks of Schneider near Fontainebleau and at Flixecourt for the textile mills of Sainte. A rather formal arrangement of straight streets and long rectangular blocks characterized the layout (Fig. 2.12). No attempt was made to integrate the contours of the site with the streets and walks. Semidetached cottages, each with its *petit jardin*, formed a line from one end of the street to the other. There were differences, however, between Menier's layout and those that preceded it. Lots on either side of the 10-meter-wide streets were staggered so that a house on one side of the street did not directly face the one opposite. Two-family houses (with a partition-wall down the center from front to rear) occupied the lots instead of less desirable four-family dwellings. The units were larger and had better light and ventilation than their midcentury counterparts at Mulhouse and Marquette. Moreover, such services and utilities as piped water, storm sewers, and gas were furnished by the company; toward the end of the century, electricity would be provided as well. And in addition to dwellings, the company built a school, library, restaurant, refectories or dining halls, bakery, and *magazine* (store). These buildings faced the place des Écoles, the square that formed a cross-axis to the three principal north-south streets. One-half kilometer west of the place des Écoles lay a church and cemetery, also furnished by the company. In contrast to the regular layout of the streets, dwellings, and public buildings was the surrounding terrain, whose curves and swells created a buffer to the new village. A small creek that emptied into the Marne and the road to Torcy bordered the village on the east, and between them was a meandering walk set within a garden. Barns and orchards and the church and cemetery lay between the housing and the winding bridle paths of the Parc de Noisiel on the west. Hence, the imposition of order and regularity within the landscape, even in the absence of a neighboring city grid, had been determined from the outset.[22]

Inasmuch as Saulnier had been placed in charge of designing the industrial site and factories, he most likely planned the housing estate that followed. He did design the houses and public buildings, and although Menier employed both an engineer and assistant engineer, he most likely entrusted the planning of the residential quarter to Saulnier. The two-family houses that later won a medal at the Paris Exposition displayed none of the structural daring or decorative exterior treatment evidenced by the turbine building. But such élan was hardly necessary: no technical feat was required, nor did the site impose unusual constraints, and although the workers and their families might have welcomed a contemporary design, they may also have expected something more conventional. Indeed, Menier may have insisted on houses of a traditional character to attract employees. In any event, the modest

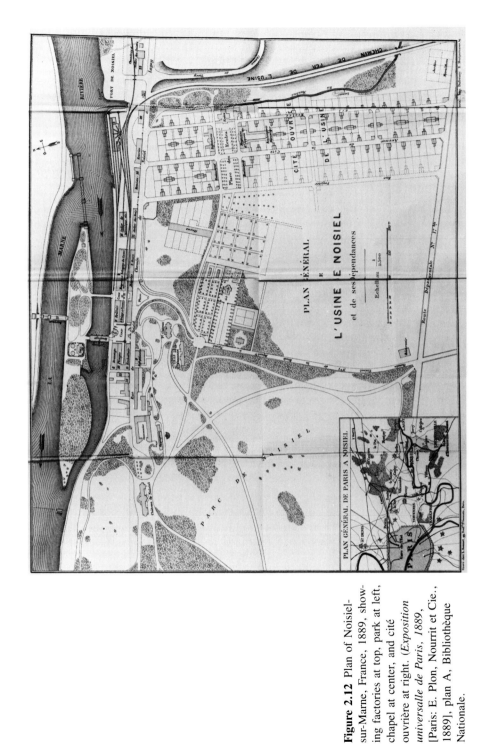

Figure 2.12 Plan of Noisiel-sur-Marne, France, 1889, showing factories at top, park at left, chapel at center, and cité ouvrière at right. (*Exposition universalle de Paris, 1889,* [Paris: E. Plon, Nourrit et Cie., 1889], plan A, Bibliothèque Nationale.)

houses exhibited few embellishments and elicited little excitement. What they lacked in style, however, they made up for in quality of construction. The foundation and walls were masonry. Stone used for the basement was from local marl and brick used above grade produced from deposits of clay on the site. The manganese in the clay produced a chocolate brown face brick. Iron Ts in place of timbers were used for the floor joists, which were decked in tile and wood parquet. Iron was also used for the window sills. Roof framing was in lumber but decked in tile and trimmed with zinc gutters and flashing. The interior walls were plastered and some rooms furnished with wallpaper. Each room above the basement had a small fireplace and at least one window. Attached at the rear of the *rez-de-chaussée* was a single-story ell that served as a laundry and outhouse. The *cabinets d'aisances* were also constructed of masonry and elevated so that the "night soil" would drop into barrels below. There were no sanitary sewers, only storm sewers that kept surface grades dry, and although water was furnished, it was delivered to an outside tap. Special attention was given to garden plots at the sides and rear of the houses. These plots, including half the house or apartment unit, measured 15 × 30 meters and provided sufficient space for cultivating vegetables and herbs. A low brick garden wall with picket fence above screened the plots from the street.[23]

The few distinguishing exterior features of the houses included beltcourses separating the first and second floors above grade as well as trim at the gables and eaves (Fig. 2.13). Quoins in corbeled brick, like those of the beltcourses, emphasized the corners and also divided the houses at center because of their placement in the middle of the front and rear walls. They also signified the dividing line or partition between the two family units. The wooden casement windows were capped with brick segmental arches. Entries were at side instead of front, offering greater privacy from the street as well as direct access to the garden. Houses at the corner of blocks were chamfered. Their angled walls made the transition between the two streets, and at the top of the corner walls were open gables with decorative finials. The corner houses and staggered lots gave evidence of Saulnier's efforts to ameliorate the otherwise repetitive rows of identical company houses. In overall appearance, given the scale of the houses, they appeared somewhat like the servants' quarters of discreet Second Empire–style châteaux, without the châteaux.

Menier's work force grew rapidly between 1870 and 1900, the period in which the housing was constructed. Before 1850, fewer than one hundred employees needed to be housed, and it can be assumed that some existing housing in the older hamlet provided shelter. During the 1860s, Saulnier constructed a few tenements for the company, but not until after 1870, when the work force had climbed to two hundred, did he design the two-family houses described. By 1873, thirteen had been constructed, and by 1875, the number had increased to thirty-seven. By 1878, the number had risen to 60; by 1889, to 100; and by 1896, to 156 houses. Despite the increasing number of houses, it did not keep pace with the work force, which climbed to fifteen hundred during the same period. Of that number, six hundred were women, and it can be assumed that many of them were married to men also employed by the company. Although some larger tenements were constructed for single workers, the two-family houses could accommodate six hundred employees

Figure 2.13 View of workers' houses facing the avenue de la Cité, Noisiel-sur-Marne, France, Jules Saulnier, 1875. (Département des Cartes et plans, Va 77, Bibliothèque Nationale.)

at best. Obviously, some managed to commute from nearby villages. But the inducement to living in the company houses was the low rent: 150 francs a year or 12.5 francs a month. Given wages of between 5 and 7 francs a day in the 1870s, the rentals were a fraction of the cost of comparable housing in Paris. Because rents were low, housing was not a money-making proposition for the company; Saulnier estimated the cost of a house at 8,335 francs in 1875, thus yielding a mere 3.6 percent return per annum on the investment. Moreover, rents remained low and were virtually unchanged as recently as 1950. But unlike Dollfus, Menier retained ownership of the housing, ostensibly to maintain control of the premises, thus denying his employees the security of home ownership. He did, however, reduce rents in stages to those who remained with the company at least ten years, until by age of retirement they lived rent-free as in the example of Scrive at Marquette.[24]

Noisiel-sur-Marne combined factories and village in a model industrial layout. It was the home of the Menier family and their base of operations, but it was not their only plant. As mentioned earlier, the company operated a factory at St. Denis largely given over to the manufacture of pharmaceuticals. It maintained offices in Paris and owned farms in the north of France, at Roye in the Somme, for the cultivation of sugarbeets, *betterave à sucre*. In London, a factory established in 1870 eventually produced more than 1 million kilograms of chocolate a year. But at Menier's cacao plantations in Central America housing was again required. In an effort by the company to control its supply of raw materials, 3,706 acres was acquired in Nicaragua in 1862 between Nandaime and Rivas and named Le Valle-Menier (Fig. 2.14). In 1865 an additional 11,120 acres was purchased near Tortugas and, like the other plantation, bordered Lake Nicaragua. Named San Emilio for Emile Menier, it brought the company's overseas real estate to some 14,820 acres. Each hectare (2.47 acres) could support fifteen hundred to eighteen hundred trees, and each tree could produce 750 grams of cacao if it received sufficient irrigation and tending. However, before the trees reached maturity and thus were able to bear fruit, they required five to six years' growth and watering at least twice a week. To tend the trees and harvest the fruit, the operations employed 312 Mozo, who were trained by an overseer and domiciled on the plantation. For their labor, they were paid 2.5 francs a day. At Le Valle-Menier a large hacienda was occupied by the overseer and his staff, and within the jungle clearing facing the hacienda were a formal garden and fountain. Across from the garden were a chapel and houses for the peasants. A large canal fed by Lake Nicaragua and its tributaries provided a basin for irrigation. From the port at Grey Town, a small fleet of ships transported the produce to France.[25]

Emile Menier (1827–1881), who took control of the company after his father's death in 1853, must be credited with transforming the operation at Noisiel-sur-Marne into a large business with international holdings and product recognition throughout the Western world. He also exercised the paternalism that governed his establishments both in France and abroad. Genuinely concerned for the welfare of his workers, he had a hand in managing every aspect of the enterprise from the cultivation of cacao plants and sugarbeets to the promotion and marketing of the final product. He exercised extraordinary business acumen in that he sought the elimination of trade barriers. As early as 1855 he protested against the *octrois*. Elected to the Chamber of Deputies in 1874, he lobbied against protective tariffs. He espoused the rights of free association for labor and equality for women. He wrote eleven books, most of which were brief tracts on manufacture but some of which were substantial endeavors that called for social and agricultural reform. In *La Civilisation moderne*, he appealed for reason and compassion over belligerence and nationalism. He echoed the eighteenth-century rationalists' call for liberty, equality, and fraternity. He believed that "a religious and militaristic civilization must be substituted by one that is scientific and productive." Machines were *égalitares*, working "peaceably for the profit of the greatest number." Individuals must not be threatened by new technologies but granted the liberty to act and to acquire security at home: "Chacun doit avoir sa place au soleil."[26]

It vexed Emile Menier to see the disparity between economic progress in France and that of other industrialized nations. In his *Atlas de la production de la richesse* (1878), he used the then-novel idea of circle and sector diagrams to illustrate exports, imports, and production quotas. Of particular interest, however, was his last diagram, which was used to illustrate "population and instruction." He drew a comparison between the United States, with a rate of only 13 percent illiteracy among its population, and that of France, with 40 percent. He equated education with national wealth and called attention to the glaring disparities in education levels

Figure 2.14 Birdseye view of the coconut tree plantation at the Valle-Menier, Nicaragua, 1862. (*Exposition universalle de Paris, 1889* [Paris: E. Plon, Nourrit et Cie., 1889], p. 25, Bibliothèque Nationale.)

among the wealthiest nations. His concern for education found expression in Noisiel-sur-Marne in the *école* designed by Saulnier (Fig. 2.15). It is significant that the school was placed at the termination of the place des Écoles, the principal cross-axis of the *cité ouvrière*. As the name of the tree-lined square in the heart of the village implies, there were two schools within one building, one for each sex. Instruction was segregated as it was throughout much of Europe: boys entered the left portal and girls the right. Visitors and staff entered the central pavilion where the school offices were located. All children of employees received free education, and by 1889 the number attending amounted to 250.[27]

Although children of workers would often follow in their parents' footsteps by accepting positions in the factory, they would do so only after a rudimentary education in reading, writing, and computation. Child labor was prohibited by the Meniers and thus school attendance encouraged. The paternalism extended by Emile Menier and his three sons, Henri, Auguste, and Gaston, the third generation to manage the enterprise, went on to include a free library, a dispensary with free medical attention, and a savings bank that returned 6 percent interest to its depositors. Comparisons made with Noisiel-sur-Marne and other villages in the region found the living conditions among the workers far superior at Noisiel, where "the maison Menier seems to have made a great effort on behalf of its workers."[28]

In conclusion, Noisiel-sur-Marne can be said to have represented the best of its type, *une ville industrielle modele*, or model company town, in which a resident employer took special interest in the physical and social setting of his enterprise. Despite the élan represented by the design and construction of the turbine building, a true monument in the history of modern architecture, the workers' village followed a familiar pattern, one that had been established in France by the middle of the nineteenth century. Even the paternalism of the Menier family was merely exemplary among several efforts by industrialists to ameliorate living conditions among their employees. It was in France, after all, that such concepts as profit sharing and cooperative ventures between capitalists and laborers found early expression. The question remains, however: to what extent did Noisiel-sur-Marne and other places of similar type influence architecture and planning for the benefit of society? The Paris Exposition of 1889 was clearly a springboard. It hosted the first international conference on housing and drew delegates from many countries, including the United States. The exhibit of workers' houses, including those designed by Saulnier for Menier, demonstrated the efficacy of improved living arrangements for working men and women provided by industry. It also launched a number of housing associations, *les habitations à bon marché*, whereby either industrialists or building and loan associations offered low-cost housing. The exhibition and conference were testament to the promotional and organizational skills of Emile Muller, and Muller's assistant, Emile Cacheux, would help sustain this initiative. A second conference was held in Marseilles in 1892, a third in Bordeaux in 1895, and every few years thereafter an international gathering was convened, until interrupted by World War I. Well-designed, inexpensive houses, set within housing estates with

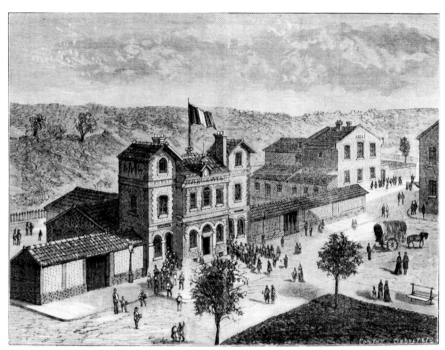

Figure 2.15 View of school facing the place des Ecoles, Noisiel-sur-Marne, France, Jules Saulnier, 1876. (Département des Cartes et plans, Va 77, Bibliothèque Nationale.)

utilities and services, were presented for discussion and then visited during excursions after the meetings. Beyond the question of housing, another influence of the *ville industrielle* was its impact on twentieth-century concepts of town planning, especially comprehensively planned new towns. They may well have influenced Tony Garnier's *Cité Industrielle*. Much has been made of the influence of Saint-Simon and Fourier, the early-nineteenth-century utopianists, on Garnier and his project. The division of society into various work forces, each accorded its place in the city and each receiving its fair share of communal earnings and social benefits, was part of the vision of a new industrial order that Garnier shared with the utopianists. But the planning and architecture embraced by Garnier borrow not from the utopianists but rather from the industrialists of his era. Clearly, Garnier was influenced by the writings of Émile Zola and other socialists who sought reform. But his linear plan and duplex housing, the public baths, libraries, and schools were modeled on those of the *cité ouvrière*. The complexity of his *Cité Industrielle* and the use of concrete and simplified Neo-classical designs share nothing with places like Noisiel-sur-Marne, which were old-fashioned by comparison. But the elements of architecture and planning exhibited in Noisiel make it a prototype for the *Cité Industrielle* and the new residential quarters that were actually built in Lyon and elsewhere in France and Germany between the world wars. Such was the legacy of the *ville industrielle*.[29]

The writing of this chapter was assisted by a Fulbright-Hays Senior Research award to France in 1979 and a follow-up sabbatical offered by the University of Illinois in 1986. For their many kindnesses, I am indebted to Michel Conan, Lion Murard, Patrick Zylberman, and Bernard Marrey.

Notes

1. Exposition universalle de 1889, Séance 17 Jan. 1887, 45; Cahier: Commission consultative de contrôle et de finance: Proces-verbaux, Séance 5 Nov. 1886, 18 [Archives nationale].

2. Antony Roulliet, *Habitations ouvriers à l'exposition universelle de 1889 à Paris* (Paris: Berger-Lavrault et Cie, 1889), 4. *Les Reflexions d'un visiteur curieux devant l'exposition du Chocolat-Menier* (Paris: E. Plon, Nourrit, et Cie., 1889), 2; Christophe Pawlowski, *Tony Garnier et les debutes de l'urbanisme fonctionnel en France* (Paris: Centre de Recherche d'Urbanisme, 1967), 7, 19.

3. Emile Muller, *Notes sur les produits, appareils ouvrages et dessins . . . Exposition Universelle de 1878* (Paris: E. Capiomont et V. Renault, 1878), 20–21. There were two American buildings erected for the Paris Exposition of 1867, a farmer's cottage and a schoolhouse. See Ellen Weiss, "Americans in Paris: Two Buildings," *Journal of the Society of Architectural Historians* 45 (June 1986): 164–67. The model tenement of the London Exposition, although relocated from Hyde Park, survives. It was built by the Society for the Amelioration of the Conditions of the Working Classes. Hippolyte de Royer de Dour, *Essai d'étude . . . en belgique* (Brusells: Societé Belge de Libraire, 1890), 23.

4. "On connaissait à Mulhouse, et dans d'autre parties du haut Rhin, ces grand bâtiments vulgairement designes chez nous sous le nom de casernes. . . . Mais cette consideration tochait peu votre comité, parce que cette agglomeration dan une même maison, d'un grand nombre de menages étrangers les uns aux autres, jouit rarement d'une paisible harmonie intérieure, et pent donner lieu à de grave desordres" (A. Penot, *Les Cités ouvrières de Mulhouse et du department du Haut-Rhin* [Mulhouse: Imprimerie de L. L. Bader, 1867], 7).

5. René Villermé, *Sur les cités ouvrières* (Paris: J.-B. Bailiere, Libraire de l'Academie Nationale de Medecine, 1850), 13, 18. Villermé's references to Mulhouse were drawn from his earlier *Tableau de l'état physique et moral des ouvriers* (1840). George Clark, *Logements modeles: System nouveau pour l'amelioration des habitations ouvriers, Propose au gouvernment français* (Paris: Imprimerie Centrale de Napoleon Chaix et Cie, 1855), 5–6.

6. "*Avec nous depuis que nous avons notre maison,*" Penot, *Les Cités ouvrières*, 11–12, 17, 21; Jules Challamel, *Compte rendu et documents du congrès international des habitations à bon marché* (Paris: Secretariat de la Societe française des habitations à bon marché, 1900), 358.

7. Scrive Frères et J. Danset, *Notes sur la situation des ouvriers de l'établissment de tissage mecanique* (Lille: L. Danel, 1851), 5–12; Lion Murard and Patrick Zylberman, *Le Petit travailleur infatigable* (Paris: Recherches, 1976), 160–61.

8. Scrive Freres et J. Danset, *Notes sur la situation des ouvriers*, 14–21; Murard and Zylberman, *Petit travailleur*, 160.

9. Letters of J.-A.-B. Menier, 5 Apr. 1844, 24 Apr. 1847, "Menier Fabricant," F12 5209, Archives Nationale; *Grand Larousse encyclopedique* (Paris: Librarie Larousse, 1963); Bernard Marrey, *Un Capitalisme ideal* (Paris: Clancier-Guenaud, 1984), 12–14.

10. T. J. Markovitch, *L'industrie française de 1789 à 1964*, vol. 7 (Paris: Cahiers de L'Institute de Science Economique Appliquee, 1966), 215–16; M. Menier, *Cacao et chocolat* (Paris: Paul Dupont, 1867), 17–18.

11. Max de Nansouty, *Les Etablissements Menier a l'exposition de 1889* (Paris: Publications du Journal le Genie Civil, 1889), 6, 8, 10.

12. Two dates have been given for the original grist mill, 1137 and 1157. It had been used to grind wheat for a nearby abbey but came into the domain of the king under Louis VII. By 1842, it had outlived its usefulness and was then reequipped with an iron water turbine. Additional repairs were made in 1853, but the size of the structure was inadequate to house more sophisticated equipment and Emile Menier had it razed in 1869 to make way for the new turbine building.

> "Au Moulin de Noisiel"
> Mille ans il a brave les vents et les orages,
> et se tint immobile en traversant les ages.
> mais la decrepitude a, d'un sillon profond,
> avec sa main de fer, enfin, marque son front.

Marie Virginie Menier, *Le Moulin de Noisiel-sur-Marne* (Fontainebleau: M. E. Bourges, 1853). See also Julien Turgan, *Les Grandes usines*, vol. 7 (Paris: Michel Levy, Frères, 1870), 97.

13. Sigfried Giedion, *Space, Time and Architecture: The Growth of a New Tradition* (Cambridge: Harvard University Press, 1941), 204–6.

14. The turbine building was not only unique in terms of construction: in exterior treatment it also departed from convention. According to some historians, "Ici la solution adoptée est l'expression d'un nouveau langage que crée un architecte rebelle à l'eclectisme de son epoque" (Maurice Dumas et al., *Les Batiments à usage industriel aux XVIIIe et XIXe siècles en france* [Paris: Conservatoirs National des Arts et Métiers et École des hautes Études en Sciences Sociale, 1978], 117–19).

15. I wish to thank Bernard Marrey for the dates of Jules Saulnier's life, which have been confused with those of his younger brother, Charles, e.g., *Macmillan Encyclopedia of Architecture*. Records in the Archives Nationale provide no evidence of Saulnier's having studied at the Ecole des Beaux-Arts. If he enrolled, he never advanced to the second class. See E. Viollet-le-Duc, *Entretiens sur l'architecture*, vol. 2 (Paris, 1863). Viollet-le-Duc's outspoken manner and emphasis on rational uses of materials, even in the restoration of Gothic cathedrals, drew the ire of more conservative factions at the École des Beaux-Arts, where he lectured for a brief period. A. de Baudot, "Usine Menier, À Saint-Denis," *Gazette des Architects et du Bâtiment* 3, no. 12 (1865): 177–82.

16. F. Liger, "Assemblages des planches, des pans de fer," *Gazette des Architectes et du Bâtiment* 1, no. 6 (1872): 41–44. The composiste wall in the *pan de fer* system exposed the iron structural members, or at least their outer flanges. The reveals created by the built-up T-sections provided a recess for the ends of the brick infill. The columns were attached to the beams by special plates or bridles; thus the column was "un filet compose de deux fers a T, . . . maintenu par des brides. . . ." M. Lanck, "Des Pans de fer," *Gazette des Architectes et du Bâtiment* 1, no. 8 (1872): 93.

17. Giedion asserts that Saulnier's turbine building was the "first building of true skeleton type," *Space, Time, and Architecture*, 204. Although published in France, the building was not reviewed in the English press; this fact surprised Giedion, who felt it might have influenced skyscraper construction. But William LeBaron Jenney's debt to France was in the

education he received and in the theory of applied mechanics. In his earliest writings and the Home Insurance Building, his first skyscraper, Jenney's search was for a fireproof means of construction. See Theodore Turak, "The Ecole Centrale and Modern Architecture: The Education of William LeBaron Jenney," *Journal of the Society of Architectural Historians* 29 (March 1970), 40–47; and "Remembrances of the Home Insurance Building," *Journal of the Society of Architectural Historians* 44 (March 1985): 60–65.

18. A detailed account of the factories at Noisiel-sur-Marne, their design, construction, and operation, was provided by Jules Saulnier in "Usine Menier, À Noisiel (Seine-et-Marne)," *Encyclopedie d'architecture: Revue mensuelle des travaux publics et particuliers,* vol. 3 (Paris: A. Morel and Co., 1874), 116–19. On a visit to the site in 1979, I was given permission to examine the turbine building. I found that the third floor had been removed together with the columns on the second floor. Steel beams of deep web design engaged the outer walls of the third floor to provide a clear span and thus open up a two-floor area to be used as a machinery shop for the plant. None of the turbines or original interior machinery remained. The exterior, however, had not been modified and remained in reasonably good shape.

19. Ibid.

20. Ibid.

21. Dumas, *Les Bâtiments à usage industriel,* 118; Saulnier, "Usine Menier, À Noisiel," 116; Commune de Noisiel: Plan du village . . . en 1825 (Département des Cartes et Plans, Bibliothèque nationale); Commune de Noisiel: Plan du village . . . en 1873 (map in the collection of Cartes & Plans, Bibliothèque nationale); *La Grande Encyclopedie,* vol. 23, pt. 2 (Tours: E. Arrault, 1905), 651–53.

22. See Emile Muller, *Les Habitations ouvrières du tous pays: Table des matieres des planches* (Paris: Baudry, 1889); Plan general de L'Usine de Noisiel et de ses dependances [1889] (map in the collection of Cartes & Plans, Bibliothèque Nationale).

23. Jules Saulnier, "Habitation pour deux maisons d'ouvriers à Noisiel (Seine-et-Marne)," *Encyclopedie d'architecture: Revue mensuelle des travaux publics et particuliers,* vol. 4 (Paris: A. Morel, 1875), 110.

24. Saulnier, "Habitation pour deux maisons . . . ," 110; Max de Nansouty, *Les Etablissements Menier à l'exposition de 1889* (Paris: Publications du Journal le Genie Civil, 1889), 19; Prosper Closson, *Etablissements Menier, Usine de Noisiel-sur-Marne, 1878* (Paris: E. Plon and Co., 1878), 13–15; Budgett Meaken, *Model Factories and Villages: Ideal Conditions of Labor and Housing* (London: Fisher & Unwin, 1905), 357.

25. Turgan, *Les Grandes Usines,* 103–6, 111; *Les Reflexions d'un visiteur curieux devant L'exposition du Chocolat-Menier* (Paris: E. Plan and Co., 1889), 23, 25–26, 29; E. Menier, *Cacao et chocolat* (Paris: Paul Dupont, 1867), 12–13, 15.

26. *La Grande Encyclopedie,* vol. 23, 651–53; E.-J. Menier, *La Civilisation moderne* (Paris: Bureau de la Reform Economique, 1876), 8, 16–17, 23–24.

27. E.-J. Menier, *Atlas de la production de la richesse* (Paris: E. Plon, 1878), map 20; Nansouty, *Les Etablissements Menier,* 20.

28. "*À Noisiel, ou la maison Menier semble avoir fait un gros effort pour ses ouvriers,*" in Philippe Bernard, *Economie et sociologie de la Seine-et-Marne, 1850–1950* (Paris: Librarie Armand Colin, 1953), 130.

29. The sources from which Garnier drew inspiration for his Cité Industrielle are many and varied, but despite the utopianist authors suggested by Dora Wiebenson, *Tony Garnier: The Cité Industrielle* (New York: George Brasiler, 1969) and Françoise Choay, *L'Urbanisme utopies et réalités* (Paris: Editions du Seuil, 1965), there can be found an underlying pragmatism or rationalism to Garnier's planning concepts based on his knowledge of previous

industrial experiments. In Anthony Vidler's "L'Acrople moderne" in *Tony Garnier: L'oeuvre complete* (Paris: Editions du Centre Pompidou, 1989), 71–79, Garnier's Cité industrielle and later work at Lyon are once again explained in terms of the writing of such authors as Émile Zola, who greatly influenced Garnier, although perhaps no more than the progressive industrialists and reformers of his day, who largely have been overlooked.

3

The Company Town in Scandinavia

MATS AHNLUND
LASSE BRUNNSTRÖM

"You should see to it that you make your first mistakes and gain your first experiences far away from home." These words of advice were given to one of Sweden's best-known architects as he was about to enter upon his professional career.[1] The idea of free and uninhibited experimentation has been closely connected with the building of company towns, especially during the first few decades of this century. Several young architects achieved fame through their design in remote resource-based company towns. This chapter discusses the Scandinavian company architects and their successes and failures, and places the company towns in historical perspective. The Swedish company STORA, founded some seven hundred years ago, claims to be the oldest limited-risk joint-stock company in the world. We cannot vouch for the truth of this claim, but Scandinavia undoubtedly has had a long tradition of building by companies (Fig. 3.1).

The earliest examples of Scandinavian resource-based towns are the mining towns (*bergstäder*) that were founded in the central parts of Sweden and Norway in the seventeenth century. The best-known are the communities that developed as a result of copper mining, such as Falun, settled in the early Middle Ages, and Røros in Norway, founded in 1646. Silver deposits at Sala and Kongsberg led to the establishment of similar communities. Falun, one of Scandinavia's first large preindustrial towns, was granted a town charter in 1641. It eventually had a population of about six thousand. Falun was considered the second most important city in Sweden and the rich copper ores were of great importance to the country's extensive military operations in Europe during the seventeenth century, when Sweden was one of the great powers. The mining operations were run by entrepreneurs, the *bergsmän*. The

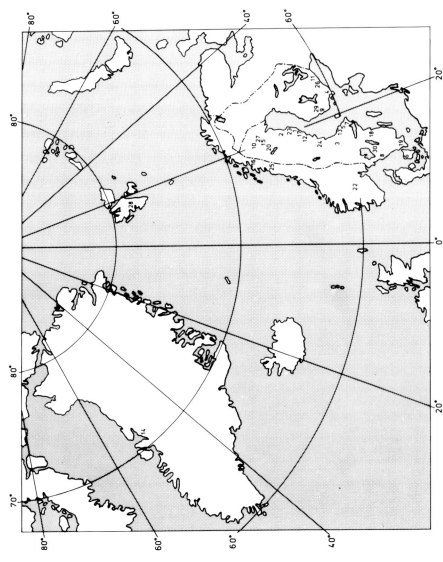

Figure 3.1 Map of part of the Northern Hemisphere, including the Scandinavian countries, Spitzbergen, and Greenland, showing the location of the towns discussed in this chapter: 1. Baggböle; 2. Boliden; 3. Falun; 4. Fiskars; 5. Forsmark; 6. Frederiksvaerk; 7. Gimo; 8. Jonsered; 9. Kauttua; 10. Kiruna; 11. Kotka; 12. Köpmanholmen; 13. Leufsta; 14. Maarmorilik; 15. Malmberget; 16. Narvik; 17. Norrbyskär; 18. Norrköping; 19. Nyvång; 20. Porjus; 22. Rjukan; 23. Robertsfors; 24. Skönvik; 25. Sulitjelma; 26. Sunila; 27. Svappavaara; 28. Sveagruvan; 29. Tampere/Tammerfors; 30. Tidaholm.

organization was quite similar to that of a modern limited company, and the company still exists under the name STORA. The houses of the entrepreneurs were situated near the copper mountain. Many of the workers lived quite close to the deposits, some may have lived in the ore storehouses. However, when Falun was granted its charter, everyone, with the exception of a few officials, moved to the newly built town nearby. In the early eighteenth century there were about six hundred permanently employed miners who were paid by their respective entrepreneur. Employees also were provided housing and some social assistance. The entrepreneurs not only ran the actual mining operations but supervised the separation of the ore into raw copper. The smelting took place in some one hundred small mills situated on nearby rivers and streams (Figs. 3.2 and 3.3).[2] As in most other Swedish towns at this time, the houses were single-story, constructed of horizontal logs, many of them unpainted and unpaneled. It mattered little whether or not they were painted, since the corrosive sulfurous gases blackened everything in the vicinity. When the well-known botanist Carl von Linné visited Falun in 1734, he reported that the ground was barren for miles around the mine and that it consisted only of big rocks. The houses were encrusted with soot.[3]

Bruk Communities

The oldest and by far the most important branch of the Scandinavian mining industry was, and still is, the mining of iron ore. Even during the Middle Ages, Swedish

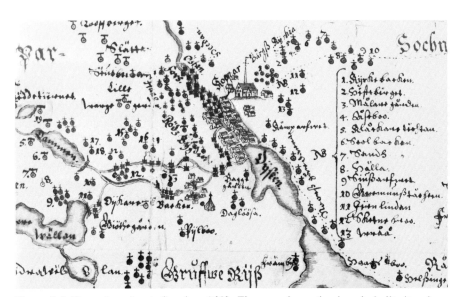

Figure 3.2 Kopparbergslaget, Sweden, 1640. The map shows the densely built city of Falun shortly before a gridiron city was developed. The copper smelting houses and hammer mills are located primarily around the streams. (Detail from "Tabula Geographica öffwer Kopparbergslaget," Archives of the National Land Survey Board, Gävle, Sweden.)

Figure 3.3 Birdseye view of the Stora Kopparberget mine in 1718. To the left of the mine shaft is Gruvstugan ("the Mine Cottage"), where accounts were kept and disputes between the entrepreneurs were settled. The building also contained a chapel. The adjacent house was the residence of the mine master. (Pen and watercolor by Johan Tobias Geisler. Hessisches Landesmuseum, Kassel, Germany. Photograph courtesy STORA, Falun, Sweden.)

iron was held in great repute in northern Europe. By the mideighteenth century, Sweden's production of wrought iron constituted 30 to 35 percent of total European production. The fact that iron accounted for more than 70 percent of the total value of Swedish exports by this period clearly indicates the significance of the industry. Even during the preindustrial period, well-known architects were employed by the large ironworks. Their primary tasks were to design manors and churches, but sometimes they also drew town plans and designed houses for the employees. Jean Eric Rehn, architect to the Crown, who was involved in the design of several "*bruk*" in central Sweden (Forsmark, Gimo, and Leufsta), is perhaps the most important figure of this era. In Finland, which was part of Sweden until 1809, the famous architects Carlo Bassi and Carl Ludwig Engel designed both the manor and some of the workers' houses at Fiskars bruk. Thus, architects participated in the building of mill towns from a very early date.[4]

Leufsta, Forsmark, and Gimo were among the so-called Walloon mills of Uppland, central Sweden. They produced a kind of bar iron that had a reputation for being the best possible raw material for the production of high-quality steel. The rich iron ore came primarily from the mining fields of Dannemora, where nearby streams and rivers supplied power. The availability of water power was the primary reason that many mills were built in this area. Yet, it should be pointed out that the milling industry did not result in an industrial revolution. The mills remained industrial islands in a primarily agrarian society. Although a great deal of research into the social and economic conditions in the mill towns has been done, there is, to our knowledge, no overall analysis of the planning and buildings of the semi-agrarian mill towns. Thus, it is not known to what extent the Continental ideal-city plans of the Renaissance served as a model for the planning of the large Walloon mills constructed during the seventeenth century. However, attempts have been made to reconstruct a town plan for Leufsta, the largest and most important seventeenth-century iron mill. Its plan was believed to have been prepared in connection with the takeover of the mill by the Dutch banker and arms dealer Louis de Geer. De Geer realized how suitable the tough Swedish iron was for the production of cannons and acquired the mines of Dannemora as well as several big Swedish mills and workshops. As early as 1627, the year in which de Geer became a naturalized Swedish citizen and was knighted, he had gained control of all of the arms workshops within the realm. Leufsta became an important link in his empire and soon grew into a sizable community (Fig. 3.4).

Plans were based on a rectangular layout, as indicated by the corner houses and the right-angle streets along which the workers' homes were situated. Their location suggests that Leufsta may have been a model town—perhaps the first example of an industrial model town. The workers' houses are small, timber dwellings with roofs covered with turf. As was common in the Middle Ages, the houses are situated

Figure 3.4 Leufsta bruk (about 160 kilometers northeast of Stockholm), ca. 1700. In the foreground is the manor and behind it the well-trimmed garden. The *bruk* buildings are in the background. (Oil painting by unknown artist, Leufsta Castle. Photograph, Map and Picture Department, Uppsala University Library, Sweden.)

close together with their gables facing the streets. The original plan of Leufsta is not extant, and thus it is difficult to say whether there is a strictly rectangular plan in the spirit of Albrecht Dürer and other Renaissance designers or whether it was influenced by French seventeenth-century *bastides*. During the eighteenth century many of the large mill towns, for example, Leufsta and Gimo, were remodeled on the pattern of French chateaux such as Vaux le Vicomte. At Gimo, a monumental baroque plan was adopted with squares, parks, and avenues to create long perspectives (Fig. 3.5). The architect succeeded in adapting the plan to meet existing conditions and yet maintained most of the old building pattern.[5]

However, because the iron industry consumed enormous quantities of charcoal, many ironworks were relocated to more thickly forested areas. It was both easier and cheaper to transport the iron ore to places where charcoal was available. This relocation process began as early as the seventeenth century and, as a result, a number of new *bruk* settlements were founded in Finland and in northern Sweden. Kauttua in southwest Finland, established in 1689, and Robertsfors in the north of Sweden near Umeå, established in the 1750s, are two typical examples of such communities. Both towns managed to adapt their production to the changing demands of the market and remain thriving industrial communities. Robertsfors was founded by the trading company of Finlay & Jennings, which owned some large mills in central Sweden. The original mill was built in a small village consisting of five farms, each enclosing a courtyard. The village structure was maintained, and by the end of the eighteenth century the *bruk* was fully completed. A map from 1799 shows the smelting-house, the German forge, and the workshops on the Ricklea River. The buildings of this community were segregated; all the workers' houses (Fig. 3.6), were located on the west river bank close to their places of work and grouped in rectangular pattern; on the other side of the river were the church and old farms, which had been made into a manor and office buildings. In addition to the production of pig iron, most of the mills also produced bar iron and various kinds of hardware. Bar iron was also sold to other major *verk* or *faktorier* (preindustrial workshops) for the production of military hardware.[6]

One of Scandinavia's more magnificent workshop complexes and company towns was Frederiksvaerk in northern Sjaelland, Denmark. It was founded in the mideighteenth century for the production of cannons and gunpowder in response to the Prussian Seven Year War. The main plan was drawn up in 1763 (Fig. 3.7) by the manager of the mill, P. H. Classen, who was also an amateur architect. Just as in Gimo, the plan is characterized by its spaciousness, magnificent tree-lined streets, and symmetrical parks. Unlike the Swedish mill towns, however, Frederiksvaerk was surrounded by baroque Continental fortifications.[7] Although more research is needed about the role of industry in the founding of communities during the eighteenth and nineteenth centuries, it appears that the early Scandinavian mills deserve more attention in a European perspective. It is true that they still had many agrarian features and were largely modeled on the châteaux and garrison towns of the seventeenth and eighteenth centuries, but they were designed on the basis of industry and thus can be seen as precursors to the planned industrial towns of Arc-et-Senans in France and Le Grand Hornu in Belgium.

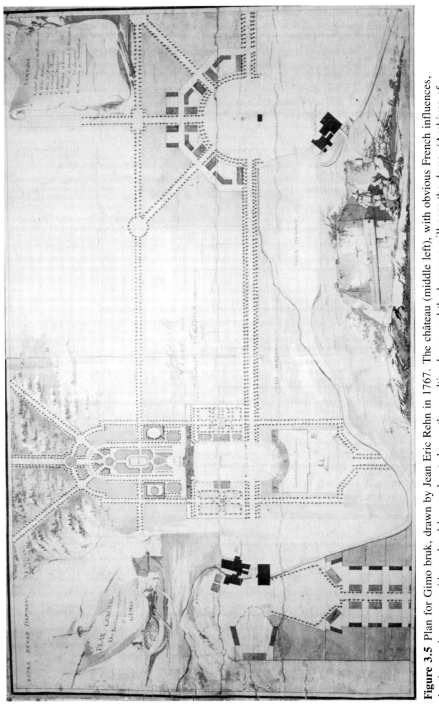

Figure 3.5 Plan for Gimo bruk, drawn by Jean Eric Rehn in 1767. The château (middle left), with obvious French influences, dominates the areas, with workers' houses located near the smelting house and the hammer mill near the dams. (Archives of Korsnäs-Marma AB, Gävle, Sweden.)

Figure 3.6 Eighteenth-century timbered family barracks for workers at Robertsfors bruk, in 1918. After a second story had been built in 1809, the building contained sixteen apartments. (Robertsfors Bruk Archives, Robertsfors, Sweden.)

Textile Communities

The textile industry also played an important role in the transformation of handicrafts and cottage industries to mass-production factories. Expansion, as in the iron industry, was supervised by foreign industrialists. Scots such as Alexander Keiller and James Finlayson will forever be associated with the emergence of the textile industry in Scandinavia. Corporate towns (or multienterprise towns) such as Norrköping (Sweden) and Tampere/Tammerfors (Finland) each claimed the title "Manchester of the North," and as far as industrial density and urban characteristics are concerned, they competed with North American cities such as Lowell and Holyoke, Massachusetts, and Manchester, New Hampshire. At Norrköping, where the majority of the Swedish wool weaving mills were located, there were no fewer than 119 textile factories in 1850, employing a total of 3,687 workers (Fig. 3.8).[8]

Less urban, although even more British in character with the row house as the basic dwelling type, are the mill towns of Jonsered, Mölnlycke, Oskarström, and Furulund. The oldest of these villages is Jonsered, near Gothenburg. Production of sailcloth and canvas began there as early as 1835 in Sweden's first single-story north-light weaving shed (Fig. 3.9). Several architects were subsequently employed to prepare plans and design various kinds of buildings. Among the first of these architects was A. W. Edelsvärd, who in 1858 designed a church in the "Scottish" style and may also have designed houses for the workers. Edelsvärd also drew the first formal plan of the community.[9]

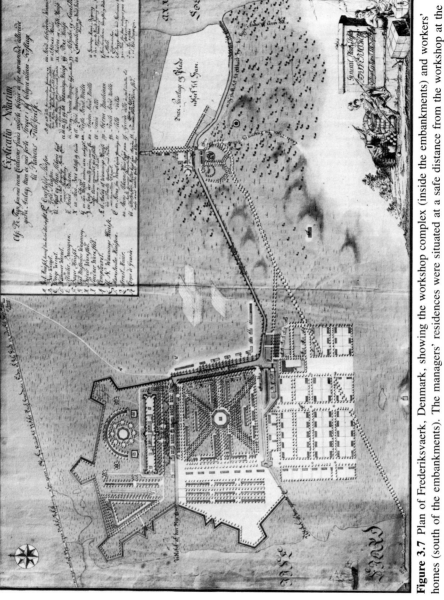

Figure 3.7 Plan of Frederiksvaerk, Denmark, showing the workshop complex (inside the embankments) and workers' homes (south of the embankments). The managers' residences were situated at a safe distance from the workshop at the far right. (Copenhagen National Museum.)

Figure 3.8 The Motala River in the city of Norrköping, Sweden, was lined with factory buildings. To the left is one of Holmens bruk paper factories, in the foreground the Kvarnholmens spinning mill. Both of these factories have external turbine houses. Photographed in 1919 during construction of a feeding tube for a new power station. (Holmen Paper Archives, Norrköping, Sweden.)

Lumber Milling Communities

Sawmilling communities did not develop until the first half of the nineteenth century, although fine-blade water-powered saws had been introduced as early as the eighteenth century. As a result of large capital investments in the lumber industry, not only did the number of thin-blade sawmills increase but they expanded to include more saw frames, which resulted in a steady increase in production. Such innovations gave rise to the timber export industry, which still, to a very large extent, contributes to the economy of Scandinavian countries. One of these export-oriented and modern water-powered lumber mills was Baggböle (Fig. 3.10), situated upstream of the medieval town of Umeå. Around 1840 Baggböle was purchased by the Gothenburg firm of Dickson & Co., and within ten years the company had built two new water-powered saws. The founder of this company was a Scottish immigrant. During the 1850s the expansion of Dickson & Co. was so great that it became the largest lumber mill in Sweden and would remain so for several decades. The company acquired control of vast forest, where the timber was logged and floated downriver to the sawmills. The sawn lumber was then floated to the coast, where the company had built its own ports for shipping, primarily to England via Gothenburg.[10] The early lumber mills often came into conflict with older village interests and traditions, especially salmon fishing.

Figure 3.9 Birdseye view of Jonsered, Sweden. The roof of the factory was a north-light sawtooth shed built in eight files. The transverse building in the background is the cotton spinning mill, built in 1854. In the distance, the church spire and the workers' rowhouses and barracks can be seen. (Sveriges Industriella Etablissementer, Stockholm, 1872.)

Residential settlements did not develop in close proximity to the lumber mills because the mills had yet to operate on a large scale. Later, the more labor-intensive loading places at coastal ports, sometimes dozens of miles from the sawmill, developed as settlements, especially after the introduction of steam-powered saws, which usually caused a relocation of the entire milling process to the ports. At the Baggböle lumber mill, water-powered saws were in operation longer than usual, and not until 1885 was a steam sawmill built at the old loading place in Holmsund.[11]

The first steam-powered lumber mill in northern Europe was built in 1849 at Tunadal near Sundsvall, Sweden. Ten years later, there were some twenty mills in the northern part of the country. Until the early twentieth century, Sweden was the world's leading exporter of sawn lumber. The development of large-scale lumber milling, however, had started in Norway and then spread via Sweden eastward to Finland and tsarist Russia. Thus, Norwegian know-how and capital were initially of great importance to the lumber industry.[12] The takeoff phase of the Industrial Revolution occurred rather late in Scandinavia, compared to countries rich in coal such as England, Belgium, France, and the United States. But the breakthrough of the lumber industry marked the beginning of rapid and intensive industrial development in Scandinavia. One obvious result was the establishment of a large number of small lumber mill communities along the coasts in the thickly forested areas in the north, especially around Sundsvall in Sweden. The industry's primary export targets were England, France, Spain, and other European countries. Attempts to refine the raw

Figure 3.10 Baggböle, Sweden, ca. 1880. In the foreground are part of the upper sawmill and the timber boom. The manor (finished in 1846), with its small polygonal pavilions, is situated on the crest of the steep riverbank, a Neoclassical ensemble designed by the assistant vicar and amateur architect J. A. Linder. The workers initially lived in large log barracks close to the river (not seen in the picture). (Västerbottens museum, Umeå, Sweden.)

material at home led to the development of a mill work industry. Several companies specialized in prefabricated houses, including AB Ekmans mekaniska snickerifabrik, established in 1858. The principal owner, Pehr Johan Ekman, was an architect and, together with his successor, the architect Frans Lindskog, he designed various types of houses. The company advertised its products in a catalog containing fifty colored drawings showing its whole range of buildings. Style was chosen with regard to the building type. Public buildings and private houses were designed in a mixture of Swiss and Old Norse styles, with dragon's heads and arabesque ornaments inspired by the Viking age. Churches were designed in the traditional Neo-Gothic style. One of these churches was delivered to Robertsfors AB and was shown on the cover of the company's catalog (Fig. 3.11).[13]

The paternalistic *bruk* community was a model for the establishment of other industrial settlements until the beginning of the twentieth century. But as traditional symbolic values were abandoned, the increasing liberalization of industrial society brought changes of its own. Secular and spiritual activities had often been manifested in a strictly axial building pattern, for example, in Forsmark. Although industrialists kept to the basic pattern, they began to emphasize work habits and education. Frans Kempe, managing director of Mo & Domsjö AB, was one of the advocates of change. In the lumber mill community of Norrbyskär (Fig. 3.12), south of Umeå, a boulevard running in a north-south direction connected the cathedrallike sawmill building at one end with a two-winged school of high architectural standards at the other. At the sawmill community of Köpmanholmen some fifteen miles south of Örnsköldsvik the two poles of the town axis consisted of a residential estate and a school/factory area. The Norrbyskär sawmill was com-

Central-Tryckeriet Stockholm.

Figure 3.11 Cover of a catalog, published by AB Ekman carpentry factory in 1890, describing the various types of houses manufactured by the company. The medals depicted were won at international exhibitions; the names of export countries adorn the frame. The inset pictures show the company's factories in Stockholm (center) and four examples of company buildings. (Archives of the Museum of Technology, Stockholm.)

Figure 3.12 Main Street, Norrbyskär, Sweden, shortly after the sawmill had started production in 1895. The workers' quarters, originally double-family houses in shingle style, were designed by a Stockholm architect, Kasper Salin. However, his designs were not followed implicitly. For example, the upper stories of the buildings were clad with ordinary vertical paneling instead of shingles. (Mo & Domsjö Archives, Domsjö, Sweden.)

paratively large in that it contained twelve saw frames. A large H-shaped lantern was built into the roof of the sawmill, providing good overall illumination, and no fewer than five thousand window panes were supposed to have been used. The furnace and engine house were constructed of red brick, primarily as a result of fire insurance requirements. Inside were mounted two compound two-hundred-horsepower steam engines. Several lavatories, including a Finnish sauna bath, were arranged close to the smokestack, for the use of the workers and their families (Fig. 3.13).[14]

The trade association of Sweden's lumber mill owners did all it could to promote regulated plans and building forms. At the Stockholm Exhibition of 1897, a detailed model at one/sixty-seven (1:67) scale of an ideal sawmill community was displayed. This strictly symmetrical model was, to a large extent, based on the layout of Norrbyskär.[15] In many ways the level of interest and ambition was higher in Norrbyskär than in other lumber mill communities at the turn of the century. Such communities were usually of a more temporary nature with large multifamily tenements of simple frame construction. Normally, one found a mixture of tenements built by the company and wooden shanties built by the workers themselves without plans and proper roads. This was true especially of the settlements in the Sundsvall area and the region around Kotka at the outlet of the Kymmene River on the Baltic Sea, Finland's most representative lumber mill district (Fig. 3.14). At Skönvik, for example, the owner's mansion, located apart from the workers' housing, as was common in New England mill towns, contrasted sharply with the rest of the community (Fig. 3.15).[16]

Figure 3.13 The two-nave sawmill at Norrbyskär shortly after its completion in 1895. (Mo & Domsjö Archives, Domsjö, Sweden.)

Figure 3.14 Workers' barracks for the sawmill company, Gutzeit & Co., at Kotka, Finland. This company, originally established in Norway, recruited experienced workers from that country and provided accommodation in Norwegian-style workers' houses with balcony access. The barracks were built in the 1870s and housed some forty families at the turn of the century. The pavilion front of the building was used as a school and a church. (Kymenlaakson maakuntamuseo, Kotka, Finland.)

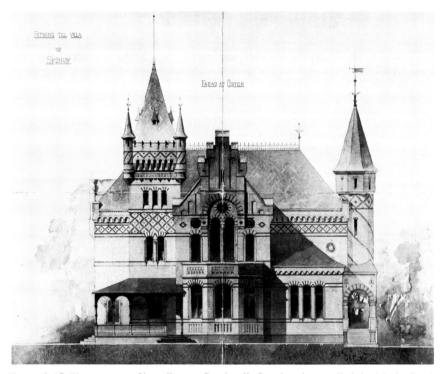

Figure 3.15 The manor at Skönvik near Sundsvall, Sweden, later called the Merlo Castle (east elevation). The brick building, inspired by medieval styles, was designed by the architect Isak Gustaf Clason in 1882 for the *bruk* manager Friedrich Bünsow. Romanesque Revival ornamentation dominates; corbel courses, patterned brickwork, crenellations, stepped gables, and tourelles. The porch with its turned posts, however, reflects Clason's interest in the American shingle style, manifested a few years later in some of his best-known detached houses. Colored ink elevation, SCA Archives. (Courtesy SCA, Sundsvall, Sweden.)

In the same way that several of the Scandinavian *bruk* were transformed into lumber mill communities, many of the latter began to produce pulp in addition to lumber thirty or forty years later. This transformation lent to the smaller communities stability that previously was found only in the major *bruk* and better-organized lumber mill communities. Hiring the services of architects and engineers for the creation of new industrial facilities or even entire communities now became more or less standard procedure. One of the architects hired to design pulp mills along the Norrland coast was Sigge Cronstedt. Ever since the advent of the chemical cellulose industry, pulp factories have consisted of a conglomeration of various buildings that called for teamwork between the architect and the building engineer. Cronstedt managed to weave together all the various units in the complex production line by careful planning (Fig. 3.16).

Alvar Aalto's contributions to the later transformation of the Finnish lumber industry during the 1930s are well known. In communities such as Sunila near Kotka and Kauttua in southwest Finland, he implemented many of the rational and socialistic ideas regarding housing that prevailed in Europe during the 1930s. However, there is no difference between the way in which Aalto masked the class hierarchy of the company town with houses laid out in a sliding scale, as in the example of Sunila, and the model company towns of the late nineteenth century. Even at the turn of the century, paternalistic industrialists used architecture and environmental design as means of creating a sense of unity and community pride. For example, skilled workers were recruited to the sawmill of Norrbyskär, and the stability, continuity, and loyalty of that work force were maintained by means of well-trimmed parks and gardens and an architectural awareness that even extended to the workers' outhouses. Neatness and everyday amenities were key ideas in those days. Aalto's most important contributions are to be found on an aesthetic plane, however: using cool modernistic designs, he designed row houses and terraced houses built of whitewashed brick and concrete and set in a thickly wooded and hilly countryside, thus creating a contrasting and beautiful landscape in the history of modern architecture (Fig. 3.17).[17]

Modern Mining Communities

The iron and lumber mill communities rarely hired the services of architects until the end of the nineteenth century. Instead, they employed master builders who both designed the buildings and directed the construction of such towns as Robertsfors. The first large company town designed by an architect was Kiruna, located above the Arctic Circle. Kiruna was built near the two mountains of Luossavaara and

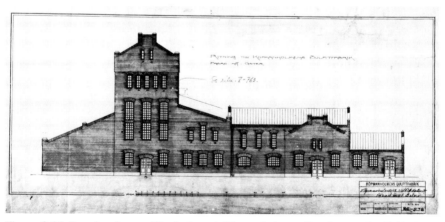

Figure 3.16 Drawing for a sulfite factory at Köpmanholmen, Sweden, on the Gulf of Bothnia. The brick building spreads in all directions from the 25-meter-high boiler house, giving the chemical laboratory process a physical representation. (Drawing by Sigge Cronstedt, 1907. NCB Archives, Köpmanholmen, Sweden.)

Figure 3.17 Alvar Aalto's terraced house in Kauttua, Finland, built in 1938. The roofs of the apartments form the terraces of the upper stories. (Courtesy Ahlstrom Oy, Kauttua, Finland.)

Kiirunavaara in a wilderness area that contained one of the richest iron ore deposits in the world, fully comparable to the mines opened somewhat earlier in the Mesabi Range of upper Minnesota. The planning of Kiruna became a matter of national interest, and the work was closely followed by the government. The state had invested large sums of money in a railroad that connected the shipping ports of Luleå on the Swedish coast of the Gulf of Bothnia and Narvik on the Norwegian Atlantic coast. Also served by this railroad, which was built between 1898 and 1902, was the large mining district and company town of Malmberget. The best Swedish architects were mobilized for the planning of Kiruna with Gustaf Wickman as chief consultant. Plans for the overall site and the service and supply town of Kiruna were drawn in 1899–1900 by the leading authority on city planning in Scandinavia, Per O. Hallman, who also designed an entirely new town plan for Robertsfors in 1901. Kiruna was the first contour plan (which had the landscape as its point of departure) in Scandinavia. Hallman had already shown an interest in the modern planning concepts of the Viennese planner Camillo Sitte. The plan for the company location with its curved narrow streets, which required no official or governmental authorization, was influenced even more by the romantic and picturesque tradition of Frederick Law Olmsted (Fig. 3.18).

Because of its architecture and planning Kiruna developed into a remarkable and much discussed community with small, architect-designed workers' homes that looked like private houses, painted in bright colors that contrasted with their often snow-white surroundings. Just as in Roanoke Rapids, North Carolina, designed by the architects McKim, Mead & White in the 1890s, different color schemes were used for each street of workers' houses. The church at Kiruna, also designed by Wickman, is both shingled and painted "Falun red." It is definitely one of Scandinavia's most interesting wooden churches and embodies a number of architectural motifs that would appear in the early twentieth century, such as, the central pantheistic interior (with no specific liturgical allusions) and the geometry of the Vienna *Jugendstil*, regionally adapted to color and form (Fig. 3.19).

The workmen in Kiruna traveled to the mine free of charge in an electric

Figure 3.18 Kiruna, Sweden. Plans for the service and supply town (above) and the company location, drawn by the architect Per O. Hallman (assisted by Gustaf Wickman) in 1899–1900. (LKAB Archives, Kiruna, Sweden.)

Figure 3.19 The church in Kiruna was designed by Gustaf Wickman and built in 1909–1912, and was sited on the highest point in town, next to the service and supply center. The structure is both shingled and painted "Falun red," traditional Scandinavian house paint produced as a byproduct in Falun since the 1760s. (B. Rönnberg, 1977.)

streetcar. In their spare time, they could visit exhibitions of modern art specially arranged for the working population, listen to lectures, or go to a concert. The company built some of Sweden's best schools with lecture halls and a well-stocked library, and in the summer the company offered school children paid holiday work in which more than two hundred boys were kept busy maintaining the streets, parks, and marketplaces of the community. Efficiency was not the company's only guiding principle; education, morality, and neatness were also part of its program. Even a progressive company encountered problems: the costs for welfare facilities had to be balanced against production and profits. Thus, Kiruna had to make do with a number of temporary or makeshift arrangements, and just as at Malmberget, there was a large shantytown in Kiruna during its earliest years.[18]

Kiruna differed from traditional mining towns in central Sweden, which were smaller and usually consisted of dispersed groups of buildings. Dannemora in the county of Uppland, for example, was primarily made up of a great number of miners' cottages consisting of one room and a kitchen with a cowshed, scattered around the sixty pits of the mining field. As decentralized, but somewhat differently organized, was the Norwegian mining community of Sulitjelma. Sulitjelma, situated on the Saltfjord at the foot of the big mountain range from which the town derives its name, consisted of about ten small, self-contained communities in the immediate vicinity of the work sites. Some were situated on the shores of Langvann (which is connected with the Saltfjord), whereas others were built high on the mountainside and could only be reached on foot or by skis. The cupreous pyrite ore was transported by means of cable cars down to the bay, where it was dressed, enriched, and transported to the coast on barges or by rail. Each community consisted of a group of houses with some two hundred to three hundred inhabitants, a shop, school, assembly halls, cinema, and so on. Many of the houses were quite tall and narrow and well adapted to the hilly countryside (Fig. 3.20).[19]

Scandinavia's largest deposits of sulfide ore containing silver, copper, and, most importantly, gold were discovered in the mountain regions of the county of Väster-botten in the north of Sweden. The gold deposits were the largest in Europe, and the prospecting and processing of these deposits received a lot of attention, as did the well-designed communities that were built in the vicinity of the mines. The chief town was Boliden, which was built in the 1920s near the largest of the main deposits. Boliden is an unusually homogeneous company town whose design is based strictly on rational principles of land use. All the buildings were constructed of wood in simple rustic forms. The town plan was drawn by the architect Tage William Olsson, and most of the buildings were designed by the architect John

Figure 3.20 The Swedish-Norwegian mining company Sulitjelma Gruber AB hired the Oslo architect Erling Nielsen to design their workers' houses at Sulitjelma, Norway. Nielsen designed this house and several other similar multifamily houses during the 1910s. Each family had an apartment that, by Scandinavian standards at this time, was quite large: three rooms and a kitchen as well as spacious storage facilities. (Lasse Brunn-ström, 1979.)

Åkerlund. The plan contained exact instructions as to the organization and future development of the town.[20]

The Scandinavian countries have very limited coal deposits. In Sweden, for example, mining capability has only occasionally exceeded 10 percent of consumption. Coal was mined primarily in Skåne in the south of Sweden and in Spitzbergen. The exploitation of the Spitzbergen deposits did not begin until the early twentieth century and was accompanied by claims from different countries for sovereignty of this strategically situated archipelago. The first company to begin mining operations in Spitzbergen was an American company, the Arctic Coal Company, registered in Boston. Its facilities in and around Longyearbyen were purchased a few years later, in 1916, by a Norwegian company in competition with Swedish investors. Norway's acquisition of Spitzbergen's largest and most important coal district was a principal reason why Norway was granted sovereignty of the archipelago in the 1920 Spitzbergen Treaty.[21]

Sveagruvan, owned by a Swedish company, was not the largest mining field in Spitzbergen. However, located at Braganza Bay, it was probably one of the better designed company towns. Construction lumber and a work force arrived there in early 1917 and the mine opened that summer. Besides miners, there were carpenters, electricians, and painters also on retainer by the company. Everything had been prepared in advance. The Stockholm architect Otar Hökerberg prepared no fewer than 150 drawings of plans and buildings for the new community. Although the building site was virgin land, surveys had been carried out during expeditions the previous summer. Workers lived on board ship until the first tenements were erected. Sveagruvan exhibits several town planning principles better suited to a temperate climate than an arctic settlement. About one hundred duplexes and row houses were laid out in picturesque surroundings. The street network included a main street, ten to twelve meters wide, that climbed a very steep slope to the manager's house. Sidewalks and lawns completed the picture of a summer rather than a winter city. The climatic response is even more surprising when one sees documentary photographs of snowed-in houses that sometimes had to be entered from the roof (Fig. 3.21). The architect of Sveagruvan was aware, of course, of the intense cold and the arctic winds, and his concern was especially apparent in the structural work requiring external walls consisting of four layers of boards, three layers of cardboard, and additional insulation material. The floors had eighteen-centimeter-thick coal insulation and, on top of that, two layers of boards with cardboard between them. For some of the houses, he designed wall buttresses to increase their stability, spacious porches and sun rooms, and entrances facing north so that northerly winds sweeping down the south slope would help keep doors free from snow. It is not known whether the plan was implemented in every detail, but we know that the broad, unprotected gables suggested in the plan had to be replaced with hipped roofs better suited to the climate (Fig. 3.22).[22]

As often the case in company towns, only a portion of the original plan for a new community was implemented. Less than one-third of the projected one hundred buildings of Sveagruvan were erected. Most of the houses were intended to be family occupied, apparently a gesture to the government. Providing work primarily for breadwinners was a policy looked on with approval during the prevailing eco-

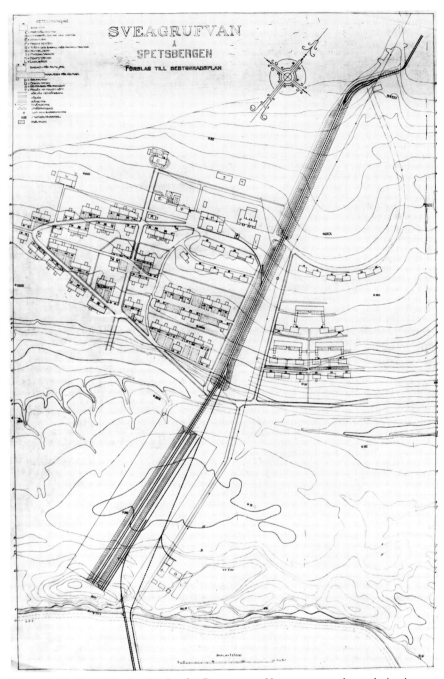

Figure 3.21 Otar Hökerberg's plan for Sveagruvan, Norway, was only partly implemented. The quay, coal store, and power station were situated near the beach and the main quarters were grouped around the canteen (F) a few hundred meters farther up. The mine lay farthest to the north. The three parts of the community were connected by railroads and cableways. (Original plan, Archives of the Museum of Architecture, Stockholm.)

Figure 3.22 Laundry and bath house in Spitzbergen, Norway, designed by the architect Otar Hökerberg in 1916–1917. Photographed in 1921. (Archives of the Science Museum [Tekniska Museet], Stockholm.)

nomic depression, and although priority appears to have been given to married workers in the recruitment of the work force, women and children stayed at home. Women were not allowed to work in Swedish mines, and the wages offered for laundry and cooking did not attract more than a handful of young women. Instead of single-family houses, the work force of about two hundred men was housed in barracks with twenty-four men in each. Although coal production never offset Swedish coal imports, great hope rested on the Spitzbergen fields during the 1910s. The rising price of coal during World War I created even greater expectations, and despite obvious difficulties, the mining of coal in Spitzbergen had certain advantages. The coal was of high quality, permafrost reduced the need for props in the drifts, and production was not hampered by water or gas. Efficiency was also four to five times higher than in English coal mines. The principal user of Spitzbergen coal was the Swedish Rail Company, and most of it was unloaded at Narvik. However, decreasing coal prices, difficult ice conditions, and, above all, an extensive fire in 1925 led to Sveagruvan's closing the same year.[23]

One name that deserves special mention among the Scandinavian architects who tried to adapt communities to an extreme winter climate is Ralph Erskine. He developed his ideas about arctic and subarctic construction in various essays and implemented them in company towns. One project that received considerable attention is the town plan and the houses of the mining community of Svappavaara, located about forty-five kilometers south of Kiruna, where an iron mine was opened in 1961. Erskine was offered the job after a town planning competition failed to produce a winning entry. An entirely new mining community was to be built next to the old seventeenth-century village. Erskine designed a town in the shape of a densely built-up bowl that would catch the sunlight and shut out the winds. Farther to the north he placed two protecting, wall-like apartment buildings with indoor streets. They were to be connected with an indoor center designed for various activities. On the south slope below the apartment houses, the scale was reduced with terraced as well as detached houses. The plan was well conceived, and the houses were designed with a goal of maximum adaptation to the long and hard winters. However, Svappavaara never became the model community envisaged. Many obstacles stood in the way of implementing the plan, but one important one was public opinion. As in the case of Le Corbusier and his design for Chandigarh, Erskine's designs were not appreciated by the people who were supposed to live in Svappavaara. The miners wanted detached homes in contrast to the close working quarters represented by the dark galleries of the mine. They associated themselves more with nature and rural habitations rather than urban ones. They wished to live in harmony with the vast expanse of mountains and to follow the succession of the seasons rather than be packed together with other people in high-density experimental houses.[24]

Thus during the past couple of decades the idea of permanent and densely settled company-owned communities has been abandoned. An example of this change in attitude can be seen in the settlement of Greenland (administered by Denmark) during the 1970s. The mining camp Maarmorilik (near the Black Angle Mine— mainly deposits of lead and zinc) was supposed to operate for only about five to ten years. The entire town was thus built with prefabricated and easily movable components. In the initial stage, simple housing containers were purchased in the United States. The operation was managed by the Danish company Greenex A/S, and the architect Klaus Johansen gradually designed a system of room-size modules that could be combined to form two-story houses. Maarmorilik was built according to the old concept of a socially differentiated mill community with a manager's house, foremen's houses, and workmen's houses separated from one another (Fig. 3.23). In this respect it differs from other modern mining camps, such as Nanisivik and Polaris in the Northwest Territories. The former community is designed according to the concept of small, self-contained houses integrated with their surroundings. In the latter, the whole company town (with the exception of the production facilities) is housed in one single building. Building a modern company town (or camp) in areas with permafrost entails not only the traditional problems of constructing suitable foundations but also difficulties above-grade. For instance, all technical systems had to be placed aboveground; thus, electrical wires and water and sewage lines run in every direction through the town. In addition, in this particular instance, there were also cable cars that crossed the fjord from Maarmorilik to the mine, which is situated at an altitude of seven hundred meters above sea level. After the deposits are mined, the structures will be removed and nature will reclaim the site.[25]

Communities Built for Hydroelectric Power

Although Scandinavia is known for its exceptional water-power resources (more than one-third the total of Europe), its harnessing of electricity did not result in the founding of new communities to the extent that the lumber milling and iron indus-

Figure 3.23 Modern-day view of the lower part of Maarmorilik, Greenland, mining camp. The early housing for the foremen, terraced container houses, each consisting of four apartments, are situated close to the beach. To the left are two pitched-roof detached houses that were built for the managers. (Photographed by Mats Ahnlund, 1990, shortly before the camp was closed.)

tries did. Hydroelectric power plants were only operated by a small number of service personnel because of the technologies employed. Many of the Scandinavian hydroelectric plants were designed by well-known and talented architects whose work served as a symbol of a modern and developing society (Fig. 3.24). The communities that were built as a result of the hydroelectric power industry can be found only in places where electrochemical and electrometallurgical industries located. A few of these communities became quite large and were for a time a subject of national interest. Rjukan, in the district of Telemark, Norway, and Porjus, in the very north of Sweden, are two examples.

The company town of Rjukan is situated in the narrow valley of Vestfjorddalen, Norway, where the sun shines only six months of the year. Its employer, Norsk Hydro, built a number of energy-intensive processing factories for the electrolysis of hydrogen, extraction of nitrogen, and production of ammonia and saltpeter. Deuterium oxide, heavy water, is its best known product. Rjukan is sometimes compared to Kiruna in regard to its combination of rapid growth and responsible architecture and may well be the most elaborately designed company town in Scandinavia. It is certainly the most magnificent, partly because of the majesty of the surrounding countryside. The community was designed in 1908 as a garden city influenced by Krupp's housing estates near Essen, Germany. About ten of Norway's

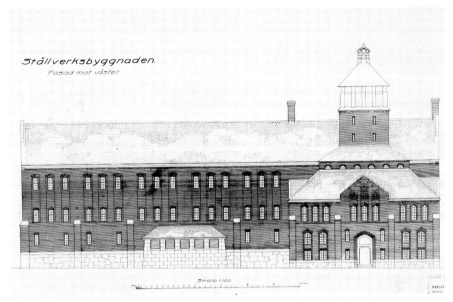

Ställverksbyggnaden.
Fasad mot väster.

Skala 1/100

Figure 3.24 Porjus power station was designed by the architect Erik Josephson. The majestic switchgear building, sometimes referred to as "the Temple in the Wilderness," towers above the subterranean machine hall. (Drawing, 1912, Vattenfall Archives, Stockholm.)

most prominent young architects were involved in the design of Rjukan, which created a community with a variety of good buildings, composed of perimeter blocks of owner-occupied detached houses of different vernacular styles, as well as those designed in the modern or functional style. In addition to monumental public buildings within the center of town, the architects were instructed to design such other structures as kiosks, bus stops, lavatories, bridges, and street lights as a matter of civic art.[26]

Porjus hydroelectric power plant is situated on the Lule River and is the northernmost of Sweden's large national power plants. It was built between 1910 and 1915 with great difficulty to provide the mines in Kiruna and especially the Iron Ore Railroad (Malmbanan) between Kiruna and Riksgränsen with electric power. Just as Kiruna, Porjus was built in an inaccessible area where there were no roads. Unlike Kiruna, however, no plan was made to supplement the power station and machinists' houses with a model company town, although nearly fifteen hundred persons were occasionally engaged in the construction of the power station. Instead, the foremen were housed in what were to become the machinists' homes and the work force in barracks. At the same time, a large shanty town grew up on private land bordering the state-owned land. It was not until contracts for the delivery of electric power had been signed with a smelting plant and a superphosphate industry that the state decided to commission a city plan. It was argued that the only chance of maintaining a steady labor force in a place so isolated and situated so far north was to offer workers the opportunity of building private homes on easy terms. The reasons for the factory owners' interest in Porjus were the rapidly increasing price of coal during World War I and the fact that Porjus could provide cheap electricity. More and more companies were attracted to the area because of the possibilities of refining iron ore, which was abundant in this part of the country. Thus the output of the power station increased in 1918, and the same year the government built another much larger power station at Harsprånget, some three miles downstream. The town plan of Porjus was published in the national newspapers in 1918 and described in high-flown terms. It was predicted that it would become an industrial metropolis of the far north and would very soon be granted a city charter.[27]

The plan of Porjus shows a garden city, typical of this period, where the blocks are zoned for different types of houses and activities (Fig. 3.25). There are two dominant areas: one for the workers' homes, grouped around a spacious park with a sports ground and various community buildings, and one much larger industrial area strictly divided into plots. The industrial area was linked to the power plant via a twenty-eight-meter-wide powerline lane, and a shopping center was planned in the area around the railroad station near the river embankment. Although plans were initiated and roads, water, sewage, and electricity lines rapidly built, Porjus did not become the industrial metropolis it was projected to be. When the general price level dropped by about 50 percent in 1920–1921, the factories had to close and Porjus never recovered from the blow. The projected power station at Harsprånget and the advanced company camp built there met a similar fate. However, construction recommenced at Harsprånget after World War II, and when the power station was opened in 1951 it became Europe's largest hydroelectric plant. The development of hydroelectric power in Scandinavia is now more or less a closed chapter. Several of the great rivers in the north are still untouched for environmental reasons, and at present there is strong political sentiment against further development.[28]

Conclusion

An important ingredient in the building of Scandinavian company towns, especially in the early years, was foreign influence. This was true in both the organization and the technology in the mining and milling industries. Skilled workers also had to be brought in from other countries, such as blacksmiths from Germany and Flanders. Continental ideas influenced the way in which preindustrial mills were planned and built. By the end of the nineteenth century, Scandinavian technology had become world-famous, especially in the iron smelting and wood-processing industries, and it was during this period that Scandinavian mills began to follow a set pattern as architects started working for industry on a regular basis. Energy-intensive blast furnaces, forge shops, and factories were always located near streams and rivers and at a convenient distance, the houses for more important workers (blacksmiths and other skilled workers) bordered straight streets to form rectangular blocks. A large square, sometimes occupied by a church, dominated the civic center. Such functional and socially differentiated planning principles continued to be applied with only slight modification well into the twentieth century. Modifications were aimed at

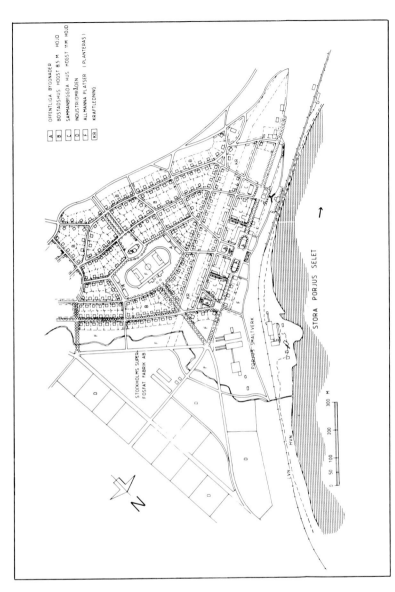

Figure 3.25 The town plan of Porjus, Sweden, drawn by the engineer Knut Plahn of the Construction Department of the State Power Board in 1917 and confirmed three years later. A. Public buildings; B. Houses, height limit 8.5 meters; C. Houses, height limit 11 meters; D. Industrial district; F. Public gardens; KR. Power line. (Drawing after the original plan in the collections of the Porjus Archives Committee, Porjus, Sweden.)

greater rationalism and at emphasis on new symbols and artistic values in town planning.[29]

Because of the northerly location of the Scandinavian countries, climate considerations naturally played an important part in planning, especially in the new mining communities. The first company that really incorporated winter planning was LKAB in Kiruna about 1900. The architect based his proposal on his own field studies as well as on thorough examination and description of existing conditions. The result was a company town located on a sheltered southern slope with a street network designed to break the winds. Natural vegetation was spared and supplemented with other weather-resistant plant species. Workers' dwellings were spacious, airy, and painted in bright colors in contrast to their surroundings. To enable the miners to travel safely and comfortably to work, a railway elevator ran up the mining mountain and connected to a streetcar network at its base. At Rjukan, the company built cable cars not only to take the workers to work but also to offer them sunshine and recreation at the top of the mountain. The most extreme climate adaptions attempted were Ralph Erskine's plans for Kiruna (the city center) in 1958 and Svappavaara in 1961–64, in which he wanted to build new compact mining communities surrounded by walls. But like his other winter-town projects, such as Resolute in Canada's Northwest Territories, these were never implemented.

Even well into the twentieth century, factory building designs were solely based on production, not on the welfare of the workers. Although working conditions varied, they were hardly better in the noisy, dusty, drafty, cold, and damp nineteenth-century sawmills, or, for that matter, the noisy, smoke-filled furnaces and forges of the eighteenth century. Nevertheless, the Norrbyskär sawmill, with its flexible timber construction, served as a model industrial building well into the twentieth century. It clearly illustrated in both architecture and technology the rapid development of steam sawmills toward wider multiaisled structures with large window walls. Sawmills were almost exclusively built of wood and not a more fire-resistant material such as brick primarily because the buildings had to withstand violent vibrations by the sawing machines. The architects' efforts, to the extent that they were engaged in factory planning, were limited. More concrete changes in working conditions were not made until the 1910s, and then not primarily by architects but by production engineers and company directors. On the basis of Frederick Winslow Taylor's efficiency principles, the manufacturing industry built new "rational" factories that were light, open, hygienic, fire-resistant, and easily expandable.[30]

Workers' houses had always been of central importance to the companies and would become subject to municipal and state guidelines during this century. There were many reasons why companies were particularly interested in workers' houses. Providing living accommodations was a matter of necessity, especially in remote areas. A well-designed community of workers' homes created a feeling of pride and attachment in a social environment that otherwise was characterized by high attrition through migration and fluctuations in the economy. At the beginning of the twentieth century, company housing had begun to be used as a means of managing labor, but an increasing number of owner-occupied houses was one of the reasons why companies eventually lost interest in building workers' homes. Resources were then concentrated on production facilities, and although companies would lose one means of controlling the workers, they found that workers were attracted by the idea of home ownership. They even supported workers who built their own homes by offering plots at favorable prices, building loans, or help with drawings. In many cases, however, the companies reserved the right to control the design of the buildings via their own architects, engineers, and administrators. At the beginning of the century, workers also received support and help from the government, which viewed the building of private homes as a means of checking emigration.

Several of the best Scandinavian architects were employed with a view to creating well-designed and practical houses. Some have been mentioned: the architects Kasper Salin (Norrbyskär), Gustaf Wickman (Kiruna), Erling Nielsen (Sulitjelma), Alvar Aalto (Sunila, Kauttua), and Ralph Erskine (Kiruna, Svappavaara). Among the many architects at Rjukan, Magnus Poulsen and Ove Bang deserve to be singled out. Other internationally known architects were also engaged in company building projects, for example, Gunnar Asplund and Sigurd Lewerentz at Tidaholms bruk (manufacture of trucks and fire engines) and Skånska Kolbrytnings AB (coal mining) at Nyvång, respectively.[31]

The oldest company towns in Scandinavia to a large extent laid the foundation for industrialization. From them, modern Scandinavia can trace its economic development. Company towns soon became important "experimental workshops" where, among other things, new types of houses and bold plans could be tested. The *bruk* communities and the model company towns have very likely been a source of inspiration for the Scandinavian welfare system that developed much later in this century. An abundance of existing company records (correspondence and collections of drawings and surveys) has, so far, been used only to a very limited extent. As a subject, the company town in Scandinavia deserves greater attention than it has received.

Notes

1. Quotation from a speech by the Swedish architect Helge Zimdal at the Nordic Architects' Conference at Kiruna in 1986. See Zimdal, *En arkitekt minns* (Göteborg: Chalmers University of Technology, 1981).

2. B. Ericsson, *Bergsstaden Falun, 1720–1769* (Uppsala: Department of History, Stockholm University, 1970), 29–35; O. Naucler, *Stora Kopparbergs gruva och kopparverk: Två akademiska avhandlingar vid Uppsala universitet år 1702 och 1703* (Uppsala: Department of History, Stockholm University, 1941), 12–53.

3. Linnés Dalaresa, *Iter Dalecarlium* (Uppsala: Hugo Gebers förlag, 1953); See also N. Sahlström, *Stadsplaner och stadsbild i Falun 1628–1850* (Falun: Stadsfullmäktige, 1961), 47.

4. E. Heckscher, *Svenskt arbete och liv* (1941; reprint, Stockholm: Aldus/Bonnier, 1965), 115, and A. Montgomery, *Industrialismens genombrott i Sverige* (1947; reprint, Stockholm: Almquist & Wiksell, 1966), 68–69; G. Selling, "Herrgårdarna och bebyg-

gelsen," *Forsmarks bruk—en uppländsk herrgårdsmiljö* (Stockholm: Forsmarks Kraftgrupp AB, 1984), 34–84; and M. Nisser, *Forsmark—ett av vallonbruken kring Dannemora gruvor: Forsmark och vallonjärnet* (Forsmark: Forsmark Kraftgrupp AB, 1987), 14–69. About Fiskars see G. Nikander, *Fiskars bruks historia* (Åbo: Fiskars AB, 1929). On Norwegian *bruk*, see, for instance, G. Thuesen, "Noen norske jernverker: Bevarte minner fra den gamle jernverkstiden," *Jernkontorets forskning*, serie H nr 15: Hyttrapport 3 (Stockholm: Jernkontoret, 1977).

5. Nisser, *Forsmark*, 14–69, B. Douhan and O. Hirn, *Smedernas Lövsta. Lövstabruk: En guide till herrgårdens och brukets historia* (Lövstabruk: Stiftelsen Leufsta, 1989), and O. Hirn, *Forsmark och Lövsta. Bebyggelsen i två kulturmiljöer: Kulturrådet* nr 5 (Stockholm: Sveriges Kulturråd, 1988), 23–35. On *Gimo bruk* see B. G. Söderberg, *Slott och herresäten i Sverige* (Uppland del I: Allhems förlag Malmö, 1967). See also "Grundritning öfwer Gimo Bruk med alla dess WÄRCK och ÅBYGNADER 1757. Archives of Korsnäs—Marma AB, Gävle.

6. B. Boëthius, *Robertsfors bruks historia* (Uppsala: Fritzes bokh, 1921). John Jennings (1729–1773) and Robert Finlay (1719–1785) were Irishmen. The 1799 map was made by A. M. Strinnholm, Robertsfors Bruk Archives.

7. J. Sestoft, *Arbejdets bygninger* (with captions in English). *Danmarks arkitektur* (Copenhagen: Nordisk Forlag A/S, 1979), 56, and *Historiske huse i Frederiksvaerk* (Copenhagen: Frederiksvaerkegnens Museum and Nationalmuseet, 1986).

8. F. Bedoire, ed., "Textilindustrins miljöer" (with an English summary, Environments of the textile industries: an introduction), *Bebyggelsehistorisk tidskrift* nr 15 (Stockholm: K. A. Lundkvist, 1988), 5–13). "Den malmcolmska verkstaden i Norrköping 1836–1868," in *Daedalus* (Stockholm: Sveriges Tekniska Museum, 1976), 33–55. For a comparison with Holyoke, see C. M. Green, *Holyoke, Massachusetts: A Case History of Industrial Revolution in America*, Yale Historical Publications, no. 34 (New Haven: Yale University Press, 1939).

9. E. Vikström, "Jonsered växer fram: Studier i Jonsereds bebyggelsehistoria" (unpublished seminar paper, Department of Art History, University of Umeå, 1978).

10. H. Wik, "Norra Sveriges sågverksindustri från 1800-talets mitt fram till 1937" (with captions in English and a summary). *Geographica* 21 (1950): 91–114, and Mats Ahnlund et al., *Äldre industrier och industriminnen vid Umeälvens nedre del* (with an English summary: Older industries and industrial monuments in the lower part of the Ume River valley), Norrländska städer och kulturmiljöer, no. 6 (Umeå: Department of Art History, 1980), 136–44.

11. Mats Ahnlund et al., *Äldre industrier och industriminnen vid Umeälvens nedre del*, 158–66.

12. F. Sejersted, *Veien mot øst: Vandringer, Festskrift til Ingrid Semmingsen* (Oslo: H. Aschehoug & Co., W. Nygaard, 1980). See also J. Björklund, "From the Gulf of Bothnia to the White Sea—Swedish Direct Investments in the Sawmill Industry of Tsarist Russia," *Scandinavian Economic History Review* 1 (1984): 17–41.

13. P. Seidegård, "AB Ekmans Snickerifabrik" (unpublished seminar paper, Department of Art History, University of Umeå, 1985). The export trade of this company was quite impressive, including sale of churches to settlers in California and delivery of a complete hospital to the sultan of Turkey. See also U. Linde, *Anteckningar om schweizerstilen* (Stockholm: AB Björkmans Eftr, 1959).

14. M. Ahnlund, "Norrbyskär—om tillkomsten av ett norrländskt sågverkssamhälle på 1890-talet" (with an English summary: Norrbyskär—the birth of a Swedish sawmill community in the 1890s), *Norrländska städer och kulturmiljöer*, no. 1 (Umeå: Department of Art, History, Umeå University, 1978), 180–83.

15. M. Ahnlund and L. Brunnström, "Bolagsbyggandet—ett försummat kapitel i arkitektur och stadsplanehistoria" (with a summary in German: Aktiengesellschaftliches Bauen—ein vernachlässigtes Kapitel der Architektur und Stadtplangeschichte)," *Taidehistoriallisa Tutkimuksia/Konsthistoriska Studier* 9 (Helsinki, 1986): 14–16.

16. H. Hultin, *Historik öfver Kotka stad* (Kotka: Kotka stads förlag, 1904), 230–53, and E. Bull, "Et norsk emigrantmiljøi Finland," *By og bygd* bind 14 (Oslo, 1960).

17. K. Mikkola, "Alvar Aalto som industrins arkitekt," *Arkitektur* 4 (1969): 14–17. Mikkola, however, tends to overemphasize Aalto's role as an innovative company architect. See also Karl Fleig, *Alvar Aalto* (1963; reprint, Zürich: Verlag für Architektur Artemis, 1965), 1: 86–95; P. Korvenmaa, "Arkitekten i industrialistens tjänst: Alvar Aaltos planer för Kauttua industrisamhälle (1938)," *Konsthistorisk tidskrift*, nr 3–4 (Stockholm, 1988), P. Korvenmaa, *Kauttua: Tuantanto ja ympäristö 1689–1989* [The shaping of an industrial community: the village of Kauttua 1689–1989] (Kauttua: Ahlström Oy, 1989).

18. L. Brunnström, "KIRUNA—ett samhällsbygge i sekelskiftets Sverige: Del I: En bebyggelsehistorisk studie av anläggningsskedet fram till 1910" (with an English summary: KIRUNA—a Swedish mining city from the turn of the century), *Norrländska städer och kulturmiljöer*, nr 3 (Umeå: DOKUMA, 1981). See also B. M. Andrén, *Konsten i Kiruna* (Umeå: Department of Art History, 1989), 62–71.

19. Brunnström, "KIRUNA," 192.

20. H. Thorelli, "Ett modernt industrisamhälle: Bolidens Gruvaktiebolags planering av bebyggelse och social organisation för Bolidens samhälle," *Affärsekonomi*, nr 15 (Stockholm, 1938), and D. Pettersson, "Boliden: Bebyggelsestudier sommaren, 1931," *Gothia* nr 1 (Göteborg, 1932), 39–69.

21. A. Hoel, *Svalbards historie 1596–1965, del II* (Oslo: Sverre Kildahl, 1966). See also H. Jakobsson and R. Kellerman, *Sveagruvan på Spetsbergen* (Stockholm: LT förlag, 1979).

22. All of Hökerberg's designs for Sveagruvan are kept in the archives of the Museum of Architecture in Stockholm.

23. E. Norlin, *Stenkol: Kort handbok om stenkol med särskild hänsyn till svensk upphandling och förbrukning* (Stockholm: Sveriges Industriförbund, 1927), 63–66.

24. Lisa Brunnström, "Ralph Erskine i Svappavaara—om en stadsplan, dess tillkomst och utförande på 1960-talet" (unpublished seminar paper, Department of Art History, University of Umeå, 1982).

25. Interview with the architect Klaus Johansen, Copenhagen, 12 Mar. 1990; letter of 16 Jan. 1990 to the authors from bjergvaerkschef (the manager) G. Lindgren, Maarmorilik. See also T. Lodberg, *Maarmorilik: Et halvt århundrede med bjergvaerksdrift i Grønland* (Copenhagen: Greenex A/S, 1990), 25–44.

26. S. Andersen, "En industriby blir till," *Byggekunst* 1 (1980): 26–38. See also Helge Dahl, *Rjukan*, bind 1: *Fram till 1920: Tinn kommune* (1981; reprint, 1988).

27. Meddelanden från Kungl, *Vattenfallsstyrelsen*, nr 15 (Stockholm: Vattenfall, 1917). See also Nils Forsgren, *Porjus Pionjärverket i ödemarken, Stockholm* (Stockholm: Arkivkommitté and Vattenfall, 1982) and H. U. Strand, "Vattenkraftsutbyggnaden i Lule älv" (with an English summary: The effect of the water power on the population in the interior parts of northern Sweden in the 20th century), *Daedalus* (Stockholm: Sveriges Tekniska Museum, 1984), 239–60; "Vår blivande nordligaste stad," *Göteborgs Handels och Sjöfarts Tidning*, Göteborg, 16 Feb. 1918.

28. Strand, "Vattenkraftsutbyggnaden," 239–60.

29. S. Montelius, "Brukshanteringens arbetarkategorier," *Fagerstabrukens historia*, del 5 (Uppsala: Almquist & Wiksell, 1959).

30. M. Ahnlund et al., "Äldre industrier och industriminnen vid Umeälvens nedre del,"

144–50; Lisa Brunnström, "Den rationella fabriken: Om funktionalismens rötter" (with an English summary: The rational factory: on the roots of modernist architecture) (Umeå: DOKUMA, 1990).

31. *Gunnar Asplund Arkitekt 1885–1940: Ritningar skisser och fotografier utgivna av Svenska Arkitekters Riksförbund* (Stockholm: Svenska Arkitekters Riksförbund, 1943), 234; E. Holmström and E. Orebäck Krantz, *Kulturhistoriskt värdefulla byggnader och miljöer i Tidaholms kommun, Tidaholm stad* (Tidaholm, 1989), 300, and J. Ahlin and Sigurd Lewerentz, *Architect* (Stockholm: Byggförlaget, 1987), 34–35.

II

COMPANY TOWNS IN
NORTH AND
SOUTH AMERICA

4

Early New England Mill Towns of the Piscataqua River Valley

RICHARD M. CANDEE

Certain generalizations continue to frame our understanding of the history, architecture, and planning of New England's textile industry. One of these key ideas was first articulated by James Montgomery, a Scottish technician who worked in New England mills during the 1830s. Montgomery differentiated between modestly capitalized factory communities centered in and around Rhode Island and larger textile manufacturing centers based on the technological organization of Waltham or Lowell to describe a landscape of northern New England corporation towns and southern New England mill villages. Just as mill owners in Rhode Island might turn to the newest mills in or around Providence to "copy their plans and style of machinery," Montgomery saw that the larger textile corporations in Maine, New Hampshire, and Massachusetts "follow the Lowell plans in the form and arrangement of the Mills, as well as the style of their machinery."[1]

The Rhode Island system relied on family labor (primarily of women and children) usually housed in modest one-, two-, or four-family tenements. These small rural factories usually were owned by a family or small unincorporated partnerships of merchants and mechanics. By 1820, a typical Rhode Island system factory might be of stone, brick, or wood—or some combination of two of these materials—and contain up to one thousand spindles. Many of these early textile mills throughout New England soon adopted technological improvements such as water-powered weaving, but generally they retained their small-scale operations and family labor system, as well as associated housing, farms, sawmill, and company store well into the middle of the nineteenth century (Fig. 4.1).[2]

Figure 4.1 View of Clayville, Rhode Island, showing the components of a small mill village about 1840, including an inn (far left), company store (center), one- and four-family company housing (right center), stone factory, and other industrial buildings (right). (Rhode Island Historical Society.)

Planned urban centers such as Lowell were controlled by a single corporation devoted to water-power development for large-scale cloth production by several independent companies. Lowell's power canals formed an industrial spine for the many textile corporations developed by the Boston Associates, those major investors who had previously developed the Boston Manufacturing Corporation in Waltham and others who later joined this select group. Although the term *Waltham system* is often used in acknowledgment of the place of origin for Lowell, Manchester, Lawrence, and other cities formed in this fashion, it may be more correct to create separate designations for Waltham and Lowell as industrial models in the New England region.

At Lowell, the mills were as uniform as the Rhode Island system factories were varied: brick five-stories over a granite foundation, they all had central stair towers on the long facade and privy towers on the rear wall above the tailrace (Fig. 4.2). The preferred roof type throughout the 1820s and 1830s was invariably the monitor, described by James Montgomery as the New England "double roof." The first factory in a mill complex featured a cupola or bell cote centered on the roof ridge. By 1840, however, Montgomery noted that several of Lowell's most recent mills

Figure 4.2 Middlesex Mills, Lowell, Massachusetts, ca. 1840. The brick woolen mill (left), with traditional monitor or "double" roof and projecting front entrance and stair tower, illustrate the standard Lowell mill of the 1820s and 1830s. The new factory (right) illustrates the plain, pitched roof and dormers adopted at Lowell in the late 1830s. (Museum of American Textile History.)

had returned to a plain pitched roof—"though the double roof has been the plan generally adopted so far, it is likely to be abandoned"—not only in Lowell but throughout its corporate hinterland. In this as in other observations, Montgomery proved to be correct.[3]

There are, however, a number of problems associated with looking at the architecture of New England's earliest textile industry communities exclusively through the success of Waltham and Lowell. First, there is a tendency to see the whole Rhode Island factory system as somehow being replaced or superseded by the corporate mills of the Lowell system. In reality, the Rhode Island system factory community continued to exist as a distinct type. The companies that survived into the late nineteenth century had to expand to meet new demands for economics of scale; several even emerged at the end of the century as the kind of model company town described by John Garner.[4] Second, the geographic distinction drawn by Montgomery's two regional "manufacturing districts" is often taken too literally. Many assume that all northern New England mill towns were of the corporate type and all southern New England factories were not. In reality, the Rhode Island system was ubiquitous throughout the region and many smaller companies continued to operate in northern New England throughout the century. Too many scholars, on the other hand, perceive that all northern New England textile corporations and the communities they created have been broadly subsumed under the more extensive analysis given to the Lowell factories, their boardinghouses, and the city plan.

What has been altogether ignored is the process of vernacular architectural design, mill engineering, and community planning that emerged during the boom of the 1820s' industrial expansion. For many industrial communities in New England this was the key decade for sorting out certain industrial design ideas and establishing their underlying town plan. However, because of the steadily shrinking number of surviving structures from this period and lack of detailed documentary case studies, there is a widespread assumption that all northern corporation towns developed on broadly similar lines. In fact, many little-known mill towns that evolved simultaneously with Lowell were financial or architectural "dead ends." The later acquisition and management of these dead-end mill towns by Boston Associate investors has sometimes led historians to characterize them as merely less-perfect examples of the Lowell corporate model. In fact, while Lowell was building a city of many interlocking corporations, others in many parts of New England opted to model their industrial community on Waltham, the Boston Manufacturing Company's successful single-enterprise town.

In an effort to set the record straight, this study examines the earliest decades of four small mill towns along tributaries of the Piscataqua River, which divides southern New Hampshire from coastal and southwestern Maine. Located in the economic hinterland of Portsmouth, New Hampshire, a colonial seaport whose early-nineteenth-century merchants furnished much of the original capital in an effort to diversify their investments, each factory center was established in the early 1820s, simultaneously with the development of Lowell but before that new industrial city could exert a strong architectural influence. Although all but one of these four corporations failed and was eventually taken over by Boston investors in ensuing decades, the variety of architectural forms created to support their industrial organization reflects both the preexisting model of Waltham's Boston Manufacturing Company and a vernacular building tradition already well established along the Piscataqua.[5]

The 1820s Mill Towns of the Piscataqua Region

The textile industry in the larger Piscataqua River Valley began with the formation of the 1812 Dover Cotton Factory, located on a small water-power site several miles above the center of the older community. Like many cotton spinning mills in the years following the embargo and war of 1812, it was a partnership of local investors from Dover and Portsmouth, New Hampshire. The cost of building their small timber-framed factory frightened the owners, and they leased it in 1815 to Isaac Wendell and his partner John Williams, successful local merchants who remained in the textile industry through much of this period. Of these two men, however, Isaac Wendell, a Quaker entrepreneur, was more significant to the industrial design and planning of Dover and Great Falls (later Somersworth) during their formative decade.

Isaac, Jacob, and Abraham Wendell were sons of a successful eighteenth century Harvard-educated Portsmouth lawyer. Isaac traveled up the Piscataqua River to Dover about 1806, and three years later he married Ann Whittier, second cousin to the Quaker poet John Greenleaf Whittier. Admitted to the Quaker Meeting in Dover nearly a year before his marriage, Isaac Wendell remained a Friend until the financial failure of his industrial empire led to his dismissal in 1829. Although he relied heavily on his brothers' wealth to underwrite a substantial part of his industrial dreams, forcing them into bankruptcy in the 1840s, Isaac Wendell's Quaker connections are a minor theme in the earliest development of several Piscataqua mill towns and suggest a link with the textile industries of both Rhode Island and Philadelphia. This is reinforced by Wendell's relocation (by way of Providence) after 1829 to "La Grange," then outside the center of Philadelphia; he died in Bustleton, Pennsylvania, in 1857.[6] In addition to the Dover and Great Falls cotton and woolen factories, Isaac Wendell was involved in several other Dover industries, including a cut nail manufactory begun by others in 1812 and incorporated in 1817 with Wendell and his partner John Williams among the local investors. About 1823 he also established an iron foundry on the nearby Bellamy River to cast the machinery for his textile factories in Dover and Great Falls.[7]

Dover Cotton Factory/Cocheco Manufacturing Company, Dover, New Hampshire

In 1810, Dover Landing, located at the head of navigation below the lowest falls of the Cocheco River, was the shipbuilding and commercial center of a town whose population totaled 2,271. From this "compact part of town," a turnpike connected the river port with Somersworth, New Hampshire, and Berwick, Maine.[8] Wendell and Williams's first cotton-spinning factory was located two miles upriver because a preexisting anchor manufactory and the new nail factory already occupied the Cocheco Falls location. With the purchase of the nail works and construction of new textile mills for the Dover Cotton Factory and its successor firms during the 1820s, industrial development along the falls above Dover Landing consolidated the community center around the mills. Here a grid of streets laid over old farms above the falls connected with preexisting portions of the older town (Fig. 4.3). Before the textile factories the town boasted a Congregational church and a Quaker meetinghouse, a courthouse and jail, a printing office, and a bank serving a fairly scattered farming and maritime population. In 1832, the mills, now reorganized as the Cocheco Manufacturing Corporation and capitalized at $1.6 million, employed more than 1,000 workers, of whom 750 were women. By 1850 Dover's population had nearly quadrupled to 8,186, of whom 500 men and 1,000 women were employees of the Cocheco corporation. Five years later, when the long-settled town was granted a city charter, there were nine different religious societies, a new bleachery across from the earlier factories, and dozens of shops, stores, and offices in the town as well as several secondary textile and paper industries on the Bellamy River, a mile away.[9]

Dover was the first of several northern New England industrial towns organized in the 1820s around the economic success of a single major textile corporation. In looking back on his ill-fated career in textile manufacturing, Isaac Wendell later

Figure 4.3 Detail, map of Dover village, New Hampshire, 1834, G. L. Whitehouse, surveyor, showing the factory quadrangle at Cocheco Falls Company, with the boardinghouses (right and upper center) surrounding the mills and commercial blocks directly opposite the factories. (Photograph courtesy Robert Whitehouse.)

noted "a Company was formed" at Dover, "mostly of Boston gentlemen and then the cotton Mills followed next. As from [the] Waltham Co. originated Lowell (then Chelmsford), Nashua, Manchester, Lawrence, Newburyport, Amesbury, &c., so from Dover may be dated the origin of Great Falls, New Market, Exeter, Salmon Falls," New Hampshire, as well as similar one-company towns in Berwick and Saco, Maine. The key difference between these two groups of textile communities is the distinction between Lowell, with its multiple corporations, and the single-enterprise towns that tried to recreate—along the tributaries of the Piscataqua—the early success of the Boston Manufacturing Company at Waltham.[10]

Great Falls Manufacturing Company, Somersworth, New Hampshire

In 1823, Wendell acquired sufficient lands at Great Falls on the Salmon Falls River for a new textile corporation, early capitalized at $1 million from local and Boston stockholders, to build his own industrial company town a few miles from Dover. A quarter-mile-long power canal laid out parallel to the river encouraged linear development of later factories. A new Main Street, soon paralleled by the railroad running beside the canal, separated the industrial complex from the boardinghouses, hotel, and shops. A small commercial node quickly emerged at the northern end of Great Falls Village to serve the influx of workers, while prominent lots along High Street were provided to several religious societies for the construction of three Protestant churches. The steep hill above this public and commercial core was crowned in the early 1850s with the first townwide high school in New Hampshire; the surrounding land soon developed into private homes for a growing middle class (Fig. 4.4).[11]

The first phase of company-built housing at Great Falls, like that in Dover, was largely destroyed by later industrial expansion. However, one row of houses for management, including Isaac Wendell's own residence, survives amid the earliest commercial complex of Great Falls. After Wendell lost control of this second industrial development to Boston investors during the panic of 1827, Great Falls agents lived among streets of corporate boardinghouses in a handsome stone house on a knoll that overlooked a small park facing the second and third mills. When these factories were completed, about 1826, they supported a new community of 1,500 people, 1,000 of whom were employed by the Great Falls Manufacturing Corporation. By 1832, after reorganization, the corporation employed 332 men and 1,050 women manufacturing not only cotton cloth but also woolen broadcloth and carpets. By midcentury there were six huge brick mills, containing 65,000 spindles and 1,680 looms. The corporation's work force, then 1,500 women and 200 men, represented almost a third of the town's population of 5,000.

Newmarket Manufacturing Company, Newmarket, New Hampshire

The Newmarket Manufacturing Company was built for Salem, Massachusetts, investors whose heirs continued to own the firm well into the twentieth century. Its original prime mover was Wendell's former Quaker mill agent at the 1815 Dover Cotton Factory, Stephen Hanson. As Newmarket's first factory agent, Hanson su-

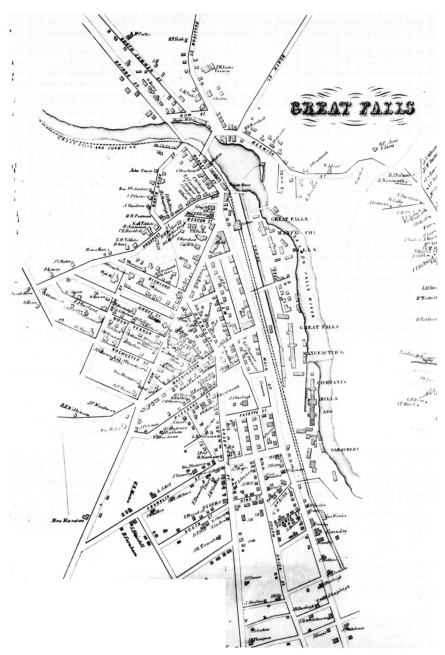

Figure 4.4 Plan of Great Falls, New Hampshire, H. F. Walling, surveyor, 1851, showing the commercial and public buildings along Bridge and High streets, the linear development of the factories, and associated boardinghouses on either side of Main Street. (Old Sturbridge Village.)

pervised the building of a cotton factory there in 1823. After leaving Newmarket, he subsequently did the same for the nearby Exeter Cotton Manufacturing Company. The small textile manufacturing village of Newmarket is located at a falls just above the mouth of the Lamprey River near its junction with the Piscataqua's bays. The company's handsome granite mills, sited just below the falls, are separated from their early company-built housing by Main Street, which parallels the mills and crosses the river between the mill agent's large brick house and the company's machine shop. While the factories and corporate boardinghouses, carefully delineated on a map of 1832 (Fig. 4.5), occupied the northern end of the village, a steep rocky ledge encouraged a linear development of the community to the south. Public buildings and private business blocks lined Main Street, while residential development quickly climbed the hillside once a stone church and school were erected on its crest. Capitalized at $600,000, in 1832 Newmarket's three mills contained only eighteen thousand spindles and employed 59 men and 613 women. Restrained by a relatively small site and limited water power, Newmarket was similar in scale to many southern New England mill villages. Yet its corporate organization, predominantly mill-girl labor force, and building forms were directly or indirectly derived from Waltham.[12]

Salmon Falls Manufacturing Company, Rollinsford, New Hampshire

The last of the four textile communities examined is Salmon Falls (Fig. 4.6), located below Great Falls in what was originally part of Dover. This small mill village was actually built for a woolen factory established in 1822 by nearby Portsmouth investors led by James Rundlett. Like most rural woolen factories in New England, it continued to follow the older model of the Rhode Island system in using "family" labor housed in two-family tenements. However, after an 1834 fire destroyed the first factory, the company and its new mill were taken over in the 1840s by the Boston commission house of Mason and Lawrence. Under the treasurer Amos A. Lawrence the village was redeveloped as a small rural version of the corporation community. Salmon Falls village was soon enlarged by a second factory and a small grid of streets for three-story brick boardinghouses and two-story brick double houses to house the families of overseers. Culminating this new growth, the village was set off from Dover in 1849 and renamed Rollinsford, New Hampshire. A true company town with very few privately owned buildings in the village, the corporation responded to another fire in 1864 by building not only a new mill but also a brick agent's house, a brick and granite commercial block, and a brick firehouse opposite the new mills.[13]

To demonstrate the evolution and the influences of industrial design ideas within and between these four corporate communities, as well as their Waltham and Lowell counterparts, we must focus on three features: Waltham-style mills and alternative factory designs, workers' housing and the development of the New England mill-girl boardinghouse, and community planning for specialized structures not directly related to the factory and its employees. All of the Piscataqua factory towns borrowed architectural ideas from recent vernacular building in nearby Portsmouth,

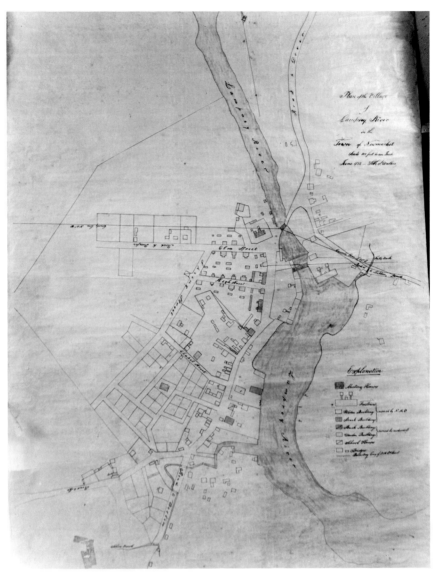

Figure 4.5 Detail, plan of the village of Lamprey River in the town of Newmarket, New Hampshire, Beth Walker, surveyor, 1832. Mills numbers 1 and 2 (left center) and Mill Number 3 (right center) occupy sites along the Lamprey River. Wooden boardinghouses line Elm and High streets; two brick rows of boardinghouses face the mills across Main Street. (Newmarket Historical Society, photograph courtesy Old Sturbridge Village.)

from new commercial architecture and engineering around Boston, and from Waltham's industrial designs. There is 'no evidence that they borrowed either industrial or residential designs from the simultaneous developments at Lowell during the 1820s. Quickly integrated into the larger network of Boston-owned factory towns, however, these new company towns provided key Boston investors and corporate managers with a laboratory in which to experiment with alternative building forms for larger industrial cities.

Factory Design

Each of the mills at Lowell's core (Fig. 4.3), like each of the 1820s factories in the Piscataqua's industrial development, benefited from earlier experiments at Waltham, Massachusetts. Beginning with their first mill in 1814 and a second built between 1816 and 1819, Boston Manufacturing Corporation managers established a specific factory type by combining several existing vernacular mill-building prac-

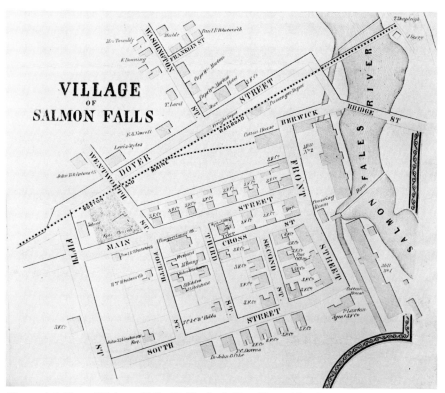

Figure 4.6 Plan of Salmon Falls, Rollinsford, New Hampshire, H. F. Walling surveyor, 1851, showing the mills with wooden family housing (1820s) along Main Street, brick boardinghouses on Second Street (1846), and family houses for management along South Street. (Old Sturbridge Village.)

tices in new ways (Fig. 4.7). They adopted brick rather than stone (preferred in Rhode Island and initially considered for Waltham), used the "double" or monitor roof form with a cupola in the middle of a slate roof, and soon added an exterior stair tower as had been done in some earlier mills.[14]

Waltham's engineers fixed on a systematic complex of machines to transform the raw cotton to woven cloth that required a considerable amount of water power to run its 3,584 spindles. This building type and its particular combination of machinery were then established as the basic "mill power" used to plan the division of water power for Lowell factory sites in 1824. In doing so, they froze the size (roughly 45 × 150 feet) and architectural form of Lowell's factory buildings for nearly twenty years to equalize the distribution of water power along the canal system. The fact that in Lowell a central holding company constructed all the buildings and machinery, as well as leased all the water power to each of the corporations, undoubtedly contributed to this uniformity over the first two decades of the city's development.

In 1819, as these mill operators sought to adopt new water-powered weaving technology, John Williams moved to Boston, where he opened a store and began to court those Boston investors whose Waltham factory had already begun to transform the industry. Meanwhile the Dover factory charter was amended to increase its

Figure 4.7 Detail, painting of Boston Manufacturing Company, Waltham, Massachusetts, attributed to Elijah Smith, Jr., ca. 1830, showing the machine shop and first mill (left), second factory (center) from the rear facing mill yard, and company housing for families of management and machine shop workers. (Photograph by Henry E. Peach. Private collection, Old Sturbridge Village.)

shares, permitting it to acquire a new power site at the lower falls of the Cocheco River and farms above the shops and wharves of the town's river landing. In 1821 Wendell and Williams hired another New Hampshire native, the lawyer Daniel Webster, to negotiate for the patent rights to copy Waltham's technology. Williams then induced "his friends in Massachusetts to subscribe liberally" to plans for corporate expansion in Dover.[15] Thus, just as the Boston Associates codified their factory design and in the very year they began to buy land and water power at Chelmsford, Massachusetts, property that would become Lowell, Wendell and Williams acquired the Waltham manufacturing system and began building their Dover Cotton Factory's Mill Number 2 (the old wooden factory upriver still being designated Mill Number 1) with John Williams acting as corporate agent.

Like its Waltham prototype, the Dover mill was 155×43 feet with three brick stories over a granite foundation, an exterior stair tower, and a monitor or "double" roof with a central cupola. In 1822 a second factory was begun with one more story just like Waltham's second factory. These mills, renamed the Dover Manufacturing Company, had immediate impact on several nearby communities as the Piscataqua's tributaries were harnessed to textile production.

In 1821 Isaac Wendell acquired his second mill site at Great Falls and erected a wooden cotton factory and machine shop, renovated a farmhouse for boarding, and established a store. There in 1823, with funding from Portsmouth and Boston investors, Wendell was installed as agent to build a brick "Cotton Factory of the same dimensions and on the same model of the Dover Cotton Factory No. 2."[16] This new mill was constructed at the upper end of a quarter-mile power canal in 1824–1825. It was four stories, 45×156 feet, with a monitor roof like its prototypes. Also in 1823 Salem investors, employing the Quaker agent Stephen Hanson (formerly Wendell's agent at the first Dover mill), began building their granite Mill Number 1 for the Newmarket Manufacturing Company. Despite its ashlar walls, this mill replicated the same industrial form in its cupola placement, roof type, and central stair tower on the long wall (Fig. 4.8). In fact, after Hanson left Newmarket for a similar position in Exeter about 1827, the brick factory he supervised for the newly incorporated Exeter Manufacturing Company was apparently of the same design.

Thus, from the inception of the Waltham factory type in coastal New Hampshire, we can see the impact of Dover as a local model and an occasional tendency among these earliest designers to alter the size or materials of the factory from its Waltham original. Such variation continued to characterize later industrial building here and in other non–Boston Associate single-company towns and stands in direct contrast to the near-uniform corporate building in Lowell.

The original contract with Waltham specifically prevented the Dover Factory Company from making printed calicoes for five years, something the Boston Associates already planned for their Merrimack Mills in Lowell. Thus in 1825, John Williams began an enormous new factory unlike anything yet seen in New England's industrial landscape. It was an L-shaped factory that extended 167 feet along the river and 245 feet along Dover's Washington Street (Fig. 4.9). This "huge works" was larger than any other New England textile mill and, together with the

Figure 4.8 Newmarket Manufacturing Company granite 1823 Mills. Mill No. 1 (left) has a clerestory roof form and central cupola. In the foreground is Mill No. 2 (1825) with skylights. (Photographed ca. 1850. Newmarket Historical Society.)

earlier Dover factories, formed a manufacturing quadrangle on the scale of those English factories that Dover's corporate spies visited while trying to obtain the new printing technology.[17] Work on this mill and print works began in April, and by September 1825 the walls were up to the fifth floor when Williams asked the Boston treasurer to send "a plan of the coving" or cornices used on Quincy Market's flanking row of stores. He thought he recalled the cornices of those Boston commercial blocks as being "built up with solid brick work and covered with wood wholly detached . . . so that should the wood burn off" it would not spread directly to the roof. Should this not be the case, Williams asked the treasurer to "please get Capt. Parris and Mr. Willard to give a draft of one which would suit our great factory. Let him know it will be seven stories high, 420 feet long on [the] outside."[18] Whether the well-known architects Alexander Parris or Solomon Willard *were* actually asked to provide a brick cornice design is unknown, but it is typical of such vernacular mill engineering that only for certain details was an architect even considered and only after the work was well advanced.

Perhaps the vast size of Dover's 1825 factory explains the urge among other one-corporation towns as far away as Saco, Maine, and Ware, Massachusetts, to build much larger mills than those in Waltham or Lowell. This was especially true of the factories that Isaac Wendell promoted along the Piscataqua, and it undoubtedly contributed to his financial failure. For example, by 1826 Great Falls had added two new huge factories, one 250 feet long, the other 390 feet long (Fig. 4.10). The one true design innovation of the 1825 Dover print works was the plain pitched roof with skylights to light the attic work space. Williams had originally planned to "raise a false [roof] . . . of sufficient height to put in one tier of square glass all along the roof." This Rhode Island roof type, often called the "trap door monitor roof," was already in local use for the Dover machine shop. Such a roof form, however, was rejected in favor of "windows flat on the roof like the Ship House at Charlestown," the naval shipyard across the river from Boston.[19] Like Waltham-type mills built in surrounding mill towns by following the first Dover models, the skylighted roof of Dover's print works also had immediate impact. In Newmarket, for example, the second granite factory begun in 1825 (Fig. 4.8) seems to have adopted this form (it later had a fire and was reroofed), as did the 1827–1829 Mill Number 3.

Inside, nearly all these factories appear to have employed the standard wooden floor framing that characterized the early New England textile mill until the late 1820s. This framing employed both large cross beams and smaller supporting floor joists that carried two layers of one-inch pine flooring. Newmarket Mill Number 3 was the earliest surviving Piscataqua factory to evidence the sudden and geographically diffuse introduction of so-called slow-burning construction. As I have tried to demonstrate elsewhere, the use of three- or four-inch plank floors on large beams without floor joists, which characterizes this new framing method, appeared almost simultaneously in southern and northern New England after 1826.[20]

Unfortunately, both the giant Dover print works and largest Great Falls factories came into production just as the financial panic of 1827 swept the country. Isaac Wendell was forced out and management of both corporations was taken over by Boston stockholders who restructured them to operate as Boston Associate corporations without the influence of local shareholders. Further capital investment in the 1840s, as railroads linked industrial satellites of Boston's financial empire, expanded the Great Falls Corporation under the direction of Patrick Tracy Jackson. In Dover the new Cocheco Manufacturing Corporation built a bleachery along the river across Washington Street from the print works. It may be that running the large

Figure 4.9 Lower bridge and factories, Dover, New Hampshire, ca. 1830, [Thomas Edward, Senefelder Lithograph Co., Boston.] showing the new printworks with skylights (center) and houses and commercial blocks opposite. (Museum of American Textile History).

Figure 4.10 Mill view at Great Falls, New Hampshire, about 1845. The first mill (center, with cupola) and later additions, office, and later factories. The artist has eliminated the power canal and railroad track to suggest a closer relationship of the mills to Main Street. (Old Sturbridge Village.)

mills of Dover and Great Falls for nearly a dozen years before the enlargement of Lowell's oldest factories began in the later 1840s gave the Boston Associates' corporate management direct experience in the benefits of substantially larger manufacturing facilities.

During the next quarter-century, however, the direction of architectural influence was clearly reversed. When Cocheco rebuilt the roof of the Dover print works, it replaced the skylights with dormers like those that had become popular in new Lowell factories in the 1840s (Fig. 4.2). Similarly, the new factories built in Salmon Falls were refitted with new machinery based on that of the Amoskeag, Nashua, and Lowell companies, and "Mr. Lawton of Lowell —the head machinist of the Massachusetts Co." was hired as their agent. Their new 1848 factory was 360 × 60 feet, with a projecting center pavilion and flat brick pilasters like those of Lowell-system factories throughout midnineteenth-century northern New England. Finally, when the Exeter Manufacturing Company enlarged its old 1820s Waltham-type mill sometime before the 1870s, it also adopted the center gabled pavilion convention originally used in Lowell to join two such mills into one during the late 1840s and early 1850s.[21]

Corporate Boardinghouses

In discussing designs for mill girl boardinghouses, it is important to emphasize that while Waltham created the New England mill-girl by abandoning child labor and paying cash wages to its workers (rather than credit in the company store), it did *not* originally build corporate boardinghouses for its single female workers. Rather, as I have demonstrated elsewhere, before the 1820s the Boston Manufacturing Company built only single- and double-family houses for its factory supervisors and machine workers and left mill-girl housing to the private local market (Fig. 4.7). Lowell's initial reliance on Waltham's housing practices is demonstrated by the similar wooden houses built before 1825 for Lowell machine shop workers and their families. Lowell's first mill-girl boardinghouses, a mixture of small wooden and brick duplexes along Dutton Street, were built for Merrimack Manufacturing Company workers.[22]

Single and double wooden boardinghouses were also built for the new Dover factories by 1824. Now that they are long destroyed, it is hard to tell how similar they were to those built between 1825 and 1829, when a new grid of streets was laid out by the corporation's civil engineer in a second phase of industrial growth. If the first wooden boardinghouses were like one surviving example built about 1826, they simply adopted certain vernacular single-family house forms found throughout the region to double houses that could be rented to boardinghouse keepers. Although Lowell's experiment with wooden boardinghouses was cut short by adoption of brick rows, the practice was both widespread and long-lived in southern New Hampshire. A number of wooden single and double houses had been built at Great Falls by 1826 for supervisory personnel, and several rows of double wooden boardinghouses like some in Dover were added for the two 1826 factories (Fig. 4.11).

Figure 4.11 Great Falls Corporation wooden boardinghouses, Broad Street, Somersworth, New Hampshire, ca. 1826–30. (Photographed by John Coolidge, late 1930s.)

Many survive today, somewhat altered after being sold by the company, and provide ample evidence of the widespread use of wooden boardinghouses in single-enterprise mill towns for a century after Lowell's brief experiment with this type.

The first brick boardinghouses in Lowell were also built on Dutton Street for the Merrimack mills. They were only two stories high, however, and seem to have been brick variants of their wooden contemporaries. In the mid-1820s Lowell resolved the problem of urban housing for literally thousands of unmarried mill girls in favor of fairly uniform rows of three-story brick boardinghouses. As Lowell factories expanded in both number and size after the 1840s, even larger brick boardinghouse rows were constructed and became the model for later factory housing in Salem, Massachusetts, and Lewiston, Maine.

Great Falls also had brick boardinghouses, perhaps like the earliest type found at Lowell, described by Isaac Wendell's son as "a row of two-storied brick houses built in 1824."[23] Moreover, the Great Falls Corporation may have built the first rows of *three*-story, multiunit brick boardinghouses of the type that soon dominated the corporation cities of Lowell and its successors (Fig. 4.12). James Montgomery later described them as "neat brick buildings, three stories in height, and each building contains four tenements; there are seven of these boardinghouses, set at equal distances from each other."[24] Whereas the original Great Falls management might have been influenced by Lowell's earlier and tentative use of brick for boarding-houses, Isaac Wendell was intimately familiar with similar three-story brick houses and commercial blocks with identical round-arched fan-lit doorways, which were still being erected in nearby Portsmouth after its devastating 1813 fire. The rows of three-story brick boardinghouses opposite the first Great Falls factories and adjoining the commercial center were standing by 1826.[25]

In Newmarket, the first corporate houses were wooden boardinghouses, now largely destroyed (Fig. 4.13). Exactly how they differed from those in Dover is impossible to tell, although the agent Stephen Hanson is widely quoted in mill-girl depositions occasioned by his attempts to lure female workers away from Dover. In 1825 Mary Firnald recalled Hanson had "stated that we should be so well satisfied at New Market that we should never want to come back to Dover[,] that he was going to have some nice women from Newbury Port and Salem to keep the Boarding Houses, who knew how to cook and treat Company."[26] Mary and her sister, Deborah Firnald, testified that Hanson implied they would lose their reputations if they stayed in Dover boardinghouses by saying "all kinds of characters were employed in the Factory and all kinds of practices carried out at the Boarding House." It appears that Dover did not initially demand gender segregation in their boarding houses, although later rules suggest this soon became common practice.[27]

Within a very few years, however, Newmarket also experimented with two brick

Figure 4.12 Great Falls Corporation brick boardinghouse rows, Main Street, Somersworth, New Hampshire, ca. 1826 (now destroyed). (Photographed by John Coolidge, late 1930s. Museum of American Textile History.)

Figure 4.13 Newmarket agent's house (center right) and corporation boardinghouses on Elm Street (left), built in the 1820s. (Photograph, ca. 1890. Newmarket Historical Society.)

three-story blocks opposite its 1825 Mill Number 2 set among the wooden boarding-houses already erected. Long destroyed by later industrial growth, these brick boardinghouses appear on an 1832 map and later maps of the new industrial community (Fig. 4.6).

To take the evolution of brick boardinghouse forms to its local culmination, we also need to look at the changes in housing at Salmon Falls. This village, originally built for an 1822 family-labor woolen mill that burned in 1834, is noteworthy for its surviving 1820s housing as well as the changes made when in 1844 it was sold to Amos A. Lawrence's commission firm. Within three months of his acquiring the company, Lawrence's diary notes that work had begun on "putting the houses in order."[28] Perhaps as late as 1846, according to local historians, brick boarding-houses and double houses for factory overseers were added along a new grid of streets that expanded the village (Fig. 4.14). Built in 1846, they were contemporaneous with similar boardinghouses erected for the first textile factories in Lawrence, Massachusetts, the Atlantic Cotton Mills, and the Bay State Mills, both 1846–1847, the latter of which was published in 1850 as a model of workers' housing (Figs. 4.15 and 4.16).[29] Thus, in expanding the sleepy mill village, the brick housing shared the progressive form of the emerging industrial city of Lawrence and, even earlier, may be seen as an experiment in boardinghouse design.

An 1854 memorandum to the directors of the Salmon Falls Company noted that

Figure 4.14 Salmon Falls Corporation boardinghouse, Second Street, built 1846. (Old Sturbridge Village.)

the "difficulty of keeping Irish and Americans together in an isolated village like ours appears to be much greater. . . . Every care must be taken to keep them in separate boardinghouses. . . . The large boardinghouse lately purchased . . . is some distance from the others and will be occupied by the Irish."[30] The social and economic changes that followed the introduction of Irish and later workers of other ethnic groups to the textile industry labor pool eventually led corporations to transfer their own responsibility for building new worker housing to private speculators. That ended the textile corporation's contribution to new urban housing forms. In rural mill towns, however, housing built for the first generation of native mill girls continued to be remodeled and used as family tenements for successive waves of workers through the depression of the 1930s and decline of the textile industry in New England.

Corporate Planning for Nonindustrial Buildings

The 1854 Salmon Falls memorandum was written to promote a number of changes to make that community "a desirable place of residence for operatives." Describing the village as "one of the best built," it noted that it lacked a number of "attractions which are most appreciated by a large class of the girls now employed in factory labor. . . . As long as the supply of hands is drawn from the country

Figure 4.15 Elevation of boardinghouse belonging to the Bay State Mills in Lawrence, Massachusetts. (Redrawn from the *Report of the Massachusetts Sanitary Survey Commission* [Boston, 1850] by Bryan Fish, 1991.)

towns . . . respectable females preferred to work in factories not far from their own homes and in many cases a preference was shown for Salmon Falls (especially by the parents) over the large towns . . . and very much over Lowell."[31] To understand the perceived needs of smaller mill villages like Salmon Falls or Newmarket, a description of the amenities offered by larger mill towns is required. In Dover, the corporation actually built its own commercial blocks, including a bank in the corner of its mill quadrangle and rows of brick stores across from the mills. Most Boston Associate textile corporations generally avoided competing with private real estate development except to sell building sites to direct private development of specific commercial locations. In all cases, however, the ability to bank or spend the cash wages of a largely female work force encouraged a certain level of commercial building that contributed to urban growth. Real estate development of commercial blocks in addition to factories and housing undoubtedly overextended the Dover company and must have been one of the reasons that Boston Associates acquired the company's physical assets during the recession of 1827. Indeed, when the corpora-

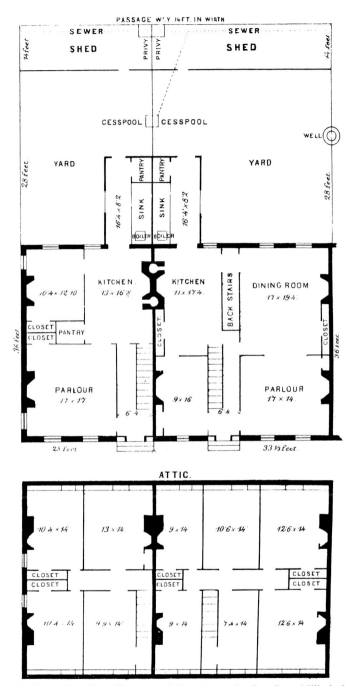

Figure 4.16 "Plans of the Boardinghouses belonging to the Bay State Mills in Lawrence," from the *Report of the Massachusetts Sanitary Survey Commission* (Boston, 1850). (Old Sturbridge Village.)

tions were asked to respond to a federal questionnaire, New Hampshire's census taker specifically noted that since the value of such buildings represented a major investment, "[i]n the returns from all the large establishments, . . . the dwelling-houses, stores, and shops belonging to them, and which afford a profitable income to the manufacturing companies, are included in the amount of capital invested in ground, buildings, waterpower, and machinery."[32]

At Great Falls the company also erected a few of the earliest commercial buildings but generally tried to profit from the sale of such real estate to private businessmen. The small block of stores later erected at Salmon Falls was another example of direct corporate investment in commercial real estate. However, because of its somewhat isolated location and the corporation's total control of property within the village, it was required to build and rent stores where such demands for commercial development could not be met by the private market as in other mill towns.

Corporations, as already noted, also provided building sites to religious organizations in these new towns. At Great Falls the Congregational Society asked the architect (and Nashua mill agent) Asher Benjamin for a church design, although it is unclear whether or not the Greek Revival church actually constructed was based on his response. At Newmarket, the first school and church—both of rubble masonry like the company's later mills—were placed atop "Zion's Hill," a seemingly symbolic site above the company town like that in so many other small New England villages. Churches were probably offered such hilltop sites when they existed, because the land had no industrial, commercial, or corporate housing value.

Education was nearly as important as religion in many mill towns. Just as Salmon Falls instituted night classes for its operatives, special legislation permitted Great Falls to create the first public high school in the state. Bringing together students from all its smaller school districts, the town built a large brick building atop the hill above the town. Within a few years, Newmarket followed suit with a similar public high school. Like many other Waltham and Lowell textile corporations, the Great Falls company also supported a Manufacturers' and Village Library as early as 1842. The library was housed for many years in the corporation's counting house located in front of the factories. As corporate support given the literary efforts of Lowell's mill girls mixed moral control with positive public relations for mill life, the Great Falls mill agent acted as the organization's librarian.[33] Some three decades later, the former Newmarket mill agent and later corporation treasurer John Webster gave his own funds to build a library for both town residents and mill operatives. Opened in 1885, the new brick library building was sited directly opposite the agent's house among the corporation's boarding-houses. This act of personal philanthropy, more commonly associated with family-owned model company towns of the late nineteenth century, suggests that life in these smaller textile corporation towns might have compared favorably with the attractions of larger urban centers even later in the century.

The study of industrial archeology in America is new and has heretofore concentrated almost exclusively on the engineering of factories, dams, bridges, railroads, and the like. As a number of younger social historians are now discovering, this is only part of the story. As John Coolidge recognized at Lowell a half-century ago, housing and corporate planning for commercial and public buildings were also significant elements of industrial development in the early textile industry.

These four case studies attempt to show that building forms established during the first blush of industrialization had a lasting impact on their company towns and may have contributed to the development of urban forms in larger industrial cities. The buildings of southern New Hampshire's early-nineteenth-century industrial communities illustrate important patterns of design. Those towns founded under the Waltham mill-girl corporate system often attempted to build much larger factories than the Boston Associates built in Lowell. Their builders also continued local vernacular domestic forms in wooden and brick housing; constructed their own commercial buildings, which were based on forms developed earlier in Portsmouth and in Boston; and sought to keep financial control of their communities in local hands. That local investors failed to maintain their leading position during economic recessions or after destructive fires should not obscure the fact that their vision of the New England textile mill town was often quite different from that of those who founded Waltham and Lowell or, later, Manchester and Lawrence. Despite new owners, later fires, rebuilding, and relocation, the basic community plan they established has remained an essential part of each community to this day.

Rather than a setting for multiple corporations fed by a common power source or designed and built by a single holding company prone to repetitive architectural solutions, the southern New Hampshire company town was an independent solution to many conflicting demands. The Waltham model of an industrial community developed around a single large textile corporation provided one set of architectural prototypes. But with different owners and builders came minor, and sometimes not so minor, variations on the themes of factory, boardinghouse, and community buildings. That the builders of one town copied the recent products of its neighbor is not unusual. In the textile towns of the Piscataqua, however, this process contributed to a regional architectural vocabulary as distinct and recognizable as that of either the Rhode Island or the Lowell factory system.

Notes

1. James Montgomery, *A Practical Detail of the Cotton Manufacture of the United States of America and the State of the Cotton Manufacture of That Country Contrasts and Compared with That of Great Britain* (Glasgow: John Niven, 1840), 14–15. The terms *Rhode Island System* and *Waltham system* may have been first applied to these different forms of industrial development in Samuel Batchelder, *Introduction and Early Progress of the Cotton Manufacture of the United States* (Boston, 1863), 73.

2. This description of the early-nineteenth-century southern New England mill village is based on the author's survey of pre-1840 textile manufacturing communities for Old Sturbridge Village between 1969 and 1975 under grants from the National Endowment for the Humanities and the Charles Merrill Foundation. Richard M. Candee, "New Towns of the Early New England Textile Industry," in *Perspectives in Vernacular Architecture*, ed. Camille

Wells vol. 1 (Annapolis, Md.: Vernacular Architecture Forum, 1982), 31–51; Richard M. Candee, "The Early New England Textile Village in Art," *Antiques* (December 1970): 910–15, provides prints and paintings of many of these factory communities. For contemporary documents of the Rhode Island system mill village, also see Gary Kulik, Roger Parks, and Theodore Penn, *The New England Mill Village, 1790–1860*, vol. 2 of *Documents in American Industrial History*, ed. Michael B. Folson (Cambridge and London: MIT Press and Merrimack Valley Textile Museum, 1982).

3. Montgomery, *Cotton Manufacture*, 15, 17.

4. John S. Garner, *The Model Company Town, Urban Design through Private Enterprise in Nineteenth-Century New England* (Amherst: University of Massachusetts Press, 1984).

5. James L. Garvin, "Academic Architecture and the Building Trades in the Piscataqua Region of New Hampshire and Southern Maine, 1715–1815" (Ph.D. diss., Boston University, 1983).

6. Microfilm, Dover Meeting, Society of Friends Mss, Dover, N.H., Public Library. A complaint that Wendell "has been so incautious and inattentive to the inspection and settlement of his affairs as to launch into business beyond his ability to manage in the truth and has contracted debts which it appears he was unable to pay . . . to the manifest injury of many and contrary to the good order and discipline of our society" led to his dismissal. Also see correspondence between Isaac Wendell and his brothers, Jacob Wendell and Abraham Wendell, 1825–1850, Wendell Mss Collection, Portsmouth Athenaeum, Portsmouth, N.H.; letter from E. French to Asa Freeman, Philadelphia, 12 Sept. 1833, among documents relating to the Belknap Manufacturing Company in the collections of the Woodman Institute, Dover, N.H.

7. I would like to thank Robert Whitehouse for providing me access to a detailed typescript history of the Dover, N.H. textile mills and their managers, no author [1916?], Woodman Institute, Dover, N.H. This documents much of the physical development of the textile industry and its metal subsidiaries. The daybook of the Dover lawyer Daniel M. Durrell, also at the Woodman Institute, indicates that sale of the nailery to the Dover Cotton Factory was considered and may have taken place as early as November 1814.

8. Robert A. Whitehouse and Cathleen C. Beaudoin, *Port of Dover: Two Centuries of Shipping on the Cocheco*, Portsmouth Marine Society Publication no. 11 (Portsmouth, N.H.: Peter Randall, Publisher, 1988), 1–30.

9. Eliphalet Merrill and Phinehas Merrill, comps., *A Gazetteer of the State of New Hampshire* (Exeter, 1817), 111; John Harvard, *A Gazetteer of New Hampshire* (Boston: John P. Jewett, 1849), 60–62; Alonzo J. Fogg, comp., *The Statistics and Gazetteer of New Hampshire* (Concord, N.H.: D. L. Guernsey, 1874), 135. Population and employment figures for Great Falls, Salmon Falls, and Newmarket are also derived from these sources.

10. "Recollections of an Old Manufacturer, From Manuscript of the Late Isaac Wendell," 4, undated imprint with mss annotations by his daughter, Ann E. Wendell, bound with "Historical Memoranda," Dover, N.H., Public Library.

11. Richard Candee, "Great Falls Industrial and Commercial Historic District," 1982, National Register of Historic Places Inventory—Nomination, typescript, N.H. Division of Historical Resources, Concord, N.H.

12. Richard M. Candee, *Newmarkert Revisited: Looking at the Era of Industrial Growth (1820–1920)* (Newmarket, N.H.: Newmarket Service Club, 1979), and Richard M. Candee, "Newmarket Industrial and Commercial Historic District," 1980, National Register of Historic Places Inventory—Nomination, typescript, N.H. Division of Historical Resources, Concord, N.H. Identification of Stephen Hansen as the agent of Wendell & Williams's first cotton

spinning factory as early as 1817 is found in John R. Ham, "Back River and Belamy River," undated late-nineteenth-century MSS, Portsmouth Athenaeum, Portsmouth, N.H., 34.

13. Strafford Regional Planning Commission, *Salmon Falls—the Mill Village Historic District Study for the Town of Rollinsford, New Hampshire* (Dover, N.H.: Strafford Regional Planning Commission, 1974). Richard M. Candee, "Salmon Falls Mill Historic District," National Register of Historic Places Inventory—Nomination, 1978, typescript, N.H. Division of Historic Resources, Concord, N.H.

14. The literature on Lowell was pioneered by John Coolidge, *Mill and Mansion: A Study of Architecture and Society in Lowell, Massachusetts, 1820–1865* (New York: Columbia University Press, 1962). For more recent analysis see Richard M. Candee, "Architecture and Corporate Planning in the Early Waltham System," in *Essays from the Lowell Conference on Industrial History 1982 and 1983*, ed. Robert Weible (No. Andover, Mass.: Museum of American Textile History, 1985), 17–43; Betsy W. Bahr, "New England Mill Engineering: Rationalization and Reform in Textile Mill Design, 1790–1920" (Ph.D. diss., University of Delaware, 1987), 1–131.

15. "Recollections of an Old Manufacturer, From Manuscript of the Late Isaac Wendell," 1; also see Wendell and Williams letters (1813–1826), Wendell Family Mss, Baker Library, Harvard Business School.

16. Great Falls Manufacturing Company, *Directors Records*, Baker Library, Harvard Business School, 1:5.

17. Richard M. Candee, "The 'Great Factory' at Dover, New Hampshire: The Dover Manufacturing Co. Print Works, 1825," *Old-Time New England* 66, nos. 1–2 (Summer-Fall 1975): 39–51. For detailed discussions of printed cottons at Dover and its contemporaries, see Caroline Sloat, "The Dover Manufacturing Company and the Integration of English and American Calico Printing Techniques, 1825–29," *Winterthur Portfolio* 10 (1975): 51–68, and Diane L. Fagen Affleck, *Just New from the Mills: Printed Cottons in America, Late Nineteenth and Early Twentieth Centuries in the Collection of the Museum of American Textile History* (No. Andover, Mass.: Museum of American Textile History, 1987).

18. *Letterbook*, Dover Manufacturing Company, New Hampshire Historical Society, vol. 1, Letter from John Williams to William Shimmin (no. 131), 23 Nov. 1825.

19. Ibid., vol. 1, Letter from John Williams to William Shimmin (no. 144), December 1825.

20. Richard M. Candee, "The 1822 Allendale Mill and Slow-Burning Construction: A Case Study in the Transmission of an Architectural Technology," *IA, The Journal of the Society for Industrial Archeology* 15, no. 1 (1989): 21–34.

21. *Great Falls Journal* 26 Apr. 1849, 4; Alfred Catalfo, Jr., *The History of the Town of Rollinsford, New Hampshire, 1623–1973* (Somersworth, N.H.: NH Printers, 1973), 287–309.

22. Candee, "Architecture and Corporate Planning," 21–23 and 35–37, and Coolidge, *Mill and Mansion*, figs. 4–5 and 8–12, illustrate several of these wooden boardinghouses. Considerable caution must, however, be exercised in using the plan of the Dutton Street wooden boardinghouse in Coolidge's fig. 5 as it was adapted from a later plan and contemporary maps suggest that the rear ell was not original.

23. "From a Letter written by Isaac P. Wendell," undated imprint annotated by Ann E. Wendell and bound with "Historical Memoranda," Dover Public Library; this was also published in the *Dover Enquirer*, 26 Jan. 1894.

24. Montgomery, *Cotton Manufacture*, 197–98.

25. *Portsmouth Journal*, 19 Aug. 1826.

26. Deposition, 11 Mar. 1825, Dover Manufacturing Company, *Letterbook*, 1: 51–52.

27. Deposition, 10 May 1825, Dover Manufacturing Company, *Letterbook*, 1: 50.

28. Amos A. Lawrence MSS Diary, box 3, vol. 1a, Massachusetts Historical Society, Boston, Mass., 16 Mar., 15 Apr., 21 June 1844; 21 Feb. and 1 Mar. 1844 also show that James Francis (the Lowell engineer), William Appleton (a major Boston Associates investor), and Lawrence's father all acquired stock in Salmon Falls. I thank Stephanie Carroll for finding the references.

29. Gregory K. Clancey, "The Origin of the Boot Boardinghouse Plan and Its Fate after 1836," in *Interdisciplinary Investigations of the Boott Mills, Lowell, Massachusetts*, vol. 3: *The Boarding House System as a Way of Life*, ed. Mary C. Beaudry and Stephen A. Mrozowski, 7–21, Cultural Resources Management Study, no. 21 (Boston: U.S. Department of Interior, National Park Service, North Atlantic Regional Office, 1989). Steve Roper, "30 and 32 Atlantic Block, 401–403 Canal Street, Lawrence, MA: Architectural and Historical Research Report," typescript, 29 Apr. 1983; "Plans of the boardinghouses built for the Atlantic Cotton Mills," c. 1847, Essex Company Collection, Museum of American Textile History. Massachusetts Sanitary Survey Commission, *Report* (Boston, 1850), appendix.

30. "Memorandum of subjects to be brought to the notice of the Directors of the Salmon Falls Co. at their monthly meeting January 18, 1854," Treasurer's Report, Salmon Falls Manufacturing Company, 1854, A. A. Lawrence Papers, Massachusetts Historical Society.

31. "Memorandum," Lawrence Papers.

32. Louis McLane, *Report of the Secretary of the Treasury*, 1832. *Documents Relative to the Manufactures in the United States*, *House Executive Documents*, 22 Congress, 1st session, Doc. No. 308, 2 vols., Washington, D.C., 1833: 1:578–83.

33. Elfreida B. McCauley, "The Manufacturers' and Village Library in Somersworth, New Hampshire," *Historical New Hampshire* 27, no. 2 (Summer 1972): 89–107.

5

Earle S. Draper and the Company Town in the American South

MARGARET CRAWFORD

In 1917, when Earle S. Draper (Fig. 5.1) opened his office in Charlotte, North Carolina, he became the South's first resident city planner. Two years earlier, his employer, the Cambridge, Massachusetts, planner John Nolen, had dispatched the young landscape architect to supervise his operations in the South, where Draper quickly saw the professional opportunities the growing economy of the New South offered planners. After failing to convince Nolen to expand the Charlotte office, Draper decided to strike out on his own.[1] His appearance in the South coincided with a major expansion in the Southern cotton textile industry. The wartime boom spurred rapidly developing production as the industry spread across the Piedmont, the foothills stretching from southern Virginia through the Carolinas to Georgia and eastern Alabama. Charlotte's central location in this region made it the hub of the industry, and mill owners were among Draper's first clients. Despite the growing profits generated by new mills and the expansion of the industry, the mill village had become a site of increasing social and cultural conflict. Mill owners hoped that Draper's planning expertise could produce a new type of mill village, one that would reconcile their economic aims with growing local criticism of village conditions and the continuing restlessness of the mill workers.

Given the task of redesigning the textile mill town, Draper confronted an economic landscape already crisscrossed by major contradictions. Rather than a tabula rasa on which a new design solution might be imposed, it resembled a palimpsest, a settlement type still bearing the imprints of the changing social and technological needs of the industry it supported. Like that of most company towns, the typology

Figure 5.1 Earle S. Draper shortly after his arrival in Charlotte, North Carolina. (From *Early Twentieth-Century Suburbs in North Carolina*, Catherine Bishir and Lawrence Early, eds. [Raleigh: North Carolina Department of Cultural Resources, 1985].)

of the textile town, with its characteristic morphology of factory and housing, initially represented the most expedient translation of the production processes and social organization of the textile mill into a settlement form. Inevitably, the town also had to adjust to accommodate the habits and interests of its residents: the mill families. Later improvements, reflecting profitable growth or imposed by social pressures, rarely altered this fundamental order. Draper's plans, intended to transform the physical order into a more acceptable image, had to be superimposed onto the already existing layers of the mill town.

This discussion of Draper's work follows a similar pattern: it begins by outlining the problems posed by the mill town, analyzing the inexorable economic logic embedded in the Southern textile industry and the social order that logic produced; it then traces the evolution of the mill village as an expression of vernacular form and a site of struggle between owners and workers. By the time Draper appeared, the mill village, under attack from outside critics and local reformers, had also taken on a symbolic dimension, becoming a cultural representation subject to conflicting interpretations. Physical planning, intervention in a situation already limited by social and economic constraints, had to satisfy complex requirements. Operating within these limits, Draper had to provide specific responses to a set of changing and conflicting demands that had been posed over the course of the fifty-year evolution of the Southern mill village. Set in the context of this regional economy and industrial culture, Draper's mill villages can be evaluated as more than just interesting answers to design problems: they also demonstrate the possibilities and the limitations of design solutions to problems whose origins lie outside the realm of design.

Maintaining Cheap Labor: The Development of the Southern Textile Industry

The "cotton mill campaign" of the 1880s, led by local merchants and professionals, launched a dynamic industry firmly grounded in the strengths of the Piedmont region (Fig. 5.2): a good supply of local capital, plentiful streams, access to raw materials, good rail connections, and, most important, a nearly inexhaustible supply of labor drawn from local tenant farms and the Appalachian mountains that marked the western boundary of the region. During the 1890s, the industry's steady growth and high profits were aided by tariff protection and virtually limitless Asian markets. This encouraged further local investment, which, in turn, accelerated the industry's growth. The area's characteristic topography, a rocky, hilly upland cut by fast-flowing streams, provided entrepreneurs with numerous mill sites to launch new textile enterprises in a vigorous effort to invigorate moribund local economies.[2]

After the Civil War, the traditionally small and self-sufficient Piedmont farmer had been increasingly impoverished by crop-lien debt, tenantry, and sharecropping.[3] The agricultural crises of the 1890s worsened this situation, forcing both farmers and tenants to leave their land in search of wage work. Promising a better life, recruiters easily enticed a steady stream of rural and mountain families to newly built textile villages, where they hoped to trade a marginal existence for the security of an hourly wage. Large families migrated to nearby mills to begin what they called "public work." These workers were a homogeneous group. From poor rural backgrounds, they shared the native-born Anglo-Saxon ethnicity and Protestant religion typical of the region. Although they lacked technical skills or formal education (most were illiterate), they were eager to work.[4]

Southern mills repeated the archetypal experience of modernization pioneered in the New England textile mills almost a century earlier: the transformation of a preindustrial agricultural population into factory workers.[5] Unlike New England mills, however, the Southern industry's late start allowed it to take advantage of new technology and increased automation to reduce the need for skilled labor. Improvements in high-speed ring spindles and new humidifiers and temperature regulators that made them practical by reducing yarn breakage enabled unskilled workers to produce far more yarn than skilled mule spinners. Automatic looms also placed a premium on unskilled labor. Combining automated technology with unskilled labor gave Southern mills the advantage they needed to expand; the industry's rapid growth—from 24 percent to the nation's spindles in 1900 to 72 percent in 1939—

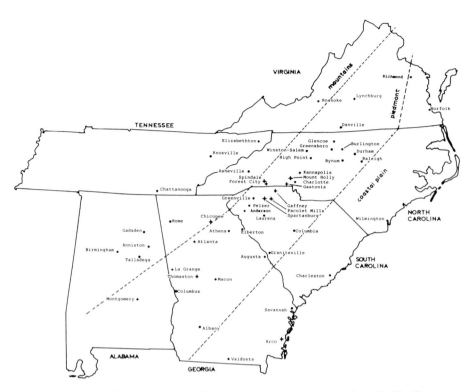

Figure 5.2 Map of the Southern textile region shows the concentration of mill villages across the Piedmont, with the densest clusters around Charlotte, North Carolina, and Greenville/Spartanburg, South Carolina. Although a few mill towns were built on the coastal plain, most were located near the mountains to be closer to sources of labor. The stars indicate mill villages designed by Earle Draper.

was largely based on the low cost of labor, which kept production costs down. Regional wage differentials were significant. From 1894 to 1927, the average Southern textile wage was 40 percent below that of other parts of the country.[6]

The family system maintained these low wages. Rather than hiring individual workers, mills purchased a family's labor as a package. Since a single mill income could not support an entire family, the family's work became the economic unit on which mill wages were based. The family system extended traditional working roles: in the mill, just as on the farm, men, women, and children worked together to sustain the family. In the early years of the industry, women and children, working at unskilled jobs for very low wages, dominated the labor force. Deprived of economic leadership in the family and unable to find work themselves, fathers occasionally had to live off their children's earnings, creating the stereotypical figure of the "lunch-pail father" or "cotton-mill drone." Even children too young to go on the payroll were used as "helpers," working alongside their mothers and sisters as unpaid apprentices. Lenient child labor laws and the absence of protective labor legislation perpetuated the system.[7]

Low labor costs significantly cut production costs, making it possible for Southern manufacturers to undercut Northern prices and take control of the textile industry. Despite the large pool of available workers, mills often faced serious problems in obtaining a steady supply of labor, as a result of what they called the workers' "moving habit." Although the sociologist Liston Pope called them "silent, incoherent, with no agency to express their needs," individualistic mill workers effectively used quitting as a personal alternative to protest or acquiescence. Cutbacks in production, the promise of better wages, disagreements with foremen, or simple restlessness could prompt a worker to quit. When one worker became dissatisfied, the entire family would quit, pack up, and move on to another mill. This pattern produced extremely high turnover rates in Southern mills: the "floating element" of nomadic workers was estimated at from 20 to 40 percent of the labor force, and, beginning in the 1890s, the annual turnover rate hovered around 100 percent.[8]

Since the industry's continuing expansion depended on adequate labor, manufacturers used every method at their disposal to maintain and discipline their restive work force. A huge pool of impoverished black workers offered an alternative source of labor, but mill owners preferred to use black workers as a threat—an ever-present reminder to white workers that they could easily be replaced at even lower wages—to enforce their terms of employment and prevent complaints about wages and hours. In the intense racial climate of the South, white workers fought back by transforming mill work into a "white right," defended with strikes and riots. As a result, blacks were hired in the mill but never for production work. Instead, they were relegated to the most menial low-wage jobs, working outdoors as loaders and drivers or as sweepers or scourers inside the mill, always isolated from contact with white women workers. This strategy effectively mobilized white workers against blacks but only temporarily quieted their discontent, leaving mill owners still searching for new means of obtaining a more permanent group of obedient workers.[9]

"Like a Family": Struggles over the Way of Life

The distinctive social order of the mill village formalized the industrial system into a way of life. The employer carefully structured the economic logic of the mill village to enable families of workers to survive even with marginal wages and frequent layoffs. The family system was built into the provision of company housing through labor quotas specifying the number of workers provided by each house: contracts usually required at least one worker per room as a condition of rental. Rents were uniformly low since subsidized housing was offered in lieu of higher wages. Some mills offered free rent, but 25 cents per room per week or a dollar a week was a more usual rent for a standard four-room house. Rents included electricity and water and were usually canceled or deferred in case of layoffs. New England textile workers usually paid a week's wages per month for housing in comparison to the one- or two-days' wages paid by Southerners. It was clearly to the worker's advantage to rent a mill house, and by the turn of the century 92 percent of Southern textile workers lived in mill villages. Although owners rarely made their homes in mill villages, residence was considered to be part of a foreman's or a superintendent's job.[10]

The mill village also functioned as an all-encompassing social system. In addition to constructing housing, mills operated a set of characteristic institutions. These included a company store, a minimum of two churches (Methodist and Baptist), and an elementary school, with both preachers and teachers hired by the mill. Some communal amenities were commonplace—baseball fields and allotment gardens cost almost nothing to provide—but more expensive facilities, such as meeting and lodge halls, libraries, and medical clinics, were rarer. Still, every mill village provided all the necessities of work, subsistence, and leisure. Even after leaving the mill, workers lived, shopped, studied, played, and worshipped in an environment created by the employer.

This nearly self-sufficient world, set apart from the larger world around it, was the product of both economic necessity and intent. Mill owners had to furnish housing to obtain a labor force, but they also used their power as the owners of the village to control their employees. In 1908, federal investigators noted, "All the affairs of the village and the conditions of living of all the people are regulated entirely by the mill company. . . . The company owns everything and controls everything and to a large extent controls everybody in the mill village." At the same time, the owner's control was mediated by the habits and customs workers brought with them to the mill. The village system evolved to accommodate the workers' patterns of daily life and to take account of at least some of their social, religious, and medical preferences. Village conditions were constantly renegotiated. If owners actively supported some after-work activities favored by the workers, such as baseball, others, like drinking and gambling, remained continuous sources of struggle.[11]

Most village institutions represented similarly uneasy accommodations between the owners' need for control and the employees' inclinations. The mill school, for example, worked both ways, offering both opportunity and regulation. In the absence of universal public education, mill schools taught the children of largely illiterate parents but at the same time developed industrial discipline and helped to prepare them for mill work. Operated by the mill outside existing school systems, the school functioned as an extension of the factory. Teaching emphasized traits such as punctuality, regularity of attendance, reliability, and respect for authority. According to one mill official, "Children who are educated become more valuable labor and are less destructive of property." When extra hands were needed at the mill, the school contained a convenient labor supply; one observer noted, "It was the custom for the overseers in the mill to send to the school house at any time of day for workers." Education beyond the seventh grade was rarely provided, since it was understood that children would then enter the mill's permanent work force. High school attendance was discouraged, because mill village children who went on to high school rarely returned to work in the mill.[12]

Churches played an even more significant role in the mill village, continuing the strong religious traditions workers took with them from their rural homes. Mill owners, as the sociologist Liston Pope demonstrated, openly acknowledged the useful role that evangelical Protestant religions played in releasing workers from the monotony of mill work and encouraging them to lead orderly and hardworking lives. To ensure a commonality of interest between mill and church, mill owners financially supported conservative faiths, bringing only Baptist and Methodist ministers to their village churches even if the owners themselves belonged to other denominations. Many played active roles in village congregations as Sunday school teachers, deacons, and ushers. Church attendance was often used as the measure of a good worker. In Bynum, North Carolina, the mill superintendent "sentenced" errant workers to attend church for a designated number of Sundays. Workers clearly recognized the connections between mill and church: "If you went to church, it had some influence on your job whether you knew it or not. . . . If there was an opening available for someone to better himself, usually the church member got the job."[13]

The pastors hired by the mills shared their sponsors' beliefs, preaching what the sociologist Harriet Herring called "doctrines which would be acceptable in the main to a capitalistic employer—a gospel of work, of gratitude for present blessings, and of patience with economic and social maladjustment as temporal and outside the sphere of religious concern."[14] The focus was on individual salvation, and the workers' acceptance of their circumstances in this world in the hope of better fortunes in the next reinforced docility and reliability. Frequent pulpit exhortations against drinking also addressed a basic problem of industrial discipline. Ministers who challenged this system quickly found themselves without church or congregation. Mill workers, on the other hand, often chose to worship outside the village, either at nearby rural or urban churches or in Pentecostal congregations. Sect churches, whose participatory services offered emotional release, although extremely popular with mill workers, were generally frowned on by owners, who considered them a disruptive influence.[15]

While mill owners used company housing, schools, and churches to address workplace issues of labor supply and discipline, they intended the company store to function as a brake on the mill worker's persistent inclination to move. Originally established as a convenience in isolated rural mill villages, company stores were often used to create an economic bond between mill and employee. Although, contrary to popular belief, company stores were rarely overpriced, they were still effective money-makers. Daniel Tompkins, the first theorist of the Southern textile industry, advised, "A mill can operate its own store and thereby get back in mercantile profit much of the money paid for wages." A more important consideration was the constant state of indebtedness created by the practice of deducting employees' store bills from their earnings. Unable to obtain credit elsewhere, employees became almost completely dependent on the mill for daily necessities. As a result, on payday many of them received either no wages or, worse, bills marked "BALANCE DUE." This continuing cycle of debt tied the worker to the employer, and if it prompted resentment, it also helped to stabilize the work force.[16]

Although mill owners often promoted the mill village as a benevolent enterprise, the federal government's 1910 *Report on Woman and Child Wage Earners* dismissed their claims that mill-owned houses and village schools, churches, and stores were philanthropic ventures. Rather, the report pointed out, the mills had to build complete communities to attract workers and counted these expenditures as normal costs of doing business.[17] In many cases, however, mill owners and superintendents exceeded these minimal obligations by devoting a great deal of personal attention to their workers. This type of paternalism, based on individual benevolence, balanced their control over the workers' lives with a direct interest in their welfare. Owners made themselves available to workers for workplace complaints as well as for advice and help for family problems or financial difficulties and performed acts of kindness such as visiting the sick, distributing Christmas presents, or helping a particularly bright child.[18]

Generosity, however, usually brought intrusiveness. As in the early New England textile mills, the demoralization of the factory worker was considered to be inherent in industrial life. Owners assumed that their paternal authority necessarily included moral guidance, so they enforced values of thrift and temperance and strict standards of sexual behavior through regulation and punishment. Bans on the sale of alcoholic beverages and even cigarette smoking in mill villages were common. In many villages, if an unmarried woman became pregnant, she and her family were immediately evicted. The owner of Bynum Mills made a practice of walking around the mill hill at nine o'clock every night to knock on the doors of those who were still up to tell them to put out the lights and go to bed. Management's zealous "protection" of their workers usually extended to the elimination of local politics, seen as a threat to stability, in the mill village. The intentionally unincorporated status of many mill villages precluded the possibility of self-government, and management often carefully supervised voting in national and state elections.[19]

To justify their control, many Southern mill owners used a distinctive ideology of paternalism that combined claims of ethnic solidarity with fellow whites, social Darwinist notions of self-selection, and a Christian sense of duty. Appropriating the heritage of the antebellum planter, they revived and adapted the pseudofeudal rhetoric of the Old South to the new industrial order. The image of the family was repeatedly invoked, its authoritarian and hierarchical discipline extended to workers "for their own good." A mill spokesman described the mill operatives: "They're all of one family. They're all of one community. They are all of the mill."[20] The fiction of "one big family" maintained the owner's control and the worker's dependence, and made unions unnecessary. Once established, this dialectic of benevolence and deference created its own momentum. In the close community of the mill village, workers often actively collaborated with paternal claims, acquiescing in their own subordination. Paternalism offered workers advantages they had never known on their Piedmont or mountain farms and at the same time produced dependence that provided further justification to continue the system.

Still, paternalism never constituted a unified approach to industrial relations in mill villages. It remained a somewhat haphazard and piecemeal endeavor erratically applied according to the inclinations of individual owners and managers. Although trade publications and the Southern press devoted enthusiastic attention to mill village paternalism, in actual practice, a variety of managerial practices prevailed in mill villages. At one extreme, Captain Ellison A. Smyth imposed a totalitarian regime of personal rule on his widely publicized "model town," Pelzer, South Carolina. A benevolent despot who provided his workers with "comfortable houses" at no charge, a lyceum, a savings bank, and impressive recreational facilities, Smyth also indulged his own prejudices by restricting after-dark activities and banning dogs from the village ("dogs are in ninety-nine cases out of a hundred worthless and troublesome"). At the other extreme were towns that furnished few amenities but imposed few controls. Many mill towns acquired reputations for lawlessness; excessive drinking and fighting in one South Carolina mill town forced workers to petition the county government for a sheriff to maintain order.[21]

The workers' own culture, created from rural habits and the shared experiences of public work, was the main barrier to the intrusions of mill owners and managers. Drawn together in the mill village for economic reasons, workers built their own networks of friendship and family to create a close-knit community. In a common situation of economic marginality, workers survived by mutual aid and communal cooperation. Sharing the produce they raised and the meat they slaughtered, families came together for seasonal tasks such as corn shucking, canning, and quilting. Women who worked in the mill shared child-raising duties with those who stayed at home. When sickness or injury struck, villages collected "love gifts" of food and money for their neighbors, a safety net in the absence of workplace benefits. These community networks not only provided security but, through a front-porch culture of visiting and gossip, enforced a self-imposed standard of behavior whose values were reinforced by religion. If the gospel taught in village churches emphasized the priorities of the mill owners, it also validated an antimaterialist ethos that emphasized virtues of caring and cooperation over monetary gain.[22]

Communities were also closely bound together by kinship. Families tended to migrate to mill villages where they had relatives, and when and if their children married in the village, they created further family ties. Even nonrelatives lived like families. Boardinghouses, run by widows and older couples, incorporated single people into the community, creating stable households that one worker described as "the nearest place to home there is." By 1920, a village like Bynum, with three generations of mill workers, could be accurately characterized as "one big family," since most residents were connected by marriage relationships. The solidarity of family ties, however distant, gave workers a collective strength and security that countered the oppressively familial relationships claimed by the mill management. Thus, in spite of its severe imbalance of power, life in the mill village reflected the contradictory needs of both owners and workers.[23]

The Mill Village: Separate and Unequal

The mill village translated these social and economic relationships into a physical environment. Instead of being modeled on existing company towns, such as mill towns in New England or other town plans or architect's designs, Southern villages evolved from vernacular principles of function and economy and relied on local building traditions and materials. Since mills depended on water power, early mill villages were located in isolated riverside sites. The Piedmont's many small but rapidly flowing streams could easily be dammed and diverted into a millrace to power textile machinery. The smallness of the streams, however, initially tended to keep mills small, scattering mill villages over a wide area rather than concentrating them in a few locations. Small size and isolation gave most villages a rural character. The most intrusive elements were the mill buildings themselves, copied from Northern prototypes. Lined up along the river, the long narrow buildings, three and four stories tall, dominated the landscape. Even in remote villages, the substantial red brick structures were embellished with decorative features that emulated those of civic and religious buildings.[24] The rest of the village was casually laid out. Factory owners hired surveyors to plot roads and lots and allowed carpenters to build according to local custom. The "mill hill," as its name suggests, was generally located on a cleared site sloping up from the riverside mill. To save money, houses were all built at the same time with identical plans and laid out in rows along roads leading from the mill. Housing followed a standard pattern, duplicating the most common and inexpensive type of rural dwelling in the Piedmont countryside. Unlike the rowhouses or duplexes common in Northern company towns, Southern mills primarily built single-family houses. These single-story frame structures, raised on brick piers to avoid damp ground, contained three or four rooms, a front porch, and often a rear kitchen extension. A small group of larger, better-built houses was reserved for mill managers or the town minister. These houses were often strategically located to keep track of comings and goings in the village. Another group of smaller houses was often set apart on the outskirts of the village for black employees. The location of other community buildings did not form any particular pattern. A store, churches, schoolhouse, and lodge hall might be clustered near the mill or interspersed with the houses without establishing a formal relationship to either. Compactness was the only planning requirement: since inhabitants walked to their daily activities, the village had to be completely accessible to pedestrians.[25]

Early villages not only presented a rural appearance but maintained rural standards of life (Fig. 5.3). Services were extremely limited. Even after 1900, few mill villages had paved or graded roads; wells and pumps shared by several families provided water, brick fireplaces provided heat, and kerosene lamps, light. Indoor plumbing was unknown, and rows of privies lined the back of lots. Rural activities were also accommodated: large lots encouraged gardening and left enough open space for pig pens, chicken coops, and cow pastures. At the same time, unlike in rural dwellings, enforcement of the "one worker per room" rule practically guaranteed overcrowded living conditions. All rooms except the kitchen had to be used for sleeping, leaving only the front porch as a family living room or a place for entertaining guests. By comparison, in New England an average textile worker's family occupied a six-room house.[26]

By 1900 the Piedmont mill village constituted a distinctive industrial landscape expressing the industrial demands and social order of the mill as well as the needs and habits of workers' daily lives. Developed by trial and error within narrow economic and environmental constraints, the basic typology of the mill village was

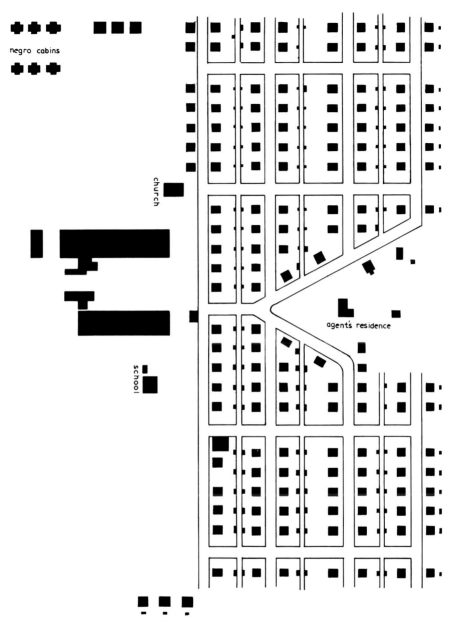

negro cabins

church

school

agents residence

Figure 5.3 Layout of a typical Southern cotton mill village. This plan, from the U.S. Bureau of Labor Statistics' survey of company housing, shows the standard features of the vernacular mill village. The mill, at the center of the plan, occupies a dominant position, flanked by school and church. The workers' houses are identical, laid out in evenly spaced rows, with outdoor privies lining the alleys in the center of each block. The supervisor's larger house is placed for maximum visibility. Segregated "negro cabins" are located behind the mill. (From Leifur Magnusson, *Housing by Employers in the United States* [Washington, D.C.: Government Printing Office, 1920].)

diffused across the textile belt. A rapidly growing group of manufacturers routinely shared information and experience, supplemented by trade publications such as *Manufacturer's Record* and *Southern Textile Bulletin*. In 1899 Daniel Tompkins codified the accumulated wisdom of Piedmont mill building and operation into a compendium, *Cotton Mill: Commercial Features*. Its seventeen chapters provided the first systematic analysis of the technology, financing, and marketing of cotton textiles written from the Southern point of view. Tompkins, a native South Carolinian trained as an engineer at Rensselaer Polytechnic Institute in New York, spoke from experience. In addition to his own mills, Tompkins's machine shop in Charlotte had designed and constructed more than one hundred textile mills all over the Piedmont.[27]

Tompkins's counsel was conservative. He advised mill owners to continue locating mills in rural areas, in spite of the freedom of movement made possible by the appearance of steam and electric power. Rural settings, he argued, offered important benefits to both workers and owners: "The whole matter of providing attractive and comfortable habitations for cotton operatives . . . [is] summarized in the statement that they are essentially a rural people. They have been accustomed to farm life. . . . [W]hile their condition is decidedly bettered by going to the factory, the old instincts cling to them." He suggested half-acre lots for each house, since gardening was "conducive to general contentment among the operatives." For the owners, the advantages of isolation included freedom from city taxes and intrusive lawyers, as well as more efficient workers, who, without the distractions of urban amusements, went to bed early.[28]

Tompkins's chapter on factory houses also repeated conventional wisdom (Fig. 5.4). Although his specifications for a four-room, $400 mill house were exactingly detailed, listing the size, material, and quality of all construction details, the plans themselves reproduced a traditional nineteenth-century house type found all over the South. A four-room frame cottage divided by a center hall, with two fireplaces and two porches, the house consisted of a basic cube broken up by two roof gables. For those interested in greater variety and architectural interest, Tompkins outlined alternative possibilities: the weatherboarding, door panels, turned porch pillars, and gable trim could be varied by pattern, shape, and color options. However, as Tompkins repeatedly emphasized, even these limited design decisions were to be made by either "the president of the company or his representative." The simplicity of these houses made them popular choices for economy-minded mill owners, and after 1900 mill houses built all over the region followed Tompkins's plans.[29]

In spite of the increasing standardization of housing and village typologies, wide variations still existed in the physical appearance and living standards in mill towns. The mill village hierarchy that emerged reflected the personal inclinations of the village owners, although differences were primarily in upkeep rather than form. Even the best villages received mixed reviews from visitors. The journalist Leonora Ellis found "cottage homes that are patterns of comfort, neatness, and sanitation" in Newry, South Carolina, and described Pelzer as "as tidy and tasteful as a good housewife's guest chamber," but the economist Richard Ely claimed that, in comparison to Northern villages, the settlement "produced a squalid and mean impres-

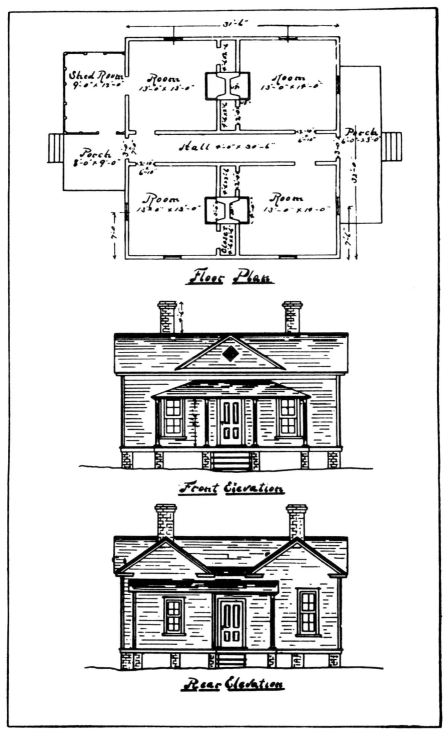

Figure 5.4 Plan and elevation for a four-room mill house. Although the distinctive gables were often eliminated, the clapboard surface, brick piers, and generic rooms became common features of subsequent mill housing. (From Daniel Tompkins, *Cotton Mill, Commercial Features* [Charlotte, N.C.: Published by the Author, 1899].)

sion." In his 1905 survey of factory conditions, the English reformer Budgett Meakin quickly passed over Pelzer, finding it well below the standards of industrial towns in other areas of the country. Newry and Pelzer were "model towns"; more typical mill villages appalled Northern reformers and Southern observers alike. The journalist Clare de Graffenried described one mill village as "horrible, built on malarial soil." In another, H. F. Garrett of Atlanta saw "houses in bad condition . . . with big cracks in them," unfit for family living. Another visitor concluded that the "villages are dirty, the streets unkept, and the very sight of the village is a horror."[30]

Almost inevitably, mill villages, easily recognizable by their distinctive morphology, became places set apart from the larger community. Isolated in the village, mill workers inhabited an increasingly closed culture; poorly educated, economically insecure, and socially restricted, they were clearly differentiated from their Piedmont neighbors. The sociologist Herbert Lahne observed that, as the industry developed and mill families tended to marry within their community, "cotton mill work [became] an almost hereditary occupation."[31] Identified as a separate caste, mill workers were treated with disdain by their urban and rural neighbors. Disparaging epithets, such as "lint head," "mill trash," and "cotton-tail," were common. The historian W. J. Cash wrote that a mill worker might wander the streets of a nearby town all day "without ever receiving a nod or a smile from anybody, or any recognition of his existence other than a scornful glance from a shop girl."[32]

"Does the Mill Village Foster Social Types?"

By the turn of the century, the conventional mill village wisdom set forth by Tompkins began to be questioned both inside and outside the factory. The success of the industry led to the rapid proliferation of mills: between 1900 and 1902, thirty-four new mills were built in North Carolina alone. With electricity providing more power, expanding mills, no longer tied to remote riverside sites, began to locate near towns, though remaining outside their corporate limits to avoid taxes and maintain control. Mill building shaped the urbanization in the Piedmont region, continuing a distinctive pattern of dispersal that produced small towns and cities rather than major centers. Even large textile towns such as Charlotte and Greenville, South Carolina, and Augusta, Georgia, never developed into dense industrial cities but remained loosely joined collections of unincorporated mill villages and suburbs surrounding a central business district.[33]

The presence of nearby mills increasingly brought factory workers to the attention of the urban middle classes, who noticed the enormous gulf separating life in the mill village from that of their communities: the "mill problem" emerged. Local reformers feared that the child labor, lack of education, and poor living conditions they observed in mill villages posed a serious threat to the social order. To the concerned middle class, the mill worker's resentment of authority, nomadic habits, and apparent lack of ambition appeared potentially dangerous, threatening the "modern" and well- regulated society of the emerging New South. Their response was to categorize the mill workers as a "social type" and an object of reform. Reform efforts focused on transforming the worker's supposedly backward culture through child labor laws and compulsory education. Although they dispensed charity and organized "uplift" work in mill villages, urban middle-class reformers, like their progressive contemporaries in other areas of the country, believed that mill village problems could best be solved by turning them over to trained and disinterested professionals.[34]

Many mill managers agreed with this assessment. They also saw their workers as primitive and unmanageable. To offset criticism and keep reformers at bay, they replaced the piecemeal efforts of paternalism with "welfare work," a rationalized approach to social welfare imported from the North. Industrial welfare work organized social services and physical improvements into systematic programs supervised by professional welfare workers. If Southern welfare advocates hoped these efforts would convert backward mill families into model workers and citizens, mill owners were more interested in "retaining a loyal work force," improving public relations, and deflecting union organization. After 1905, in response to the severe labor shortage created by the industry's rapid expansion, which had depleted the labor supply, Southern mills increasingly turned to welfare work to foster "permanency of residence and regularity of work." Unfortunately for the mills, however, the easy availability of jobs induced mill hands to move even more frequently than usual, and by 1907 the annual rate of turnover was 176 percent. Although welfare programs were expensive, between 1905 and 1915 eight Piedmont mills ranked among the nation's leading practitioners of company-sponsored welfare work.[35]

Welfare work directly attacked the workers' culture by reeducating workers as both producers and consumers. Mill employees trained in social work, teaching, and public health extended and institutionalized paternalist traditions. Some programs, such as subsidized medical clinics, group insurance schemes, parks, and playgrounds, represented genuine improvements; others were designed to integrate the workers' lives into the functioning of the firm. Welfare workers reorganized informal baseball games, for example, into mill teams and factory leagues that not only structured leisure time but served as object lessons in discipline and obedience to rules. By sponsoring a favorite pastime, owners hoped to transfer the workers' loyalty from the team to the mill. Programs for women, such as child-care classes, mother's clubs, and domestic science courses, instructed them in middle-class values, habits, and aspirations. Home economists taught young women how to sew fashionable clothes and cook fancy meals. The house functioned as an object of particular attention. Workers were encouraged to identify with their house as a home rather than as simply a part of their wage. Mills distributed flower seeds and shrubs, then held contests for the most beautiful garden. Neat housekeeping was promoted, and stylish interiors with upholstered furniture were held up as an ideal. Intended to narrow the cultural gap between mill and town, these efforts ignored the economic fact that, even if the mill families wanted these improvements, they were beyond the means of most (Fig. 5.5).[36]

Professional expertise was also replacing personal authority inside the mills, as the systematic and impersonal methods of the modern corporation gradually elimi-

Figure 5.5 A street in Pelzer, South Carolina, an "improved" mill village. Rows of neat whitewashed frame cottages, provided rent-free to workers, reflect Capt. Ellison A. Smyth's desire to make Pelzer a "model" textile town. In spite of Smyth's intentions, however, the town's repetitious order maintained the grim monotony typical of most company town planning. (Photographed by author, 1991.)

nated the old-fashioned management styles typical of family-owned mills. The enormous growth of local enterprises and the increasing relocation of Northern mills to the Piedmont imposed new standards of efficiency and profitability. Other Northern imports, such as scientific management, focused on increased productivity with techniques that substituted objectively determined rules and standards for agreements previously negotiated by foremen and workers. As the pace of production was rationalized, workers were continually assigned larger production quotas—a process called the "stretch-out." A new generation of college-educated mill men, many of whom had been trained in Northern business schools or in the textile colleges founded by Daniel Tompkins and his contemporaries, introduced these techniques. Experience no longer guaranteed advancement: supervisors did not rise up through the ranks but were hired straight from business and engineering schools, eliminating the possibility of upward mobility from within the mill.[37]

After 1914, Southern mills faced a series of challenges that tested their newly rationalized methods. The European war generated an enormous demand for textiles, producing boom conditions in the industry and exacerbating already severe labor shortages. Lucrative military contracts offered mill owners unprecedented profits, but to realize them they had to recruit and maintain increasingly scarce labor. In response, manufacturers raised wages to new heights and supplemented them with a bonus system designed to entice reluctant mill hands into working longer hours. Workers acted on their newfound economic power, and union organization, dormant since the 1901 American Federation of Labor defeat in Danville, Virginia, reared its head in the South once again. The Union of Textile Workers began to organize Southern mills, and between 1918 and 1920 a series of strikes erupted in mill towns across the Piedmont.

Not surprisingly, welfare activities, widely advertised as a panacea for virtually all industrial relations problems, also reached a peak during these years. The *Southern Textile Bulletin*, representing the cutting edge of the industry, published a series of "Health and Happiness" issues in 1917, 1919, and 1923, extolling the virtues of welfare work, demonstrated by photographs of smiling children in manicured villages (Fig. 5.6).[38] During this brief period of extraordinary prosperity, huge profits from the wartime boom funded ever more elaborate programs designed to ensure a steady work force and promote industrial harmony. Despite high expectations, the actual results were disappointing. Many mill families, suspicious of the condescending implications of welfare activities, refused to participate. Others, instead of showing gratitude, suggested that they would prefer a larger paycheck. Even those who took advantage of services did not necessarily repay the mills with the loyalty anticipated.[39]

Design as a Solution: Earle Draper's Planned Mill Villages

Professional planning proposed yet another solution to the contradictions accumulating in the mill village. Far more than welfare workers, who, after all, were company employees, independent professionals such as Earle Draper hoped to mediate the conflicting demands of the mill owners' needs, the reformers' concerns, and, most of all, the workers' resistance. Draper's approach was initially biased toward the interests of the first two groups, since, like most professionals, he shared many of their values. He saw mill village design, first, as a demonstration of the value of professional planning and civic design and, only as a result of that, as an opportunity to upgrade the lives of mill workers. Although Draper compared the mill village to an industrial plantation, he did not question the mill owners' sincerity in requesting improvements. Like many Southern observers of the textile industry, he was convinced that properly designed mill villages could offer vastly improved living conditions to workers from mountain cabins and tenant shacks, but only if implemented through the goodwill of the mill owners. Yet, as he attacked the physical problem of redesigning the mill village, Draper was forced to confront the social and economic contradictions embedded in its forms and functions. By taking physical control of the village, he removed decisions about the workers' way of life from the mill owners' hands and altered the balance of power and control in the mill village. Given the already conflicting expectations of his professional role, the use of design to resolve these problems inevitably produced contradictory results. Still, even if Draper's designs were unable to produce a lasting solution to the problems of the mill village, they demonstrated a more profound understanding of a situation that could not be resolved.[40]

Through his planning work and his own residence in Myers Park, Charlotte's

SECTION TWO

SOUTHERN
TEXTILE BULLETIN

VOLUME 25   CHARLOTTE, N. C., THURSDAY, NOVEMBER 22, 1923.   NUMBER 13

HEALTH and HAPPINESS Number 1923

Figure 5.6 Cover of the 1923 "Health and Happiness" issue published by the *Southern Textile Bulletin*. Widely distributed to schools, public libraries, and chambers of commerce, these special publications were an important publicity vehicle for the Southern textile industry. Showcasing welfare work in Southern mills, they featured a full range of industry-sponsored "improvement" efforts. (Photograph, Library of Congress.)

most desirable suburb, Draper established close social and professional contracts with the textile families who settled there. When they turned to him for professional advice, Draper, whose own family was connected with the New England textile industry—his grandfather had owned cotton mills near Stoughton, Massachusetts—was sympathetic to their concerns. The mill owners' demands were primarily technical: they needed to upgrade the physical environment and amenities of the mill village to improve their public image and help them attract and retain steady workers. Better living standards for employees would finally, they hoped, "secure an attachment for the village to decrease the migratory tendency." A mill president suggested that new mill villages would make "more loyal, better workers, better contented with their lot . . . those mills will have the best class of labor and more of it in times of stress." Physical improvements might also divert the workers' and the public's attention from more fundamental issues, such as conflicts over wages and hours or the right to organize, which threatened profits.[41]

Draper's success in meeting the mill owners' requirements bolstered his professional standing, and he quickly established himself as the only local "expert" on mill village planning. As the Southern industry grew, he prospered. By 1920 he employed more than a dozen professionals and operated a field office in Atlanta, a planning practice comparable to the largest offices in the country. His professional stationery listed community and mill village developments at the top of the firm's list of services, and from 1917 to 1925 mill villages provided the bulk of Draper's commissions. Beginning with the Spencer Mills in Spindale, North Carolina, his office planned more than one hundred villages, developing, extending, or improving mill villages in every Southern textile state. Unlike most planning firms, Draper's controlled the entire planning process, providing comprehensive design and development services. It took responsibility for the town's layout, the grading and landscaping of the site, engineering of roads, drainage and utilities, and location of building sites. The firm's working relationships with two important textile engineering firms, J. E. Sirrine of Greenville, South Carolina, and L. W. Roberts of Atlanta, allowed it to play an even larger role in determining the nature of the town, by collaborating in designing and constructing mills and housing on sites selected by Draper.[42]

The mill owners' confidence allowed Draper, paradoxically, to claim a more independent role that gave him the power to set and enforce his own priorities in the mill villages he built. By insisting on his own standards, which were considerably higher than the norm, he was able to improve physical conditions significantly in the mill towns he designed. Because he had more work than he could handle, he often refused commissions, turning away mill owners who proposed towns with less than what he considered to be minimum standards of light, water, electricity, sanitary conveniences, housing, and roads.[43] These substantial improvements in living conditions, subsidized by profits from the wartime boom, offered reformers immediate visible proof of the benefits of professional town planning. Unlike earlier model towns, Draper's were genuinely attractive—they did not require exaggerated descriptions to convince observers of their merits. Although town planning was originally intended to be an adjunct to and a setting for welfare work, planned mill villages increasingly became a substitute for other types of welfare programs.

Although remedying the technical deficiencies of the mill village satisfied the limited objectives of mill owners and reformers, Draper defined his task more broadly. Without directly challenging the industrial premises imposed on the mill town, he interpreted the workers' point of view by adding a level of meaning to the town, a conceptual overlay on top of its productive order. Although Draper's writing about mill village planning focused almost exclusively on practical issues, his towns, as both designs and real places, reveal another dimension: Through site planning, landscape design, and provision of housing and community services, they offered the families living there an alternative reading of their situation, one based not only on industrial determinants but on a more sympathetic understanding of their cultural heritage and rural origins.

Nothing in Draper's background had given him the design tools for this task. He was forced him to discover his methods empirically, and he gradually perfected his distinctive style of rural community planning in the course of building mill villages. Educated in the landscape architecture program at Massachusetts College, he had soon gravitated to the infant profession of city planning, then known as "civic art." His work for John Nolen ranged from exclusive subdivisions such as Myers Park to the industrial new town of Kingsport, Tennessee, but Draper chose not to follow Nolen's beaux arts example. Instead, he located himself solidly in the naturalistic planning tradition originated by Frederick Law Olmsted. He also drew on more recent developments in town planning and industrial housing through his familiarity with the English Garden Cities designed by Parker and Unwin, the picturesque industrial villages of Bourneville and Port Sunlight in England, and the Krupp towns in Germany. Although he adopted many of their formal techniques, such as cul-de-sacs, greenbelts, and pedestrian circulation systems, when inserted in the mill village's completely different social and physical setting, they acquired very different meanings.[44]

Although Draper accepted the social order dictated by the mill owners, he challenged their assessment of the workers' culture. Rather than urbanizing workers or homogenizing their environment, as reformers urged, he, like Daniel Tompkins, emphasized their rural origins. Unlike Tompkins, however, he refused to subordinate this rural identity to the mill. In planning textile towns he created a new cultural landscape that negated their exclusively industrial premises. Instead, he reversed the physical conventions of the mill village to allow the villagers symbolically to reclaim their own turf. His plans created a separate living sphere to offset the workers' restricted industrial roles and supplied them with open space, housing, recreation, and pleasant surroundings out of sight of the mill. This both sustained and expanded lives narrowly focused around family and religion. Draper developed landscaping and site planning techniques to reconnect residents to the familiar natural setting of the Piedmont, thus validating their rural and mountain origins. Improved housing began to erase the social boundaries between living conditions in mill villages and those of urban areas and gradually included mill workers in the Piedmont culture. Unlike the standardized and normative improvement efforts of welfare capitalism, Draper's carefully detailed and site-specific plans gave mill workers an image of dignity derived from their own heritage.

Draper's planning style was most visible in two noteworthy textile towns, Pacolet Mill Village, South Carolina, built in 1919, and Chicopee, Georgia, his last textile project, built in 1925 (Fig. 5.7). The unusual advantages of large budgets and cooperative management in both towns allowed Draper to demonstrate the main elements of his approach fully. Pacolet Mills, one of the earliest large mills in South

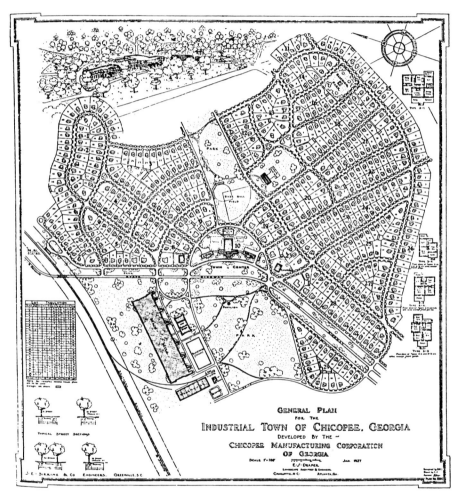

Figure 5.7 The plan of Chicopee, Georgia, 1925, illustrates many of Earle Draper's planning trademarks: loosely winding tree-lined streets, parkland buffers, and extensive recreation facilities, all focused on the town center. Note the complete separation of the mill from the rest of the village. (From Arthur Comey and Max Wehrly, "Planned Communities," *Supplementary Report of the Urbanism Committee*, vol. 2, *Urban Planning and Land Policies* [Washington, D.C.: Government Printing Office, 1939].)

Carolina, expanded operations by building a completely new mill village down-stream from the town of Pacolet on the Saluda River in Spartanburg County. Strong financial backing from a well-established family firm allowed the owner not only to follow but also to encourage Draper's suggestions (Fig. 5.8).[45] Johnson & Johnson, a major producer of medical supplies, was typical of Northern firms that, experiencing labor problems and legally mandated wages and hours, increasingly relocated in the South—in this case, transferring gauze production from the grimy textile town of Chicopee, Massachusetts, to Georgia. The firm had been a pioneer in welfare work—since 1906, its New Jersey headquarters had offered medical, legal, and social services as well as low-cost housing to employees—and it intended to continue this tradition by building a model textile village in the South.[46]

Draper's most significant departure from previous mill village practice is immediately evident in both towns: the mill is no longer the focal point of the village.[47] In Pacolet, the mill, screened by trees, is set apart from the village; in Chicopee, it has been completely eliminated. Located across the main highway, separated by parkland and wooded areas, the Chicopee mill, the earliest single-story plant built in the

Figure 5.8 A street in Pacolet Mill village, South Carolina. To avoid the mud and dust created by the red clay soil, Draper provided an elaborate drainage system with paved streets and sidewalks and stone gutters. Terraces and retaining walls built of local stone took advantage of the town's hilly topography so that mill cottages could be placed at irregular elevations. This greatly reduced the uniformity usually found in mill villages. (Photographed by the author, 1991.)

South, is barely visible from the village.[48] Draper's loosely curving street patterns underlined the distinction between mill and town: instead of directly connecting the mill to the housing, the dominant circulation routes led to the semicircle that forms the village center. The only formal gesture in the plan, this pattern focused the town around a compact grouping of communal services: shops, churches, clinics, and community buildings. The town center's intersection with the belt of recreation space and parkland formed the conceptual and aesthetic lynchpin of Draper's plan, suggesting that the village had an existence independent of the mill and encouraging a community identity separate from the workplace.

The essence of this community was its rural nature. Since his goal was to recreate a microcosm of the Piedmont landscape in every village, Draper's primary design consideration was the search for the correct site (Fig. 5.9). Avoiding the bare red fields used by plant engineers and surveyors, Draper selected sloping and irregular sites, readily available in a region of hilly uplands. He preferred wooded sites and retained stands of second-growth timber as much as possible, because of his conviction that "a certain percentage of wooded area is always important in the South."[49] To maintain the natural topography, he made extensive use of terracing, retaining walls, and steps, usually constructed of stones found on the site. Draper organized Pacolet's hilly terrain into a series of stone terraces that gradually step down from the ridges to the riverside mill below. This practice not only respected the natural contours of the site but varied the shape of the lots and allowed buildings to be placed at irregular intervals and elevations, a three-dimensional solution to the basic design problem of the mill village: tedious uniformity.

Such sites always contained a large proportion of land too hilly or wooded to build on, so Draper joined these areas together into a continuous system of green spaces and parkland. Salvaged woodlands, creek beds, and bottomlands were then used as buffers to isolate different parts of the village and to maintain natural vistas. In Pacolet, the parkland system, incorporating hills, creeks, and trees as it moved across the site, broke up blocks into irregular shapes. Large house lots with room for garden plots lowered housing density. To discourage adjacent development and preserve the physical integrity of the villages, Draper also encouraged mill owners to buy sites much larger than the area of the mill village: both Pacolet and Chicopee are surrounded by large greenbelts that help maintain their distinctly rural appearance. Extensive woodlands, winding roads, and low-density housing, all adjusted to the existing terrain, belie their careful planning by projecting the image of an open landscape.

Draper encouraged engagement with this landscape by using site planning as a way of shaping the residents' experiences. In Pacolet, he drew attention to the village's scenic location above the Saluda by siting houses along the bluffs overlooking the river. To take advantage of spectacular views, he constructed an elaborate scenic overlook just above the river dam, with a series of steps and landings descending to the riverbank, providing workers with opportunities to appreciate the native landscape as part of their everyday activities. To accommodate the mill town's daily pedestrian traffic of workers to the mill, children to school, and housewives to the store, Draper, following Olmsted's example, furnished separate

Figure 5.9 Entering Chicopee, Georgia. A broad green common lined with shade trees separated the mill village from the plant and served as a buffer between community and industry. (Photographed by the author, 1991.)

pedestrian paths, with dense rows of trees separating the wide sidewalks from the winding streets. The trees lining the street offered shade and a microclimate that were important amenities in the Southern heat.

Increased leisure time, made possible by the reduction of the workweek to fifty hours, provided opportunities for other communal experiences away from the workplace. Draper's park systems expanded to include more recreational facilities, with baseball diamonds, playgrounds, picnic areas, and even, in Chicopee, a swimming pool. In order not to disturb the landscape, they were always unobtrusively sited. In the wooded hills above Pacolet, Draper hid an elaborate two-level park. Set into a natural slope, an open-air amphitheater, entered from above through a pergola-covered walkway and surrounded by grassy meadows, created a secluded setting for community gatherings and events.

Draper sought a careful balance between modern improvements and traditional images. His attempts "to blend modern forms with the long-existing living habits and social customs of the locality"[50] became more intense as new technology such as the automobile and the radio, appeared in the mill village, gradually changing its relationship to the wider society. By 1920 many mill workers could afford to purchase an automobile, even if it was "a limping old jalopy." At Chicopee, Draper provided group garages hidden at the end of blocks. Automobiles helped lessen the isolation of the mill village and, as families took weekend drives to visit friends and relatives on distant farms and in mill towns, strengthened the cohesiveness of the mill culture by connecting the extensive network of Piedmont mill villages into a regional community. The radio, found in virtually every mill home, not only put mill workers and their families in touch with the developing mass culture but validated their own musical tastes by broadcasting the traditional music played by string bands and fiddlers. On Saturday night, mill families listening to the "Grand Ole Opry" could hear Fiddlin' John Carson or the North Carolina Ramblers, once mill workers like them, sing of experiences that resonated in their own lives.[51]

Even the functional improvements that Draper always insisted on, such as drainage, modern utilities, and paved roads, were never allowed to undermine the rural character of the villages. To defeat the notorious red clay soil of the area, which regularly changed from mud to dust, both Pacolet and Chicopee had elaborate drainage systems, with street gutters and storm drains faced with local stone. Automobile roads were limited to a minimum width and followed the natural contours of the land in gentle curves that were also used to provide additional drainage. To disturb the natural landscape as little as possible, power lines and utilities were either placed underground, as at Chicopee, or at the rear of the lots.

Housing also integrated modern improvements with traditional habits. Buildings were fitted into the natural landscape as much as possible (Fig. 5.10). Although Draper did not design housing, he exercised considerable control over the choice of housing type; he favored the ground-hugging bungalow as an improvement over the frame mill house on piers. The bungalow style, which easily lent itself to innumerable variations in detail and finish—in Chicopee, thirty-one different types were built—undermined the uniformity of company housing. The popularity of the ubiquitous bungalow in the South also removed much of the stigma attached to easily identifiable mill houses, suggesting equality of mill workers with their neighbors. Chicopee's brick houses, which featured indoor plumbing, electricity, and hot water, established a standard of accommodation much higher than that of most of the housing in nearby Gainesville. If large front and rear porches remained standard features, they no longer had to be used as primary family living spaces, since the plans for four- and five-room houses now differentiated space into private and public zones, just as middle-class dwellings had a quarter of a century earlier.[52]

There were still fundamental problems that design could not address, and even

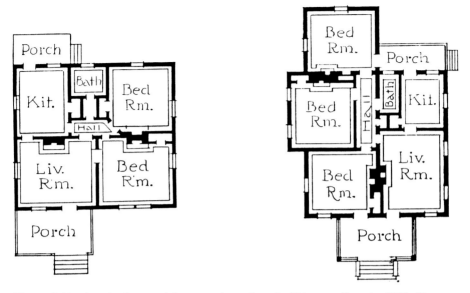

Figure 5.10 Plans for four- and five-room bungalows in Chicopee, Georgia, 1925. The organization of the rooms follows middle-class models by separating public from private spaces. Indoor plumbing has become a standard feature. (From Johnson & Johnson, *Chicopee* [Chicopee, Ga.: Johnson & Johnson, 1979].)

Draper's most successful villages retained clear social limitations. Blacks were assigned smaller and cruder dwellings than the rest of the workers and remained segregated on the outskirts of the village. Social control was still very much in evidence, even if impersonally administered within a corporate structure. At Chicopee, Johnson & Johnson imposed cleanliness and health as the guiding principles of the town (Fig. 5.11). Objecting to dirt produced by workers' cows, the mill instead opened a model dairy farm to supply free milk to each house. Resident nurses employed by the mill conducted regular inspections to enforce the village's extensive list of regulations, governing everything from cleaning toilets to supervising children.[53] By 1925, as the textile industry went into an extreme depression, abruptly curtailing his mill village practice, it was clear that, despite the excellence of his designs, Draper's imagery and amenities could not efface the reality of the mill village system.

Postscript: The Mill Village in the New Deal

The 1929 depression worsened the situation of the already ailing textile industry. To survive in a contracting market, mills continued to rationalize production, extending the stretch-out even further. But even such extreme measures had little effect, and in 1932 the Roosevelt administration's new program for economic revitalization, the National Industrial Recovery Act (NIRA), first directed its attention to the cotton textile industry. The Cotton Textile Code, designed to stimulate production, represented the mill owner's interests but also contained labor provisions imposed by prolabor New Dealers. Clauses that required minimum wages and hours and gave workers the right to collective bargaining clearly threatened the owners' control of the mill villages. The code also struck at the heart of regional wage differences and the "mill problem" by suggesting that Southern mills dispose of their villages.[54]

To textile workers, the benefits promised by the NIRA proved to be illusory. The stretch-out worsened, minimum wages were rarely met, and the legal right to organize was negated in practice by mill owners who fired any worker who joined a union. In spite of this, membership in the United Textile Workers (UTW) grew from 40,000 in September 1933 to 270,000 in August 1934, and the atmosphere in mill villages grew tense. On 13 February 1934, workers in Spindale, North Carolina, residents of an attractive village designed by Earle Draper, were the first to walk out (Fig. 5.12). Although the outraged mill owner, K. S. Tanner, fought back by firing union members, Spindale union leaders warned that a general strike was inevitable. By Labor Day, the UTW had led more than 400,000 mill workers off the job, the largest single labor conflict in American history. UTW "flying squadron" automobile convoys sped from mill to mill organizing walkouts, and radio talks by union leaders spread strike news across the Piedmont. When the news reached Chicopee, a violent wildcat strike shut down the plant. The management responded by calling in the National Guard and completely closing down production.[55]

In spite of this dramatic outburst from previously silent workers, the strike ended in defeat and did not lead to subsequent unionization. At Chicopee, striking workers were fired and evicted, and the plant resumed production only when a completely new set of workers and managers was brought in. Workers returned to their jobs, but the mill village system gradually dissolved as its social and economic rationale disappeared. The NIRA was declared unconstitutional, but other New Deal legislation, such as the Wagner Act, maintained labor's right to organize. Owners turned to other methods to fend off the threat of unionization. The spread of automobile ownership allowed workers to commute, ending the need to provide housing to attract labor. In the wake of the general strike, mills began to dismantle their villages and sell off their housing; ten years later, Harriet Herring was able to catalogue the "passing of the mill village." Today, with a few isolated exceptions, the cotton mill village as an institution is dead, the final chapter in the history of the American company town.[56]

The New Deal also gave Earle S. Draper the opportunity for the ultimate expression of his rural planning style, the Tennessee Valley Authority (TVA) town of Norris, Tennessee, begun in 1933 (Fig. 5.13). Although he was unknown outside the South, Draper's familiarity with Southern conditions and his extensive mill village experience led to his selection as the physical planner—Director of Land Planning and Housing—for the newly formed TVA, a position many planners considered the most desirable job of the decade. Draper's plan for Norris both summed up and transcended his mill village designs. Norris, a government-sponsored company town, was intended first to house workers on the Norris Dam and then to become a permanent community based on a new social concept combining small-

Summing Up

Starting with a perfectly clean slate in mill, in village and in every home, the Chicopee Manufacturing Corporation of Georgia has taken every possible precaution to assure the COMFORT, SAFETY, HEALTH, HAPPINESS and WELFARE of its workers. In return for these provisions, we ask every employee and every member of his family to:

> KEEP CLEAN
> KEEP WELL
> KEEP THE PEACE
> KEEP STRICT OBSERVANCE OF THE FOLLOWING HOUSEHOLD, VILLAGE AND MILL REGULATIONS—

Household Regulations

1. Keep wash basins, bath tubs and water closet clean. (Special brushes are provided for this purpose.)

2. Keep your cook stoves and ice boxes *clean.*

3. Keep walls and ceilings *clean* in every room.

4. Keep porches *clean.*

5. Keep screens in windows through the summer.

6. Report at once any trouble with the lights or plumbing.

7. Keep grass on lawns cut, and grounds around house clean and free from rubbish.

8. Do not allow garbage or ashes to collect upon the premises. Put them in the cans provided for this purpose. These cans will be collected and their contents disposed of daily without charge.

9. Do not waste water and electric current. Turn off all electric lights, water faucets and electric stoves or heaters as soon as you are through with them.

10. Follow all directions of the visiting nurse when she makes her regular inspection of the premises.

Village Regulations

1. Keep sidewalks swept.

2. Help to keep all streets, parks and playgrounds clean. Do not scatter papers or other rubbish on any part of the property.

3. Never park an automobile in front of a fire hydrant.

4. Do not tamper with fire hydrants or the village telephones.

5. Do not damage trees, shrubs, roadways or any other public property.

6. Cows, mules, horses and goats must not be kept upon the property and household pets must not include a vicious dog or any other animal which can menace or annoy your neighbors.

7. Know where your children are and what they are doing when not in school or in charge of a director at the playgrounds.

8. Use village telephones to instantly report an outbreak of fire.

9. Report immediately to the trained nurse in every case of sickness.

10. Report all public nuisances, disturbances and violations of the law to the Department of Public Safety.

11. Use village telephones to report accidents.

Figure 5.12 The 1934 general strike led by the United Textile Workers. During the height of the Depression, more than 400,000 textile workers walked out of the mills, the largest single strike in American history. Although the strike ended in defeat for the workers, it marked the beginning of the end for the mill village. (From Robert Dunn and Jack Hardy, *Labor and Textiles* [New York: International Publishers, 1931].)

scale industry and subsistence farming. Just across the Great Smoky Mountains from the Piedmont cotton belt, Norris, situated in a rural upland settled by a homogeneous Appalachian population, addressed a set of regional conditions similar to that of the Piedmont.[57]

Given a free hand by the TVA and without the social and industrial constraints of textile production, Draper created a town plan that pushed the techniques developed in mill villages toward even greater regional specificity (Fig. 5.14). Adapting his informal planning to the uneven topography of the heavily wooded site produced a loose road pattern, with roads running along ridges and into valleys, often culminating in cul-de-sacs. One of Draper's mill town trademarks, the parkland buffer, was expanded to include an enormous greenbelt circling the town and a limited-access parkway to Knoxville, intended to act as a woodland barrier against strip development. The town's rural character was emphasized by large and irregular lots to be used for gardening. The generous provision of green space further reduced the density of the housing. House sites were related to topography rather than street lines. Draper laid out the sites not by drawing them on a plan but by

Figure 5.11 List of household and village regulations distributed to residents of Chicopee, Georgia. Note the emphasis on cleanliness and the implied role of the company nurse as enforcer of these regulations. (From Johnson & Johnson, *Chicopee*.)

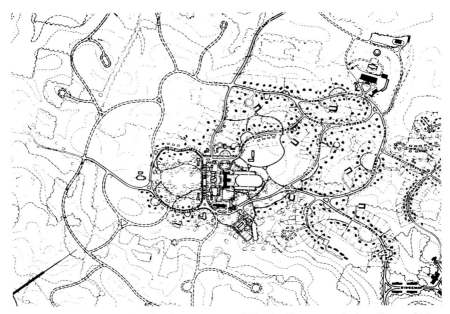

Figure 5.13 Draper's design for the TVA town of Norris, Tennessee, is the climax of his rural planning style. At the center of the plan, a tightly organized formal core is mirrored by a huge green common. The rest of the town follows a loose pattern of roads along the top of ridges. Houses were sited according to topography rather than standard setbacks. (Courtesy of the Tennessee Valley Authority.)

walking the site and staking them out. As in Chicopee, house plans were varied—thirty different plans for 294 houses—but now housing styles based on indigenous types replaced generic bungalows, referring to the previous vernacular of the area, which had been submerged under Norris Lake. Dogtrot plans and traditional materials such as hickory shakes split by hand echoed the log cabin tradition and, although criticized by modernists, offered familiar images of shelter, now supplied with fully electric kitchens.[58]

At the center of the plan, a fourteen-acre green common circles Norris's only monumental building, the consolidated school, which had now replaced the mill as the symbolic heart of the town, signaling a completely new set of social intentions. Other informal community buildings formed a civic cluster scattered around the central common. Even more than the gradual disappearance of the mill village, Draper's plan for Norris signifies the true ending of the textile mill village. The TVA's project of state-sponsored rural electrification and recreational development proposed a new social and economic paradigm as an alternative to the exploitation and cultural disruption of Piedmont industrialization, opening up a new era of development that would once again transform the economic landscape of the South.[59]

Figure 5.14 A street in Norris, Tennessee. In comparison to Draper's mill towns, Norris presents an even more rural image. Houses, sited in relation to topography, are dotted along streets that wind through woodlands. (Photographed by author, 1991.)

Notes

1. Charles E. Augur, "Earle S. Draper: Unsung Hero of American Planned Community and Regional Development" (Paper presented at the Second National Conference on American Planning History, Columbus, Ohio, 25 Sept. 1987); Thomas W. Hanchett, "Earle Sumner Draper, City Planner of the New South," in *Early Twentieth-Century Suburbs in North Carolina*, ed. Catherine W. Bishir and Lawrence S. Early (Raleigh: North Carolina Department of Cultural Resources, 1985), 79; Earle Draper, interview with author, Vero Beach, Fla., 19 Mar. 1984. As Augur's title suggests, Draper's work is just beginning to be studied by historians of urban planning. See also Norman T. Newton, *Design on the Land* (Cambridge: Harvard University Press, 1971), 486–89.

2. Broadus Mitchell, *The Rise of Cotton Mills in the South* (Baltimore: Johns Hopkins University Press, 1921), is the classic account of this process; more recent work has challenged Mitchell's assessment of the philanthropic motives of Southern textile entrepreneurs: Melton A. McLaurin, *Paternalism and Protest* (Westport, Conn.: Greenwood Publishing, 1971).

3. The post–Civil War shortage of cash forced small farmers to turn to local merchants for cash or credit. To guarantee their investment, lenders demanded a lien on the crop. The crop-lien system, legalized in 1866, increased cotton crops while decreasing prices. Unable to repay their loans, indebted farmers lost their land and turned into tenants, cultivating shares of land that they had once owned. Mill work provided one way out of this continuing cycle. McLaurin, *Paternalism and Protest*, 13.

4. In 1910, Southern mill workers born of foreign parents constituted 0.4 percent of the labor force, foreign-born operatives 0.3 percent. Ibid., 20.

5. For a detailed account of this process, see Jacquelyn Dowd Hall et al., *Like a Family: The Making of a Southern Cotton Mill World* (Chapel Hill: University of North Carolina Press, 1987), 44–113.

6. Herbert Lahne, *The Cotton Mill Worker* (New York: Farrar and Rinehart, 1944), 41.

7. Although, by 1913, most Southern states had laws that prohibited the employment of children less than twelve years old, these regulations contained many exemptions and were rarely enforced. The 1907–1908 Bureau of Labor study found that 92 percent of mills in South Carolina, for example, ignored child labor regulations. Many Southern mill owners fought against federal legislation, a battle that culminated in the suit brought by a Charlotte mill worker against the Keating-Owen Child Labor Bill of 1916, which resulted in the overturning of federal laws against child labor. Child labor, however, did decline, and by the 1920s less than 10 percent of mill workers were less than sixteen years old. McLaurin, *Paternalism and Protest*, 22; Hall et al., *Like a Family*, 58–61.

8. McLaurin, *Paternalism and Protest*, 8; David Carlton, *Mill and Town in South Carolina 1880–1920* (Baton Rouge: Louisiana State University Press, 1982), 152.

9. McLaurin, *Paternalism and Protest*, 60–67.

10. Lahne, *Cotton Mill Worker*, 36–39.

11. Hall et al., *Like a Family*, 115.

12. Lahne, *Cotton Mill Worker*, 61; Hall et al., *Like a Family*, 127–29.

13. Hall et al., *Like a Family*, 126. The classic study of religion in the mill village is Liston Pope, *Millhands and Preachers* (New Haven: Yale University Press, 1914).

14. Harriet Herring, *Welfare Work in Mill Villages* (Chapel Hill: University of North Carolina Press, 1930), 99.

15. Pope, *Millhands and Preachers*, 126–140.

16. Tompkins, *Cotton Mill: Commercial Features* (Charlotte, N.C.: Published by the Author, 1899), 35.

17. *Report on the Condition of Woman and Child Wage Earners in the United States*, vol. 645, 61st Congress, 2d Session (Washington, D.C.: Government Printing Office, 1910), 596.

18. McLaurin, *Paternalism and Protest*, 38.

19. McLaurin, *Paternalism and Protest*, 45. The political career of Coleman L. Blease provides a rare instance of mill workers' effective participation in the political process. Much of Blease's support was provided by mill workers, who responded to his attacks on modernization and urban middle-class values. See Carlton, *Mill and Town*, 215–272.

20. McLaurin, *Paternalism and Protest*, 43–48.

21. Richard Ely, "An American Industrial Experiment," *Harpers Magazine* 105 (1902): 39–45; McLaurin *Paternalism and Protest* pp. 33–34.

22. Hall et al., *Like a Family*, 14.

23. Ibid, 140–45.

24. Brent Glass, "Southern Mill Hills: Design in a Public Place," in *Carolina Dwelling: Towards Preservation of Place: In Celebration of the North Carolina Vernacular Landscape*, ed. Doug Swaim (Raleigh: North Carolina State University School of Design, 1978), 139. See also Catharine Bishir, *North Carolina Architecture* (Chapel Hill: University of North Carolina Press, 1990), and Catharine Bishir, *Architects and Builders in North Carolina* (Chapel Hill: University of North Carolina Press, 1990).

25. Glass, "Southern Mill Hills," 140–42; Jennings Rhyne, *Some Southern Cotton Mill Workers and Their Villages* (Chapel Hill: University of North Carolina Press, 1930), 7–19; Dale Newman, "Work and Community Life in a Southern Textile Town," *Labor History* 19

(1978): 212; Leifur Magnussen, "Southern Cotton Mill Villages," in *Housing by Employers in the United States*, Bulletin no. 263, U.S. Department of Labor, Bureau of Labor Statistics (Washington, D.C.: Government Printing Office, 1920), 139–60.

26. Hall et al., *Like a Family*, 127.

27. Tompkins, *Cotton Mill*, 117–21; Allen Toullos, *Habits of Industry* (Chapel Hill: University of North Carolina Press, 1989), 157–61.

28. Tompkins, *Cotton Mill*, 117.

29. Ibid., 121.

30. Leonora Ellis, "A Model Factory Town," *Forum* 32 (1901–1902): 60–61; Ely, "American Industrial Experiment," 40; Budgett Meakin, *Model Factories and Villages* (London: T. Fisher Unwin, 1905), 392–93; Clare de Graffenried, "The Georgia Cracker in the Cotton Mill," *Century Magazine*, February 1981, 483; Hall et al., *Like a Family*, 119.

31. Lahne, *Cotton Mill Worker*, 66.

32. W. J. Cash, *The Mind of the South* (New York: Vintage, 1941), 274.

33. Catherine W. Bishir, introduction to Bishir and Early, *Early Twentieth-Century Suburbs in North Carolina*, 3.

34. Jeannette P. Nichols "Does the Mill Village Foster Any Social Types?" *Social Forces* 2 (March 1924): 350–57; Carlton, *Mill and Town*, 171–200.

35. Hall et al., *Like a Family*, 107, 131–32; Harriet Herring, *Welfare Work*, 108–10. Two basic sources on welfare work are Daniel Nelson, *Workers and Managers* (Madison: University of Wisconsin Press, 1975) and Stuart Brandes, *American Welfare Capitalism* (Chicago: University of Chicago Press, 1976).

36. Herring, *Welfare Work*, 135–39, 206.

37. Hall et al., *Like a Family*, 210.

38. Herring, *Welfare Work*, 115, 123–24, 126.

39. Hall et al., *Like a Family*, 133–39.

40. Earle Draper interview, author.

41. Auger, "Earle Draper," 214; Hall et al., *Like a Family*, 264.

42. Draper interview, author; Earle S. Draper, "Southern Textile Village Planning," *Landscape Architecture* 18 (October 1927): 1–27; Earle S. Draper, "Community Work in Southern Mill Villages," *Southern Textile Bulletin*, 8 May 1919, 31.

43. Draper interview, author.

44. Although Draper does not mention them, undoubtedly he was also aware of the extensive landscape, company town, and suburb planning done in the United States beginning in 1919 with Forest Hills Gardens, designed by Grosvenor Atterbury. Most of these plans were prominently featured in architectural and landscape journals of the period, and many of them were collected in Werner Hegemann and Elbert Peet's *The American Vitruvius*, published in 1922 (New York: Architectural Book Publishing Company). Draper interview, author; Auger, "Earle Draper," 214–20.

45. Draper interview, author.

46. Lawrence G. Foster, *A Company That Cares* (New Brunswick, N.J.: Johnson & Johnson, 1986), 34–35.

47. Glass, "Southern Mill Hills," 145.

48. Johnson and Johnson, "Reflections—Chicopee, Georgia" (Chicopee: Johnson & Johnson, 1979), 11–12.

49. Draper, "Southern Textile Village," 20.

50. Earle S. Draper, "Applied Home Economics in TVA Houses," *Journal of Home Economics* 27, no. 10 (December 1935): 632.

51. Cash, *Mind of the South*, 274; Hall et al., *Like a Family*, 259–61.

52. Johnson and Johnson, "Reflections," 33; Hall et al., *Like a Family*, 127.

53. Johnson and Johnson, "Reflections," 42–44.

54. James A. Hodges, *New Deal Labor Policy and the Southern Cotton Textile Industry* (Knoxville: University of Tennessee Press, 1986), 10–11.

55. Johnson and Johnson, "Reflections," 14.

56. Harriet Herring, *The Passing of the Mill Village* (Chapel Hill: University of North Carolina Press, 1949), 9.

57. Arthur Morgan, the first TVA director, described the concept behind Norris in terms that echo Draper's, suggesting a sympathy in their aims: "The mountain regions of the South are the last great bulwarks of individuality in America. . . . The Southern Highlander is different. He likes rural life. His income has been and is very small. Agriculture alone will not support him. Today great industries are settling in his midst. Some of these factories tend to destroy his type of civilization. The Southern Highlander is often regarded merely as cheap labor to be exploited rather than as the representative of a valuable type of culture to be encouraged and protected." Quoted in Walter Creese, *TVA's Public Planning: The Vision, The Reality* (Knoxville: University of Tennessee Press, 1990), 251–52. For another general discussion of TVA planning, see Phoebe Culter, *The Landscape of the New Deal* (New Haven: Yale University Press, 1985). More specific discussions of Norris include Earle S. Draper, "The New TVA Town of Norris, Tennessee, *American City* 48, no. 12 (December 1933): 67–68; Tracy Auger, "The Planning of the Town of Norris," *American Architect* 128 (April 1926): 19–26.

58. Draper interview, author. Earle S. Draper, Jr., "The TVA's Forgotten Town: Norris, Tennessee," *Landscape Architecture* 78, no. 2 (March 1988): 96–102.

59. An extensive literature critically addresses the question of whether the TVA fulfilled the hopes of its early sponsors. See Phillip Selznick, *TVA and the Grass Roots* (Berkeley: University of California Press, 1949); Thomas K. McGraw, *Morgan vs. Lilienthal* (Chicago: Loyola University Press, 1970); *TVA: Fifty Years of Grassroots Bureaucracy*, ed. Erwin Hargrove and Paul Conklin (Urbana: University of Illinois Press, 1983).

6

Company Towns in the Western United States

LELAND M. ROTH

The story of company towns in the American West differs from that in the East in some significant respects. First, the area west of the Mississippi measures nearly fourteen hundred miles east to west, and more than twelve hundred miles from the Canadian border to the southern extremity of Arizona (Fig. 6.1). By comparison, the more heavily industrialized Northeast, from Massachusetts Bay to Wisconsin, and from the Adirondacks to the Chesapeake Bay, is less than 860 by 370 miles. Moreover, in the early years of this century, this area was crisscrossed by a dense network of rails, whereas in the West only a few trunk lines ran from east to west, making movement from north to south difficult over the long, rugged distances. Second, the climatic regions in the West differ in the extreme, from the cool, damp coastal conifer forests of the Pacific Northwest, to the high uplands of the Rocky Mountains, to the hot, arid deserts of the Southwest. In large measure these climatic differences also circumscribe the two major industries of the West: lumbering in the coastal mountains and mining in the Rockies and the desert Southwest. To a greater extent than elsewhere, these industrial activities continue, although in diminished capacity and under different circumstances, reflecting advances in productivity in all industries in the past quarter-century.

Types of Western Company Towns

Planning of industrial communities and housing in the East and in the West has received relatively little attention since the mid-1960s, when two important works appeared: a small book by historian James Allen and a doctoral dissertation by

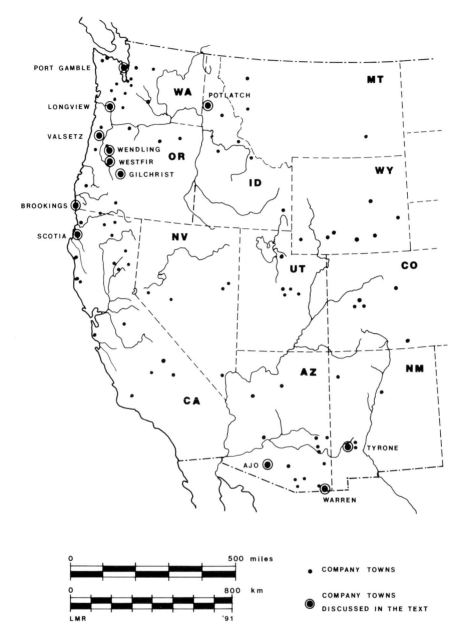

PORT GAMBLE

WA

POTLATCH

MT

LONGVIEW

VALSETZ

WENDLING

WESTFIR

OR

GILCHRIST

ID

WY

BROOKINGS

SCOTIA

NV

UT

CO

AZ

NM

CA

AJO

TYRONE

WARREN

0   500 miles

0   800 km

LMR   '91

• COMPANY TOWNS

⊙ COMPANY TOWNS
  DISCUSSED IN THE TEXT

Figure 6.1 Map of western United States showing company-owned and -operated towns. (L. M. Roth)

historian Kenneth A. Erickson.[1] In contrast, Eastern industrial settlements have been the subject of several books, mostly devoted to individual planned communities.[2] As Allen notes, Western towns fall largely into three groups: (1) coal-mining towns (primarily in the region of the Four Corners Monument, where the borders of Utah, Colorado, New Mexico, and Arizona cross at right angles); (2) copper-mining towns (largely in the southern quarters of Arizona and New Mexico); and (3) lumbering towns in the Northwest (in the Coast Range and on both sides of the Cascade Range, through Washington, Oregon, and northern California).[3] This order also corresponds to the degree of attention given by companies to planning and building design, for, as Allen notes, coal-mining towns as a group were those least often given the benefit of forethought and usually had the fewest amenities.[4] Copper-mining towns, by comparison, included more examples of carefully planned street layouts and buildings, even if some plans existed only on paper or were interrupted in the course of development. Slightly larger, perhaps, was the number of planned lumber towns. In all three groups, however, the small number of planned towns was far surpassed by countless thrown-together work camps, temporary villages, and even permanent settlements that grew of their own accord.

A few towns were developed for other activities, but this group is relatively small compared to the scores of towns of the three types already defined. One of the better known today—and also the most atypical in its time, so far as the industry and planner were concerned—was the original plan developed by Frederick Law Olmsted in 1873 for the terminus of the Northern Pacific Railroad at Tacoma, Washington. The proposed site was on steeply sloping land, on a bluff overlooking Commencement Bay at the southern extremity of Puget Sound. Olmsted submitted a street plan that followed the topography, with streets gently inclined on the steep grades and including ample public parklands. Railroad officials summarily rejected Olmsted's scheme, sputtering that there wasn't a straight line or right angle in it; that the blocks were "shaped like melons, pears, and sweet potatoes"; and that one long block looked like a banana. As the planning historian John Reps has noted, "Westerners conditioned to hundreds of settlements west of the Mississippi were simply unable to conceive of a town not composed of the simplest of rectangular elements."[5] The company had its railroad engineer, Isaac Smith, prepare a more conventional plan of two-angled grids colliding at Division Street, producing in the city as built impossible grades on the streets plunging downhill.

Another specialized company town in the west was Parco (later Sinclair), Wyoming, built in the 1920s for an oil refinery. Several towns based on the manufacture of cement were created, including Boettcher, Colorado, founded in 1926 by the Ideal Cement Company, and Davenport, California, built in 1906–1907 by the Santa Cruz Portland Cement Company. Because of the need to keep explosives manufacture away from settled towns, the DuPont Company established two isolated towns, at Louviers, Colorado, and DuPont, Washington. A particularly large operation was the creation of Litchfield Park, Arizona, built in 1916 on twenty-six thousand acres outside Phoenix by the Goodyear Tire and Rubber Company for the production of long-fiber cotton used in tire cords. Specialized mining operations resulted in the development of two towns in the 1920s: Climax, Colorado, where molybdenum was mined, and Trona, California, established by the American Potash and Chemical Company.[6]

Company Town Taxonomy

What constitutes a company town? One definition would be that it is a community devoted to a single industry, with all land and buildings owned by the company and all housing rented to employees. Another definition would include communities with one or more industries that may have owned all the land at one time but gradually sold off the land to other businesses and homeowner-employees. For the purposes of this chapter—because of the limited number of planned wholly owned company towns in the West—a definition closer to the second will be used. In his survey of Western company towns, James Allen counted 191 communities in eleven states (Washington, Oregon, California, Nevada, Idaho, Montana, Utah, Wyoming, Colorado, Arizona, and New Mexico).[7] If these same town sites were surveyed today, the total would be much lower, for many Western towns have closed or have been razed. This is a further contrast to what has happened to Eastern company towns in the near-century since company town building began in the West. Many Eastern industrial communities, now hedged in by the expanded megalopolis of the Eastern Seaboard, have become desirable sites for "gentrification," as has happened in Lowell, Massachusetts. In the West, however, the industrial towns have remained largely isolated, so that absorption into surrounding communities has rarely been possible. Moreover, since nearly all these Western industrial towns were based on extractive processes (whether cutting trees or mining ore), the raw materials have become depleted so that economic factors have caused the abandonment of many of these settlements, even those carefully designed by professional planners and architects. In fact, a number of temporary lumber camps consisted of small buildings built on skids or of bunkhouses built in boxcars so they could be moved to a new location as soon as the trees were clear-cut in one tract. The entire town of Shevlin, a lumber "settlement" in Oregon, was famous for being moved from site to site in Klamath and Deschutes counties until it was closed and the peripatetic post office discontinued in 1951.[8]

Another distinction between Eastern company towns and those in the West is their chronology, for the great majority of those built in the Rockies and farther west were begun after the turn of the century. Even those few planned and designed by professionals have nearly all been closed, dismantled, or obliterated after little more than fifty years of existence.

Company towns fall into roughly six categories, beginning with those with street layouts made by the corporation, company engineers, or company-hired engineers, and with buildings and housing built by company crews or local speculative contractors and based on prevailing vernacular housing types.[9] In the East this type appeared early in Lowell, Massachusetts, begun in 1822; in the West it is extremely well represented by one of the first lumber towns, Teekalet (later renamed Port

Gamble), begun in 1853 on an inlet in Puget Sound, Washington (then the Oregon Territory) (Fig. 6.9).

A second company town type had streets laid out by company engineers, but houses and other buildings designed by an architect. In the East, this type is represented by the creation of Echota, Niagara Falls, New York, in 1891–1895, laid out by the engineer John Bogart, with houses and community buildings by the celebrated New York architects McKim, Mead & White.[10] In the West there are few examples of this kind of development, one of which is the small lumber town of McCormick, on State Highway 6 in Lewis County, Washington. Developed by J. E. Wheeler in 1912–1915, the street plan was laid out by company officials, but Wheeler's local residence, the company store, and the town church were all designed by Ellis F. Lawrence of Portland, Oregon, one of the most esteemed architects in the area[11] (Fig. 6.2).

The third type of company town has a street and landscape plan laid out by a professional landscape architect, with housing and other buildings by local contractors or others hired by the company. In the East this is found at Hopedale, Massachusetts, where Warren H. Manning, an assistant of Frederick Law Olmsted, was engaged by the Draper Company as early as 1889.[12] In the West, however, there appear to be no comparable examples; in the few instances where professionals were engaged to develop a landscape plan they were also engaged to design the buildings (this is discussed later).

The cases in which a pair of professional designers were engaged to lay out the town and to design the major public buildings and housing represent the fourth type of company town. A good example in the East is Kohler, four miles west of Sheboygan, Wisconsin, planned by Werner Hegemann and Elbert Peets, with later modifications by the Olmsted brothers and English Arts and Crafts–like houses designed by the architects Brust & Philipp.[13] One particularly ambitious Western mining community begun in this way was the proposed model town of Warren, Arizona, laid out by Warren H. Manning, a former associate of Frederick Law Olmsted, with buildings and housing design by the architects Applegarth & Elliott[14] (Fig. 6.3).

Somewhat more numerous in the west were examples of the fifth type of company town, in which both site plan and buildings were designed by a single individual. Excellent examples in the East include the communities designed by Grosvenor Atterbury, including Indian Hills, Worcester, Massachusetts, and Erwin, Tennessee.[15] Several comparable industrial communities were started in the West, most notably the copper mining town of Tyrone, New Mexico, designed almost wholly by Bertram Goodhue, and the lumber town of Brookings, Oregon, whose street plan and initial buildings were designed by Bernard Maybeck but were never fully realized[16] (Figs. 6.7 and 6.11).

The final type of planned company town is that developed from an existing settlement, either one converted to industry or expanded and replanned around an existing but smaller industrial site. An Eastern example developed from a rural village converted to industry is Naugatuck, Connecticut. For a century, this was a local trading point that, by the midnineteenth century, became the center of both the

Figure 6.2 McCormick, Lewis County, Washington; photographed ca. 1913–1914. Buildings by the architect Ellis F. Lawrence include the McCormick Lumber Company offices, 1912 (lower right, with front colonnade), and the J. E. Wheeler house, 1912 (top center). Later, on the open land between buildings, Lawrence built the Presbyterian Church, 1914–1915. (E. F. Lawrence Collection, courtesy of Special Collections, Knight Library, University of Oregon.)

rubber and malleable iron industries.[17] A most interesting Eastern example of an enlarged industrial site is Midland, Pennsylvania, whose original rigid grid plan was expanded with curvilinear streets adjusted to the hilly terrain by Albert H. Spahr in 1916.[18] Evidence available so far suggests that there are no comparable Western examples. The reasons are several: in mining towns, there was no pressure to encourage retention of skilled labor by providing amenities as there was in the East, where workers moved from place to place; the distances between Western mining communities largely precluded easy relocation by workers, whether skilled managers or laborers. Much the same was true of lumbering communities in the Northwest. Once rudimentary settlements were begun, as in the mining camps of Bisbee or Jerome, Arizona, there was little incentive for the parent corporation to make significant improvements in street layout or buildings.

Mining Towns

Coal-Mining Towns

The detailed study of coal-mining towns undertaken by Leifur Magnusson of the U.S. Government Bureau of Labor in 1919–1920 underscored the poor esteem this industry had earned because of its Western mining settlements.[19] James Allen reiterates that coal-mining towns had a well-deserved reputation as the dirtiest and least well-planned and constructed of the Western industrial communities. The great majority of these coal camps had been started to provide fuel by the transcontinental railroads. Those later owned and operated by Colorado Fuel and Iron Corporation, in particular, were among the more unsightly and unsanitary. Given such poor working conditions, it is understandable that the coal industry was greatly beset with labor unrest, culminating in the massacre at Ludlow, Colorado, in 1914. One of the few coal towns that received positive comment was Dawson, New Mexico, owned and operated by the Phelps-Dodge Company as a source of fuel for the trains it used in its copper-mining operations. It was closed in the 1940s; nothing of it remains today.

Copper-Mining Towns

The strike and subsequent deaths at Ludlow, Colorado, indicate the general labor unrest that periodically swept through the Western states in all three of the major industries.[20] The greater attention given to the layout and building design of several copper-mining towns can be interpreted, perhaps, as an effort of Eastern-based management to obviate some of the conditions that gave rise to labor unrest. Copper mining appeared early in the Southwest. One of the earliest efforts was by the Spanish at the presidio of Tubac in Arizona, which was taken over by the Sonora Exploring and Mining Company in 1856 but abandoned four years later because of Apache threats. Tubac and later operations in Arizona were little more than ragged mining camps. Even subsequent mines opened by North Americans later in the

nineteenth century that became boom towns—Jerome, Clifton, Morenci, Bisbee—
had no planning or organized building: they simply sprang up with buildings erected
on stilts along the sides of steep ravines.

Morenci, Arizona, was first settled in 1872 by William Church, who formed the
Detroit Copper Mining Company and began the first buildings there in 1880.
Seventeen years later the Detroit Copper Mining Company was absorbed into the
Phelps Dodge Corporation, based in New York City. Run by white Americans
(Anglos), it had a labor force increasingly made up of laborers imported from
Mexico; these Mexican *mineros* were paid a lower wage than Anglo laborers, laying
the seeds of repeated strike attempts by the *mineros* in the next two decades. The
proliferation of hillside shanties, saloons, dance halls, and other buildings formed
the picture of the archetypal Western mining town. When a fire destroyed the oldest
part of Morenci, it was rebuilt by Phelps Dodge with somewhat more attention to
visual order. The same pattern was evident at Bisbee, Arizona, where a mining
camp appeared in 1877, and in Jerome, Arizona, begun in 1876.[21] An attempt at
creating a more ordered environment was made at Clarkdale, Arizona, built by the
United Verde Copper Company in 1914 to be the smelter for ore from the Jerome
mines. Named for the senator from Montana, William A. Clark, who owned part of
the United Verde Copper Company, the town's unvaried ranks of housing units were
far from the city planning ideal and could hardly have been more distant from the
florid ostentatiousness of the mansion that Clark hired the architects Lord, Hewlett,
Hull & Murchinson to build for him in New York City between 1898 and 1904.[22]

The City Beautiful ideal was rather ambitiously taken as the model for a new
housing community near Bisbee, Arizona, to be called Warren after George Warren,
one of the early prospectors of the deposits that later came to be called the Copper
Queen Mines and were acquired by Phelps Dodge in 1881.[23] Located just four miles
southeast of Bisbee, Warren was to have every benefit that Bisbee lacked. The
venture was proposed by Henry Hoveland, H. A. Smith, and C. W. Van Dyke in
1905, and Warren H. Manning of Boston was hired to lay out the general plan. After
a visit to the high desert site in spring 1906, Manning developed the wedge-shaped
plan, fitted to the valley floor and focusing on a civic center at the southern end
(Fig. 6.3). Later that year, Manning arranged for the architects R. A. Applegarth
and Huger Elliott to design the major public buildings and to develop housing
prototypes. Applegarth and Elliott used a Spanish Mediterranean theme for the post
office, railroad station, and commercial buildings (Fig. 6.4). A simpler version was
used for the houses: villas for the Anglo managers and even simpler one- and two-
bedroom houses for the Mexican workers. Manning carefully devised the street
system to divert the rapid runoff of occasional heavy rains, and he proposed using
landscaping materials drawn from the desert. By late 1906, the basic infrastructure
was established, with the rail line from Bisbee completed, as well as the water
system and sewers. Early in 1907, however, an attempt at cornering the copper
market by New York speculators caused a deep but short-lived financial panic and
created confusion in the industry. Meanwhile, the architects met local resistance
regarding the clarity mandated by proposed building restrictions in the plan.
Applegarth and Elliott had hoped for a uniform building type and color scheme,

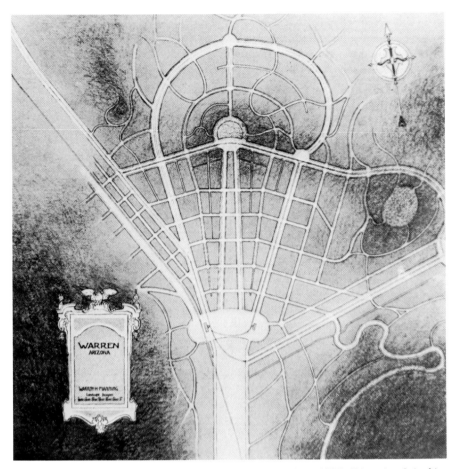

Figure 6.3 Warren, Arizona; plan by Warren H. Manning, ca. 1905. (*[American] Architectural Review* 15 [September 1908].)

with cream-colored stucco walls and red-brown tile roofs playing against the varied colors of the desert, but the first builders opted for their own designs and color choices. The ideal city scheme was largely ignored.

Far more successfully realized was Ajo, Arizona, 180 miles west of Bisbee and Warren, in the middle of the Sonoran Desert, which became part of the United States with the Gadsden Purchase of 1853.[24] *Ajo*, which can be used as an expletive in Spanish, fairly describes the miserable summer conditions in the desert; this and the very low grade of the surface ores there prevented exploitation of the deposits. By the end of the nineteenth century, the various abandoned claims in the region had been purchased by the New Cornelia Copper Company. Encouraged by the extension of the railroad to Gila Bend at the turn of the century, New Cornelia attempted in 1906 to start commercial mining, cut short by the panic in 1907. In 1911, the Calumet and Arizona Company bought a controlling interest in New Cornelia and

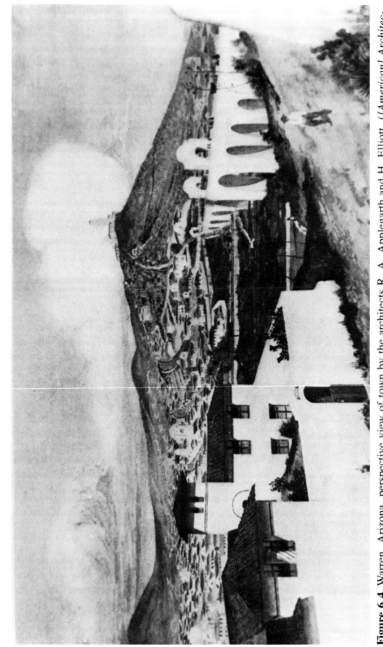

Figure 6.4 Warren, Arizona, perspective view of town by the architects R. A. Applegarth and H. Elliott. (*[American] Architectural Review* 15 [September 1908].)

began further explorations (in 1931, Phelps Dodge absorbed both the New Cornelia and the Calumet and Arizona companies). New tests revealed a rich lode of copper sulfite under a thick overburden of low-grade ore, and preparations for opening a large open-pit mine began. New chemical separation methods also made the Ajo project feasible, and the construction of an on-site smelter would make the venture centralized and more economically profitable. (In southeastern Arizona, around Bisbee and elsewhere, for example, ores were carried by rail to separate smelters.) The town project got under way when a deep well, six miles north of the town site, yielded abundant water. With 5 million gallons of water being produced a day, there was plenty for a flotation ore separation process, as well as for irrigation of the extensive landscaping and planting proposed for the new community.

The town plan was devised by the architects and planners William Kenyon and Maurice Maine (Fig. 6.5). Using zoning, they divided the settlement into four discrete sections, segregating not only the smelter from the workers but the employee ethnic groups from each other, with separate sections for the smelter, an Anglo section containing the town center with its shops and public buildings, a section for Mexican miners, and another for Papago workers.[25] The Anglo section

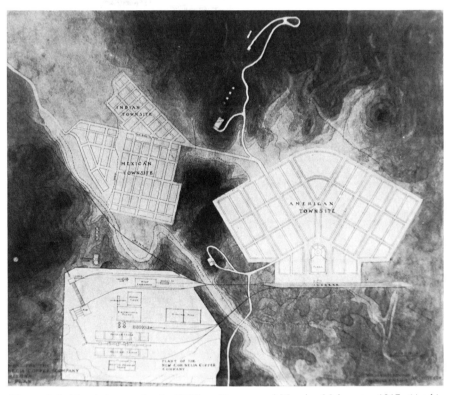

Figure 6.5 Ajo, Arizona, plan by William Kenyon and Maurice Maine, ca. 1917. (*Architecture* 39 [January 1919].)

focused on a town center, with buildings enclosing a plaza complete with bandstand and graced with palm trees and oleanders. At the opposite end of the plaza was the railroad station, whose Spanish Mediterranean style was used for the entire community (Fig. 6.6). The extended business blocks on either side of the plaza provided space for the company store, other shops, a moviehouse as well as a vaudeville theater, and a restaurant, bank, and post office, all connected by long arcades opening out to the plaza. These buildings, and others in the Mexican and Papago sections of the town, were of stucco-covered hollow clay tile construction. Altogether, more than $11 million (1919 dollars) was expended on building the new plant and town, which in the 1920s reached a maximum population of eight thousand.

The most architecturally elaborate of all the new copper towns was Tyrone, New Mexico. As the price of copper gradually rose after the panic of 1907, and especially as the European war artificially inflated the price of copper after 1914, the low-grade ores in the Burro Mountains of southwestern New Mexico appeared commercially minable. Between 1904 and 1913 Phelps Dodge purchased rights to more than one hundred old claims in the area; in another two years, the company had acquired rights to another two hundred. As the European war commenced in 1914, the New York–based company engaged the prominent New York architect Bertram Goodhue to design the town and its major buildings (although a hospital and courthouse were begun before Goodhue was hired). Wives of two company officials took a special interest in the plans for the new model community and pushed for the selection of a good architect.[26] Goodhue seemed an especially suitable choice since

Figure 6.6 Ajo, Arizona, view of central plaza in the American (Anglo) quarter, Kenyon and Maine, architects, ca. 1918–1919. (*Architecture* 39 [January 1919].)

he had attracted considerable attention with his elaborate Spanish Colonial Revival buildings for the Panama-California Exposition (San Diego, 1915) and had quickly been given other commissions in southern California.[27] The commission gave Goodhue an excellent opportunity to explore ideas on the planning of small communities and the design of modern dwelling units.

On the broad floor of a ravine or arroyo, Goodhue placed a formal plaza, his conception of an ideal Mexican village (Fig. 6.7; the plan is drawn upside down, with north toward the bottom). The open plaza, punctuated by a bandstand and a fountain, measured 140 × 250 feet and was enclosed by shops and public buildings connected by continuous arcades. An axis ran through the plaza, aligning it with the arroyo, and arranged around the plaza were an open-air train station (its waiting area consisting of a court surrounded by covered arcades), shops, heating plant, company department store, workers' club, theater, offices, and hotel (Fig. 6.8). Largest of all was the company department store (with a separate warehouse to the rear), described as the "Wanamaker's of the desert."[28] Beyond the plaza to the east was a large public school. To the south, and placed higher up the slope of the ravine, was a church modeled closely on the Spanish Colonial theme building Goodhue designed for the San Diego fair in 1915. Meandering out from the plaza and up the hillsides were roads along which the housing was arranged. To the southwest of the plaza were to be single-family houses for the Anglo managerial staff. To the south and

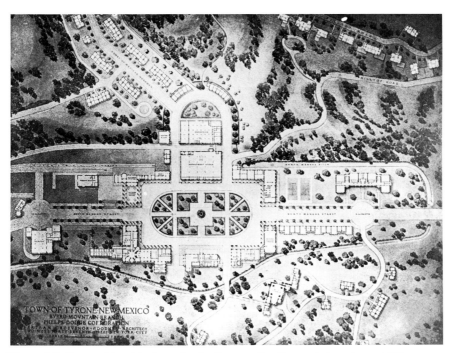

Figure 6.7 Tyrone, New Mexico, plan by Bertram Goodhue and Associates, 1915. (*[American] Architectural Review* n.s. 6 [April 1918].)

Figure 6.8 Tyrone, New Mexico, aerial perspective of plaza looking west, office of Bertram Goodhue, ca. 1915–1916. (*[American] Architectural Review* n.s. 6 [April 1918].)

southeast, roads climbed up to the four-unit row houses of the Mexican workers. The public buildings at the town center were decidedly Spanish Revival, but for the housing Goodhue tended to use simpler forms based on shelters he observed in Mexican villages in the region and on the ancient pueblo structures; he was also greatly influenced by the work of Irving Gill that he had seen in San Diego.[29] Some of the houses at Tyrone were built on the slopes of the steep arroyos that permitted two levels, the lower unit opening onto the arroyo and the upper unit facing the road. All the buildings were of hollow clay tile covered with two coats of stucco, the outer coat mixed with various pigments ranging from salmon, pale green, cream, to light brown (the Mexican houses were unpigmented).

Data for the housing at Tyrone are more detailed than for any other single Western company town, since it was the subject of a study conducted early in 1917 by Leifer Magnusson of the U.S. Bureau of Labor.[30] He reported that 124 individual dwelling units had been built for the Mexican laborers in 1916, with rents varying from $6 a month in a six-dwelling building to $12 a month for freestanding single-family dwellings. At the time of his study, sixty-seven dwellings had been built for the Anglo staff during 1914–1916. All single-family dwellings, they ranged from three to five rooms and were rented at $15 to $30 per month.[31] The total expenditure by the company on all buildings and improvements stood at $689,547 by the end of 1917. Unlike in Ajo, no intensive irrigation system was planned for Tyrone, and Magnusson notes that all the existing native vegetation was carefully preserved by Goodhue. Magnusson concluded that Tyrone, as it then stood, was exceptionally well maintained and, although it had just been built, already had good public amenities, including a baseball club and a band and orchestra that played for weekly dances held either in the moviehouse or on the concrete dance floor built in the plaza.

Shortly after Magnusson made his study of Tyrone, the price of copper plummeted with the end of the First World War, as U.S. copper companies found themselves suddenly with a surplus of 800 million pounds. Phelps Dodge alone dropped production from 186 million pounds in 1918 to less than 21 million pounds in 1921, and the first mines to be shut were those of lowest yield, among which were the Burro Mountain mines at Tyrone. In a few years, the still-incomplete model town was abandoned, except for a caretaker, and the buildings gradually became a romantic ruin. When copper production was resumed at Tyrone in 1966, the method employed was open pit mining, and within a few years the pit had spread beneath Goodhue's noble experiment. The post office was moved, the buildings demolished, and where once was a beautiful, if fragmented, planned town, there opened up a vast hole. Tyrone was no more.[32]

Lumber Towns

Coastal and Deep Water Lumber Towns

The lumber towns of the Pacific Northwest never approached the extravagance of the copper towns of the Southwest, although at least one that was proposed, Brookings, Oregon, approached the distinction of Tyrone. The lumber towns fall into two general categories: larger mill towns and lumber shipping centers located on rivers, estuaries, or ocean bays, and smaller lumber mill towns placed deep in the middle of forest lands owned by the parent company.

One of the earliest waterfront lumber towns is also one of the oldest, Port Gamble, on the Hood Canal in Puget Sound, Washington. Port Gamble (initially called Teekalet, the name used by the local Chemakum native Americans), was selected as a lumbering and shipping port by Captain William C. Talbot in 1853.[33] He had sailed from East Machias, Maine, where the Pope & Talbot lumbering and shipping company had prospered for several generations. Now, however, the company sought new timber sources for lumber to be shipped to nearby Seattle, Olympia, and—more important—to the burgeoning towns of California exploding in the rush for gold. Surrounded by dense forests of huge firs, the new town of Port Gamble was ideally located on a heavily wooded peninsula jutting out into the upper reaches of the Hood Canal. The first mill was framed in a few days and was ready for the second ship from East Machias carrying the first sawing machines, which arrived a few days after Talbot had selected the site. Within several years, backed by the considerable resources of the Maine-based company, Port Gamble was one of the largest producers of lumber in the Pacific Northwest. Port Gamble's streets followed a simple grid aligned to the compass (which also, coincidentally, fitted nicely into the end of the peninsula) (Fig. 6.9). The trim, white-painted workers' houses, built by the company, and the other town buildings had strong New England characteristics. The initial building materials were imported from Maine, as were two complete house frames. The company-built church, moreover, was a virtual duplicate of the Congregational Church of East Machias. Even the maple trees lining the streets had been grown from cuttings shipped from Maine.[34]

One other waterside town must be mentioned here, even though it does not conform to the strict definition of a company town wholly owned by one company and devoted to a single industrial activity. Longview, Washington, was planned at first solely as a large lumber-based town but was soon modified in scope to become a multi-industry city. It certainly had the most detailed planning and the most ambitious architectural development of any of the industrial towns of the American West. Just as the Pope & Talbot company, based in the East, had looked westward for new opportunities in the midnineteenth century, so too did R. A. Long, founder of the Long-Bell Lumber Company of Kansas City, look to the West for a new start in 1918. At age sixty-eight, Long decided to sell everything he owned in Kansas City and begin anew. He proposed creating a new city closer to better timber reserves in the Pacific Northwest. During 1919 and 1920, Long and other company officials scouted various tracts in Washington and Oregon, eventually deciding that a location along the Columbia made the most sense for their proposed new city.[35] As company officials looked closely at the level land just west of the Cowlitz River opposite Kelso, Washington (and close to the seventy thousand acres of fir forest they purchased in Cowlitz County), the detailed report of the company engineer Wesley Vandercook alerted them to several considerations and problems, especially the labor situation in the Northwest, which differed from that in the Southeast where Long-Bell had been cutting timber. In the Northwest, mill workers were unionized,

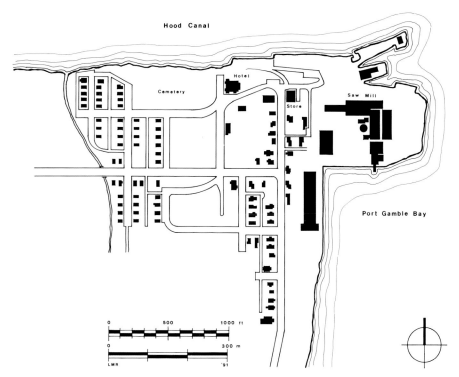

Figure 6.9 Port Gamble, Washington, plan of original settlement, as of 1860. (L. Roth after K. Erickson, "Morphology of Lumber Settlements" [Ph.D. diss., University of California—Berkeley, 1965].)

and many belonged to the strident Industrial Workers of the World (the I.W.W., or "Wobblies"). Relations between workers and management had been deteriorating progressively since 1900.[36] This warning persuaded Long to attempt a higher standard in the West, both in town planning and in public building and housing.

Land at the junction of the Cowlitz and Columbia was purchased in 1921, but by then it had been decided to build two huge mills, employing nearly four thousand men and entailing a community of nearly fifteen thousand people; hence, additional lands were acquired, eventually totaling fourteen thousand acres. Gradually R. A. Long enlarged his view, so that instead of a medium-sized mill town he would build an industrial city. He went back to Kansas City to confer with his friend J. C. Nichols, the developer of the highly successful Country Club district of Kansas City. When Nichols visited the proposed site, he persuaded Long to expand his view further: to aim for a city of fifty thousand, to consider land use carefully, to practice strict zoning, to establish building standards, and, above all, to follow a well-prepared plan. At Nichols's urging, Long engaged the landscape architects and planners Hare and Hare, in association with George Kessler, all of Kansas City, the same people Nichols had used for the Country Club district.[37]

Since the site was relatively flat, a straightforward grid was used with important deviations (Fig. 6.10). To the west was a curved slough that was dredged and turned into the long, crescent-shaped Lake Sacajawea, enclosed in public parkland. Between this parkland and the Cowlitz River was the town's center, its grid aligned with the Cowlitz and bisected by Broadway, leading to the passenger station at the tracks along the Cowlitz. The focus was on a six-acre civic center around Jefferson Park in the middle of the grid, from which major boulevard arterials extended on the diagonals. In fact, this was perhaps the only industrial town of its period planned with consideration of the impact of the private automobile by providing major arteries running circumferentially around the principal residential zones. To the west and south, beyond Lake Sacajawea, were additional residential districts and a central manufacturing district. The lands along the Columbia and Cowlitz were reserved for industrial development; where the two rivers joined were to be two new mills of the Long-Bell Lumber Company.

Street grading began in 1922, lots were sold in 1923, and at the same time work commenced on the first commercial building, the six-story concrete-frame Georgian brick Hotel Monticello facing Jefferson Park. The hotel was designed by the architects Hoit, Price & Barnes, as were the public library and passenger depot, all of matching brick with cream-colored terra cotta trim details. By 1932 the town had 12,000 residents, 2,700 homes, and several apartment buildings, plus a public library donated by Long, four schools, a hospital, nine churches, and 160 acres of developed park land. Thirty-one different industries located there, employing 3,000 workers beyond those employed by Long-Bell.[38] The homes and buildings, as well as the plan itself, were not exceptionally innovative for their time but were all carefully and competently done. Although the town grew with dramatic speed at first, it never achieved the 50,000 that had been planned (it stood at 31,100 in 1980); as a result, commercial development occurred closer to the actual center of population rather than around Jefferson Park and along Broadway. Nonetheless, Longview today retains a clarity of plan and a high quality of architectural character that remain as Long's legacy.

The only other lumber town with a deep water port planned by a professional designer was Brookings, Oregon. Another totally new community, it was begun by J. L. Brookings, whose family operated lumber mills in Oakland, California. The Brookings company was considering expanding operations into the southern coastal region of Oregon, and in 1913, J. L. Brookings approached Bernard Maybeck of San Francisco to design the town and its first buildings.[39] Brookings sought out Maybeck because of his participation in the international competition for Canberra, Australia, and his design of the western end of the Panama-Pacific Exposition, particularly the palace of Fine Arts. The site was a protected bay on the southern Oregon coast near the mouth of the Chetco River, with the settlement to be on a plateau rising forty to sixty feet from the cobble beach. The mill and loading dock were built by the company in 1914, while Maybeck was developing his street plan for the town and designs for a hotel and employee houses (built) as well as a YMCA and school (unbuilt).

Maybeck was successful in persuading Brookings of the value of a comprehensive plan, carefully adjusted to the irregularities of the terrain (Fig. 6.11). The

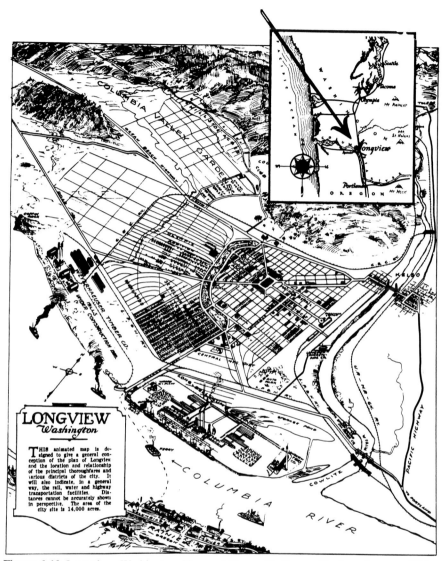

Figure 6.10 Longview, Washington; Hare and Hare with George Kessler, planners, 1921–1922. (From J. B. McCleland, . . . *the Story of Longview* [Longview, Wash., c. 1976].)

irregular parcels were reserved for public buildings and parks, and all the steeper slopes were set aside as parkland.[40] By 1922, with the mill in full operation and house lots being sold, the population rose to twelve hundred. Without warning, in 1925, the mill closed as a result of financial difficulties experienced by the parent company. The population dropped sharply to perhaps a few hundred persons by the time of the depression in the 1930s. Kenneth Erickson credits the eventual resurrection of Brookings as a plywood manufacturing town to careful planning by a

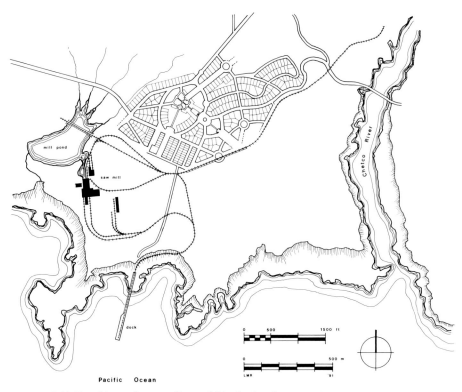

Figure 6.11 Brookings, Oregon; Bernard Maybeck, planner and architect, 1913–1914. (L. Roth, after K. Erickson, "Morphology of Lumber Settlements.")

professional.[41] Regrettably, the later construction of U.S. Highway 101 through Brookings destroyed a good part of Maybeck's intricate street scheme, but by the mid-1960s many of the small ceder-shingle-covered employee houses survived, although changed by later additions and alterations. Erickson further credits Maybeck for having given the houses a pleasant shingled resort character that contributed to their preservation until the recovery of the town after 1951.

Inland Lumber Towns

None of the inland lumber towns approached the size of Longview or the design sophistication of Brookings. Longview has endured and prospered because of its diversity of industry, its separation from timber supplies, and its relative closeness to other cities, most notably Portland. By contrast, most of the smaller inland lumber towns were placed in the midst of stands of giant coastal redwoods and firs or on the high plateau east of the Cascades among large stands of Ponderosa pine. This has meant that, as these timber resources have disappeared, the towns have shrunk or vanished altogether. Such a prospect was evident even in the early years of the century, when most of these towns were established but little attention was given to street layout and building design, much less to provision of public open space. Many of these inland towns did not even have cemeteries, so that eventual removal of the buildings and replanting with trees would not introduce the problem of disturbing graves. A great many of these settlements were rough camps. One, called "Dollar Camp," now long gone, has been described by two former residents.[42] Located at the end of a single rail line extending up the Calapooia River from Sweet Home, Oregon, the camp had ten to twelve dwellings, some with four to five rooms for families; others were simple two-room houses, little more than shanties, for single men. There was a simple roundhouse at the end of the line for rotating the steam engine that pulled trains of logs into Sweet Home for milling. Soon after the last trees had been clear-cut, about 1967, the rails were pulled up. By 1981 only one dwelling remained standing. As the hillsides reverted to scrubby trees, the abandoned buildings gradually disappeared.

Even larger and more settled lumber towns eventually vanished. Two good examples in Oregon were Wendling and Valsetz. Wendling was begun as a camp by two timber cutters, Jordan and Holcomb, before the turn of the last century, at the point where the Mill and Wolf creeks merged about twenty miles northwest of Springfield.[43] By 1900 the town, now bearing the name of George Wendling, an early settler and mill operator, had been taken over by the Booth-Kelly Lumber Company and was reached by a branch line of the Southern Pacific that carried rough lumber back to Springfield for further milling. At its maximum, Wendling had about nine hundred inhabitants. There was no particular attention given to street layout or building design; indeed, the streets were paved only with sawdust and mill waste until about 1910, when plank roads and sidewalks were laid. By the early 1940s, more then forty-two thousand acres of old-growth Douglas fir had been clear-cut and it was evident that the little town had no future. Cutting and milling continued through the Second World War, but in early 1946 the mill shut down, and in September of that year it burned. By 1961, the land was owned by Georgia-Pacific, which created a small public park at the eastern end of the rapidly disappearing town. Soon after 1961, the remaining buildings were removed and the land was converted into a tree farm. Today, the park is all that remains in a landscape of short trees and a few scattered foundation stones; a paved road runs up the Mohawk River and Mill Creek valleys to a spot that is still identified on current maps as Wendling.

The obliteration of Valsetz, Oregon, once a far more handsome and vital community, has been absolute. Valsetz was created in 1919 by the Cobbs and Mitchell Company, which had been logging on the eastern side of the Coast Range with its base at Falls River, about twenty-one miles east of Salem, the state capital. The company pushed cutting westward and extended its subsidiary Valley and Siletz Railroad up the Luckiamute River deep into the Coast Range to an isolated valley, where it built Valsetz (a contraction of the railroad's name). The rail line and a single gravel road were all that connected Valsetz to the outside world. Although hardly more than a camp, it was neatly laid out in the narrow valley along the single road, roughly four thousand feet in length, lined by trim houses (Fig. 6.12). A broad cross street led to the church and the principal company buildings. In the 1920s, the

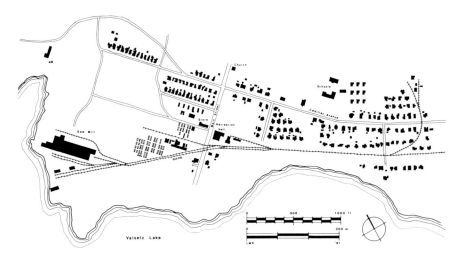

Figure 6.12 Valsetz, Oregon, plan ca. 1919–1925. (L. Roth, after K. Erickson, "Morphology of Lumber Settlements.")

population numbered about 300, yet with no increase in production the population doubled by 1940 with the growth of families; around 1950, the population peaked at roughly 1,000, with 260 men in the mill and another 125 in logging.[44] Although a general store, a school, and a combination recreation hall/post office were the only facilities provided by the company, the community was stable and people who had grown up there cherished the solitude and the near-absence of crime. After 1960, with the reduction of good timber and the conversion to plywood manufacture, the population dropped to 300 people. By the early 1980s, as at Wendling, the old-growth timber was gone and the new owner, Boise-Cascade, determined to close the mill. It proved a wrenching experience for the expelled residents, one of whom remarked that the company had once been "like our father."[45] In 1984 the buildings were demolished, the debris bulldozed away, and the land replanted with shoots awaiting a new harvest in eighty years. Even the gravel road was removed, so that current maps of the region show nothing at all.

Another mill town, Westfir, Oregon, forty miles southwest of Eugene-Springfield on the Middle Fork of the Willamette River, has fared somewhat better. Unlike Valsetz, which sat isolated in the middle of densely wooded mountains, Westfir was built as an adjunct to the existing town of Oakridge. Both lay on a much-traveled state highway and a trunk line of the Southern Pacific Railroad that extended from Eugene to Oakridge, and that, in 1926, was completed over the Cascades, connecting ultimately to San Francisco. In 1923, the U.S. Forest Service offered to sell timber from the Willamette National Forest along the North Fork of the Willamette River, but the contract of sale stipulated that a "stable community be established to provide decent living conditions and to encourage family life," as well as "opportunities for a permanency in a well-balanced lumber operation."[46] George Kelly (brother of John Kelly, the co-founder of the Booth-Kelly Company) was successful in obtaining the contract, forming the Western Lumber Company. The initial mill, built in 1923, was followed by a larger facility in 1925; meanwhile, houses and other necessary buildings were constructed to meet the conditions of the contract.

Most of the housing, owned by the company, was built along two parallel streets, Sunset Avenue and Hemlock Road, with a community building at the far east end of the linear town. Financial difficulties arose almost immediately, perhaps because the cost of constructing the mill plus the town exceeded early estimates. Outside funding was procured, but economic problems increased with the onset of the Depression. Another reorganization in 1935 and creation of a new Westfir Lumber Company simply postponed the sale of the company and town to the Edward Hines Lumber Company of Chicago in 1944. For a time, production improved through modernization of the plant, even though population declined as a result of automation. But the Edward Hines Company eventually had to sell the plant and town in 1977, prompting the four hundred residents to incorporate early in 1979. Later that year, however, the plywood mill burned and the future of the town has been in question since that time.

Fortunately, the presence of Oakridge and the relatively easy connections to other communities have prevented total disappearance of Westfir, although it has ceased to be a true company town. Although it may eke out an existence and not disappear as have so many other towns, the statistics are not encouraging. Several guide books and historical studies list fifteen lumber "ghost towns" in Oregon alone.[47] The moving town of Shevlin, Oregon—at the end situated about three miles east of present-day Lapine—quickly disappeared when its mills were shut down in 1951 and no longer appears on any maps. In his survey of Western company-owned towns, James Allen cites a number of lumber towns operating normally in the early 1960s, among them Kinsua, Oregon (about seventy-five miles southeast of the Dalles on the Columbia), where the mill was closed in 1978. Included in this list, too, is Valsetz, now vanished. As a local newspaper printed in commenting on the demise of Kinsua: "WHEN SAWMILL DIES, TOWN DIES."[48] Other lingering company towns Allen mentions include Vaughn, Wauna, and Westfir in Oregon; all have had their mills closed and company property sold since the mid-1960s and their futures look dim. Although the names of some small Oregon towns remain on current maps, all but one, Gilchrist, have ceased to exist as true company towns.

Nonetheless, some lumber communities survive. Potlatch, Idaho, has managed to endure despite the closing of its mill in 1981. Created in 1906, it is a good example of the influence of lumbering interests that, having cut over Michigan, Wisconsin, and Minnesota, moved to the still-lush forests of the Pacific Northwest. When the two Northern transcontinental railroads were completed from Chicago and Duluth to the Pacific in 1894, the relative ease of shipping lumber to Eastern markets made exploitation of Western forests by Great Lakes lumbermen a virtual certainty[49]; in 1899, Frederick Weyerhaeuser and a number of his associates scouted Idaho, Washington, and Oregon for virgin forests. Weyerhaeuser's original fortune had come out of the forests of Wisconsin, and the prospects of additional wealth presented by the great stands of white pine in the West were substantial. In 1903 the Weyerhaeuser interests formed the subsidiary Potlatch Lumber Company to establish mills in the Northwest and two years later created the new town of Potlatch, Idaho, on the North Fork of the Palouse River, about six miles east of the Washington state border.[50] The Potlatch Lumber Company built there the largest mill for white pine in the world, capable of turning out 500,000 linear feet of finished lumber in a single day's ten-hour shift.

Simultaneously, the company's engineers laid out a town on a regular grid oriented to the points of the compass. To the north of the principal east-west street was the neighborhood of the workers; to the south, on a rise, dubbed "Nob Hill," was the area where the managers lived (Fig. 6.13). The public buildings and the houses were designed by Clarence F. White, a well-known architect based in Spokane, Washington, the nearest major city, about eighty-five miles to the northwest.[51] In these buildings, however, White adhered to well-established vernacular types rather than attempting anything particularly innovative. An initial group of 201 houses, capable of accommodating fifteen hundred people, was built. The residences ranged in cost from $400 to $2,000 for the mill workers, and up to $6,340 for management residences, although the average for the houses on Nob Hill

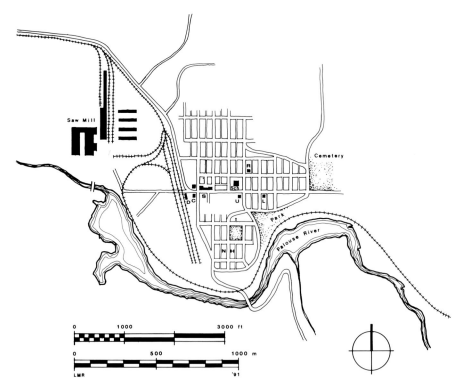

Figure 6.13 Potlatch, Idaho, plan ca. 1960. (L. Roth after K. Peterson, *Company Town: Potlatch, Idaho.* . . . [Pullman, Wash., 1987].)

was $3,060 (Fig. 6.14). During 1907–1908, the company also built two churches (Roman Catholic and Union Protestant); the Lutherans built their own church at the same time. The company also constructed a school, hospital, jailhouse, ice house, department store, hotel, and railway depot.

Overall, the company is said to have taken as its inspiration the model company town of Pullman, Illinois, not in form so much as in provision of public services and the solidity of company-built housing.[52] In this way, the business hoped to obviate labor unrest, which continued to grow among fallers and mill workers throughout the Northwest. In contrast to the Pullman Palace Car Company, which was forced by the courts to sell all nonfactory properties after the notorious strike and riot of 1894, the Potlatch Lumber Company continued to practice a diminishing paternalism until the 1950s, when it concluded that paternalism really did not pay. Houses were sold to residents and a minor construction boom ensued when the new purchasers began renovations and customization of the once-company-owned houses.

To say that paternalism did not pay is perhaps putting too great an emphasis on the "bottom line," for certainly in the lumber towns discussed here there was a certain reluctance among laborers to strike. Fallers in one of the Potlatch Lumber Company remote camps, however, were among the first to strike in the opening moves of the great walkout that swept the entire Northwest in 1917; eventually the workers in the town of Potlatch were involved as well, but they were not among

Figure 6.14 Potlatch, Idaho, manager's residence, ca. 1906–1907, Clarence F. White, architect. (From K. Peterson, *Company Town: Potlatch, Idaho. . . .* [Pullman, Wash., 1987].)

those most eager to strike. In Gilchrist, Oregon (built in 1938 and discussed later), workers were even more reluctant to stop work. Although the Gilchrist labor force was unionized, it elected at first not to participate in the strike that swept the region in 1945–1946; Gilchrist Timber Company management offered to increase wages, but union officials insisted that Gilchrist workers honor the regionwide strike.[53]

Another survivor is Scotia, in northern coastal California, formerly one of several such towns in California, including Weed and McCloud. In both Weed and McCloud, the founding lumber companies were taken over during 1956–1963 by larger companies, which then quickly sold off company-owned houses. Both are on major tourist routes into the Mount Shasta recreational area in northern California, and this traffic, plus their diversified industrial bases, has enabled those towns to endure. Two other communities, Albion and Graegle, were already being converted to new uses—resorts in the cases of Albion and Graegle—when Allen was making his survey in the early 1960s.[54] Scotia, California—so named because of the lumbermen brought from Nova Scotia at the town's founding in the 1880s—has remained wholly owned by the Pacific Lumber Company, which cuts and processes the redwoods of the northern Pacific coast. Lying about thirty miles south of Eureka on coastal highway U.S. 101, Scotia has changed little since it was created, except that Pacific Lumber has leased the business enterprises it once owned, including the store, theater, bank, hospital, and butcher shop. Tourism along U.S. 101 enables Scotia to maintain some contact with the outside world, but residents still like the relative solitude and isolation. A recent social study by Hugh Wilkerson, *Life in the Peace Zone: An American Company Town*, documents the view of residents. Wilkerson's assessment is that in Scotia, where frustrations are few, so are fantasies. A clergyman, new to the town, says he has yet to encounter an alcoholic, and no one can remember a major Scotia crime. No one sinks, but no one soars. What Scotia is really offering those dismayed with the world outside is also the tie that pulls back men who vowed to leave: not the promise of fulfillment but an assurance of moderation, the possibility of living a humane life in a humane community. And for that, there will always be a waiting list.[55]

The case of Gilchrist, Oregon, is similar; it is apparently the very last wholly company-owned lumber town in either Oregon or Washington. Lying astride U.S. Highway 97, Gilchrist is located nearly fifty miles south of Bend and not quite one hundred miles north of Klamath Falls. It was created by Frank W. Gilchrist (1903–1956) in 1937–1938, the result of a family's century of activity in the lumber business. Gilchrist's great-grandfather, Albert, of Concord, New Hampshire had begun lumbering in 1850, first in New Hampshire, and then in Michigan. His son, Frank William (1845–1912), greatly enlarged operations in Michigan, and then, with business associates, expanded even farther into Wisconsin, southern Illinois, Tennessee, and, in 1907, Laurel, Mississippi. In turn Frank William's son, Frank R. (1871–1917), operated the business in Mississippi, at the same time buying up timberlands in northern California, eastern Oregon, and Idaho, accumulating sixty thousand acres in the area around the future Gilchrist, Oregon, by the time of his death. Frank R.'s son, Frank W. (1903–1956), only fourteen when his father died, began working in the Mississippi operation; control of the company passed temporarily to his uncle, Harry E. Fletcher.[56]

As the depression of the 1930s worsened, the Gilchrist-Fordney Company in Mississippi faced uncertain prospects as their timber supply dwindled. Frank W. Gilchrist, Fletcher, and other company officials began examining closely their holdings in the West and finally, in 1937, decided that they had to make a fresh start. (By this time Frank W. Gilchrist was general manager of the company and had married; his son, Frank R. [1924–1991] had been born in Big Rapids, Michigan.) The decision was to move the entire company operation to Oregon and build a smaller mill capable of producing up to 1 million board feet of lumber a year. The company would also need to build a self-sufficient town for its workers, as distances to towns of any size were too great for commuting laborers, given the roads and automobiles of the day. Indeed, company officials decided to create an attractive residential community to correct the problems they had had with itinerant mill hands in Mississippi.[57] Construction of the new town, to be named Gilchrist, began in April 1938, and the first phase was completed by September before winter set in. It was situated roughly in the middle of the eighty-five thousand acres of Ponderosa pine now owned by the company and divided into two zones separated by Highway 97, the mill, yards, and mill pond on the west side of the river and the business and residential sections on the east side (Fig. 6.15). A simple grid, aligned with the highway, was developed by the architect and planner Hollis Johnston of Portland, who also designed the business buildings and the initial group of houses. His overall plan would provide services and homes for a maximum of fifteen hundred people, and his goal was to create a "civic personality which promotes a spirit of respect and affection in the inhabitants."[58]

The easterly residential section of Gilchrist was divided by a central community and business district. Fronting the highway were two business blocks, with all the facilities gathered under their two broad roofs: restaurant, cocktail lounge, barber shop, beauty shop, bowling alley, grocery store, theater, and post office. All the buildings were severely plain, with a few details in cupolas and trim that suggest that Johnston may have been looking at contemporary Scandinavian architecture. This is further emphasized by the painted Scandinavian stencil patterns (sometimes called Swiss) that embellish the two commercial buildings.[59] Behind the two business buildings is the combined school with a separate apartment building to house the teachers. In 1938, 128 houses of two and three bedrooms were built; these were rented in 1938 for $25 per month (Fig. 6.16). Moreover, provisions were made for the construction of more houses in later years as need required. A group of California-style bungalows built in 1951 brought the number to 140.[60] The first houses were rapidly filled, for more than half the labor force decided to move to Oregon from Mississippi (one still hears slight traces of a Southern drawl in Gilchrist). The houses, and all other buildings in the town, were painted a rich chocolate brown with cream-colored trim. The company also provided a three-man maintenance crew, whose jobs included completely repainting all buildings every five years.

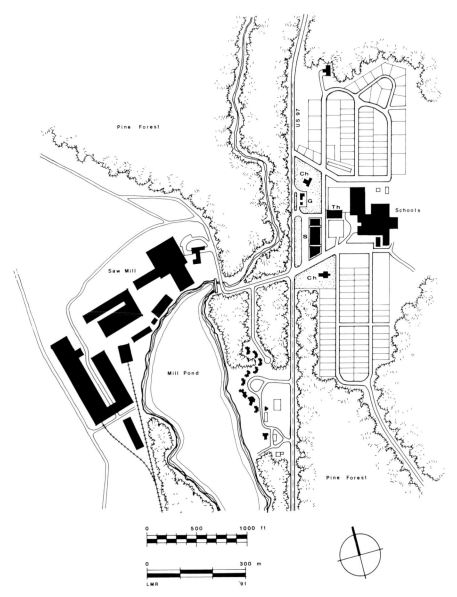

Figure 6.15 Gilchrist, Oregon, plan 1937–1970. (L. Roth, after information supplied by the Gilchrist Lumber Company.)

The town of Gilchrist, whose population had risen from 350 in 1940 to about 500 in 1988, has no elected government, since virtually everything is operated and owned by the company. Nonetheless, the paternalism practiced there differs from that which undermined so many other earlier communities. The company deeded ten acres to Klamath County for the school site. Today, although the company itself operates the movie theater, gas station, and bowling alley, other businesses are leased to private operators. Scrip has never been issued, although in tough times credit was extended, and unlike so many other company towns of the past, Gilchrist is not dry. According to statute, the liquor store is operated by the state, but the cocktail lounge is leased to a private operator. The company provides an office for a state patrol officer (said to be one of the most coveted posts among the state police). A building is also provided to Klamath County for a branch of the county public library. And the company provided lots at no cost for the construction of three churches: Methodist, Roman Catholic, and Mormon.[61] Why so many workers and residents have remained in Gilchrist so long is explained in part by economic advantages. In 1972 one mill worker, Bud Koewn, with fourteen years' experience with the company, was earning $9,600 a year when rents for houses in the town peaked at $85 per month. Even if Koewn paid this highest rate, his cost of housing was only 10.6 percent of his gross income. Eleven years later, in 1983, the highest house rent had increased to only $90 per month.[62] No wonder that for youths in Gilchrist the greatest aspiration is to graduate from high school and go immediately into the mill.[63] John Driscoll's assessment in 1984 (at the end of a particularly serious recession in the Northwest lumber industry) was that "in the 1980s, as was the case in the 1930s, the Gilchrist Timber Company is providing its employees with employment and inexpensive housing during a period when both are scarce."[64]

The late Frank Gilchrist (1924–1991) was quoted in 1981 as saying the mill and town "will be here forever." In early 1991 the entire Gilchrist operation—timber

Figure 6.16 Residence, Gilchrist, Oregon, ca. 1937–1938. (Photography by L. M. Roth.)

lands, mill, and town—was put up for sale by stockholders who outvoted members of the Gilchrist family. In October 1991 the sale was completed, with the timber lands and mill property being purchased by Crown Pacific Inc. of Oregon, centered in Portland. The town and all its buildings, however, was sold separately to nephews of the late Frank Gilchrist (Gil, John, and Will Ernst) and a fourth un-named investor, who plan to operate the town for current residents who will con-tinue to work in the adjacent mill. Gilchrist is no longer a company town in the strict sense, but it will continue as a community; it may, if the timber lands are harvested sensibly for a sustained yield as they have been for a half century, continue to exist as an idyllic enclave well into the next century.[65]

Notes

1. James B. Allen, *The Company Town in the American West* (Norman, Okla., 1966); Kenneth A. Erickson, "The Morphology of Lumber Settlements in Western Oregon and Washington" (Ph.D. diss., University of California-Berkeley, 1965).

2. Three examples can serve as illustrations: John Garner, *The Model Company Town: Urban Design through Private Enterprise in Nineteenth-Century New England* (Amherst, Mass., 1984), devoted largely to Hopedale, Massachusetts; Richard M. Candee, *Atlantic Heights: A World War I Shipbuilder's Community* (Portsmouth, N.H., 1985); and Edward G. Roddy, *Mills, Mansions, and Mergers: The Life of William M. Wood* (North Andover, Mass., 1982), which focuses on Shawsheen Village, a textile industrial community built near An-dover, Mass., after World War I.

3. Allen, *Company Town*, 9, 14, 33, and 50.

4. Allen, *Company Town*, 51. A comparison of the list of company towns, given by Allen in the appendix to his book, with current maps of the coal-mining states also reveals that, as a group, coal-mining towns have the highest order of closure and obliteration. These towns were clearly not planned for any long-term habitation.

5. For Tacoma, Wash., not mentioned in Allen, see John W. Reps, *Cities of the Ameri-can West: A History of Frontier Urban Planning* (Princeton, N.J., 1979), 565–71, and his *The Making of Urban America* (Princeton, N.J., 1965), 406–13.

6. These miscellaneous Western company towns are surveyed briefly in Allen, *Com-pany Town*, 70–78. For Litchfield Park, see Hugh Allen, *The House of Goodyear: A Story of Rubber and of Modern Business* (Cleveland, 1943), and Susan M. Smith, "Litchfield Park and Vicinity" (M.A. thesis, University of Arizona, 1948).

7. Allen, *Company Town*, 146–84, lists company towns and camps alphabetically by state. Many of the listings include commentary not repeated in the text. Allen also notes whether the towns were closed, sold off, or in transition to some other use.

8. Allen, *Company Town*, 168.

9. I first sketched out this taxonomy in my essay, "Three Industrial Towns by McKim, Mead & White," *Journal, Society of Architectural Historians* 38 (December 1979): 317–47; see esp. 320–21. I have expanded on this in my *Concise History of American Architecture* (New York, 1979).

10. Roth, "Three Industrial Towns," 321–28.

11. Michael Shellenbarger, ed., *Harmony in Diversity: The Architecture and Teaching of Ellis F. Lawrence* (Eugene, Oreg., 1989), 28–29, 44, 68–69.

12. Garner, *Model Company Town*, 152.

13. "The Town of Kohler, Wisconsin: A Model Industrial Development; Brust and Philipp, Architects," *Architecture* 51 (April 1925): 149–54. For the street plan, see Reps, *Making of Urban America*, 430.

14. Huger Elliott, "An Ideal City in the West," *[American] Architectural Review* 15 (September 1908): 137–42.

15. Charles C. May, "Indian Hill, an Industrial Village at Worcester, Massachusetts," *Architectural Record* 41 (January 1917): 21–35; and Lawrence Veiller, "Industrial Housing Developments in America, pt. 4; A Colony in the Blue Ridge Mountains at Erwin, Tennessee," *Architectural Record* 43 (June 1918): 547–59.

16. For Tyrone see "New Mining Town of Tyrone, New Mexico," *[American] Architectural Review* 6 (April 1918): 59–62. For Brookings see Kenneth H. Cardwell, *Bernard Maybeck, Artisan, Architect, Artist* (Salt Lake City, 1983), 191–96, 243.

17. I have discussed the replanning and architectural embellishment of Naugatuck in "Three Company Towns," 331–47.

18. "The Town of Midland, Pennsylvania: A New Development in Housing near Pittsburgh," *[American] Architectural Review* 4 (March 1916): 33–36.

19. Leifur Magnusson, "Company Housing in the Bituminous Coal Field," U.S. Bureau of Labor, *Monthly Labor Review* 10, no. 4 (April 1920): 1045–52. See also his "Sanitary Aspects of Company Housing," *Monthly Labor Review* 8, no. 1 (January 1919); 288–89.

20. For Ludlow, see Howard M. Gitelman, *Legacy of the Ludlow Massacre* (Philadelphia, 1988), and Zeese Papanokolas, *Buried Unsung: Louis Tikas and the Ludlow Massacre* (Salt Lake City, 1982). For labor strikes and violence in the other Southwestern industries see James W. Byrkit, *Forging the Copper Collar: Arizona's Labor Management War of 1901–1921* (Tucson, Ariz., 1982); Norman Clark, *Mill Town: A Social History of Everett, Washington, Beginnings to the Present* (Seattle, 1970); and Robert Tyler, *Rebels in the Woods: The I.W.W. in the Pacific Northwest* (Eugene, Oreg., 1967).

21. For Jerome, see J. Carl Brogdon, "The History of Jerome, Arizona" (M.A. thesis, University of Arizona, 1952). For general information about other properties of the Phelps Dodge Company see Robert G. Cleland, *A History of Phelps Dodge, 1834–1950* (New York, 1952).

22. For an illustration of the Clark mansion, see Nathan Silver, *Lost New York* (New York, 1967), 125; the house was demolished in 1927. By 1953 the ore at Jerome was exhausted; Clarkdale was then sold and converted to the manufacture of cement.

23. Elliott, "Ideal City in the West," 137–42.

24. Cleland, *History of Phelps Dodge*, 122, 266, 229–337

25. William M. Kenyon, "The Town Site of the New Cornelia Copper Company," *Architecture* 39 (January 1919): 7–10.

26. This claim is made by Robert B. Riley, "Gone Forever, Goodhue's Beaux Arts Ghost Town," *Journal, American Institute of Architects* 50 (August 1968): 68.

27. Richard Oliver, *Bertram Grosvenor Goodhue* (New York, 1983), 151–54.

28. Quoted by Riley, "Gone Forever," 70.

29. Gill's influence is noted by Oliver, *Goodhue*, 154, as are Goodhue's research trips to Taos and other sites in the vicinity of Tyrone. Goodhue's plans and building designs, including a number of representative house plans, are well presented in two articles: "The New Mining Community of Tyrone, N.M.," *[American] Architectural Review* 6 (April 1918): 59–

62; and "Tyrone, New Mexico, the Development of the Phelps-Dodge Company," *Architectural Forum* 28 (April 1918): 131–34.

30. Leifur Magnusson, "A Modern Copper Mining Town," U.S. Bureau of Labor, *Monthly Labor Review* 7 (September 1918): 754–60.

31. In *Housing by Employers in the United States* (Washington, D.C., 1920), 123, Leifur Magnusson notes that in the six towns studied in metal mining, only 857 of 5,398 miners (15.9 percent) were housed in company-built dwellings; the remainder lived in tents or houses erected on lots rented from the company.

32. Production figures from Cleland, *Phelps Dodge*, 102, 159–161, 199–200, 302; and Orris C. Herfindahl, *Copper Costs and Prices: 1870–1957* (Baltimore, 1959), 90–99, 162, 202–13. For the end of Tyrone, see Riley, "Gone Forever," 68–70.

33. Edwin T. Coman and Helen Gibbs, *Time, Tide, and Timber: A Century of Pope and Talbot* (Stanford, 1950), 51–56.

34. Ibid., 168–70.

35. For the development of Longview, see Norman T. Newton, *Design on the Land: The Development of Landscape Architecture* (Cambridge, Mass., 1971), 479–83; John B. McCleland, Jr., *R. A. Long's Planned City: The Story of Longview* (Longview, Wash., c. 1976); and Michael Neuschwanger, "Longview: In the Spirit of the City Beautiful," *Cowlitz Historical Quarterly* 28 (1986): 3–41. I must thank my colleagues Norman Johnston and Philip Dole, respectively, for alerting me to the last two obscure references. See also the coverage in Steven Dotterer, "Cities and Towns," in *Space, Style, and Structure; Building in Northwest America*, 2 vols., ed. T. Vaughn and V. G. Ferriday (Portland, Oreg., 1974), 2: 463–66.

36. McCleland, *Long's Planned City*, 4–10.

37. Ibid., 21–22.

38. In February 1991, the news media announced construction of a new deinking plant at Longview, part of a major regional paper-recycling operation.

39. For Brookings, Oreg., see Erickson, "Morphology," 267–75, and Cardwell, *Bernard Maybeck*, 165, 191–96, 243.

40. Cardwell, *Bernard Maybeck*, 191–92.

41. Erickson, "Morphology," 270.

42. Jack Jeppsen and Kelly Spencer, interviewed by Clarence Hubert, summer 1981, as part of a class conducted by the author.

43. Shannon Kracht, "Wendling, a Company Town," *Lane County Historian* 20 (Spring 1975): 3–16.

44. [Portland] *Oregonian*, 21 Nov. 1954: 40–41.

45. Lisa Strycker, "Valsetz, Oregon, 1919–1984," [Eugene] *Register-Guard*, 28 May 1984: 1A, 4A.

46. Quoted in the *Comprehensive Plan for Westfir* (Westfir, Oreg., 1980); 2.1–2.5. Other information regarding Westfir is also drawn from this document and from research conducted by William Lenart, summer 1981, in a class conducted by the author.

47. Lambert Florin, *Oregon Ghost Towns* (Seattle, 1970); also see Oregon Historical Society, *Oregon Ghost Towns and Other Historic Communities* (Portland, Oreg., 1970), among other studies. Wendling, Oreg., is included in this group, as is Mabel, now gone but once Wendling's equally busy neighbor about five miles to the north.

48. *East Oregonian*, 27 January 1978. Allen's list of prospering company-owned lumber towns is found in *Company Town*, 29.

49. For the westward migration of Great Lakes lumber interests, see Richard L. Williams, *The Loggers* (New York, 1976), 195–205.

50. For a remarkably detailed study of Potlatch, see Keith C. Petersen, *Company Town: Potlatch, Idaho, and the Potlatch Lumber Company* (Pullman, Wash., 1987). Data regarding the design and construction of the town are found in chap. 5, "Building a Company Town."

51. Clarence Ferris White (1867–1932) was born and educated in Chicago and studied architecture there for six years. He relocated to Spokane, Washington, in 1890 after that city suffered a disastrous fire, sensing opportunity in its reconstruction. He formed a partnership with C. B. Seaton and carried on a highly productive practice based in Spokane; his work, however, remains largely unknown. In his later years, ironically, he switched to operating a wrecking company. Sources of biographical information concerning White are noted in Petersen, *Potlatch*, 242 n. 15.

52. Petersen, *Potlatch*, 86.

53. For labor disputes affecting Potlatch, see Petersen, *Potlatch*, 159–69; for events in Gilchrist, see Driscoll, "Gilchrist," 146.

54. Allen, *Company Town*, 149–55.

55. Hugh Wilkerson, *Life in the Peace Zone: An American Company Town* (New York, 1971), 106. A similar appraisal is found in Frank J. Taylor, "Paradise with a Waiting List," *Saturday Evening Post*, 233 24 Feb. 1951: 36–37, 103–4, 106–7.

56. This family chronology, paralleling that of other Great Lakes lumbermen such as Frederick Weyerhaeuser, is based on information given in Jim Fisher, *Gilchrist: The First Fifty Years* (Bend, Oreg., 1988), the most complete source of information on the founders, the company, and the town. I am immensely grateful to Joan Kelly, who unearthed a number of the published sources dealing with Gilchrist, Oregon.

57. Allen Nacheman, "Company Town," *Columbus* [Ohio] *Dispatch*, 12 May 1972, 18A.

58. Johnston, quoted in Fisher, *Gilchrist*, 20.

59. In a detailed study of Gilchrist, "Gilchrist, Oregon, a Company Town," *Oregon Historical Quarterly* 85 (Summer 1984): 135–53, John Driscoll writes that the buildings were built "using a modern Norwegian architectural style" but does not explain further.

60. Driscoll, "Gilchrist," 139, 147; Mike Thoele, "Mill Town Takes Care of Its Own," [Eugene] *Register-Guard*, 23 May 1988, C1–C2.

61. Nacheman, "Company Town," 18A.

62. Jane Seagrave, "Company Town Life Survives in Gilchrist," [Portland] *Oregonian*, 5 January 1983: B2.

63. Driscoll, "Gilchrist," 152–53; Thoele, "Mill Town Takes Care of Its Own," C2.

64. Driscoll, "Gilchrist," 153.

65. Eugene *Register-Guard*, 10 October 10 1991: A1, A6.

7

Company Towns of Chile and Argentina

OLGA PATERLINI DE KOCH

The urbanization of many Latin American countries was a response to special industrial activities that occurred during the second half of the nineteenth century and beginning of the twentieth. Company towns were founded to process sugar, tannin, nitrate, and meat—the more significant exports. Although developed with variations in different Latin American countries, such as Chile, Argentina, and Brazil, the planning and architectural features that identify company towns were similar to those found in Europe and the United States. Many company towns remain active, although they have lost some of their economic and social importance. Workers and their families have migrated to larger cities to look for better jobs. Residential layouts often did not take into account traditional customs and social relationships, and those who worked in company towns had to accept a company-imposed routine and pattern of living. The company towns of Latin America provide a rich source of information for those interested in indigenous resources and communal patterns of behavior. The purpose of this chapter is to outline briefly regional resources, town planning, and architectural design.

The nitrate towns of Antofagasta in the northern part of Chile, and the tannin towns of El Chaco, sugar towns of Tucumán, and Liebig's meat-packing factory of Entre Ríos in northern Argentina are representative company towns (Fig. 7.1). There were no prevailing urban patterns in these provinces, nor did governments impose regulations about how to build streets or houses to ensure sanitary conditions and the health of workers. But examples of foreign development were studied. Robert Owen and Jean-Baptiste Godin, among others in Europe, had already developed enlightened industrial villages that may have influenced those who built indus-

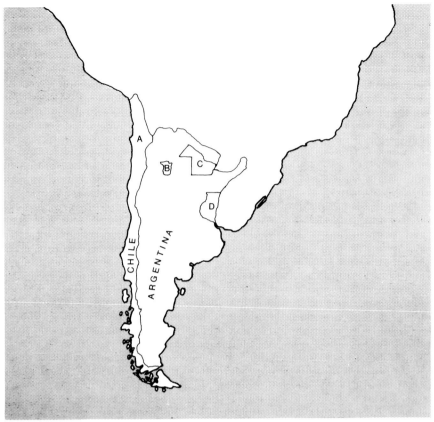

Figure 7.1 Map of South America showing Chile and Argentina and the provinces in which the company towns discussed are located: A. Antofagasta, Atacama, Tacma, and Tarapaca; B. Tucumán; C. Chaco; D. Entre Ríos.

tries in Latin America. Despite the absence of underlying patterns of building, there were a few sensitive (although pragmatic) men who, as architects, engineers, and owners of factories, introduced modern European and American processing machinery to Latin America. At the same time, they built new towns in rural and sometimes wilderness locations. In many instances, they demonstrated concern for the moral and physical welfare of their workers, who would, in return, render a straightforward economic advantage to them. To some extent, the industrialists perceived that their profits would be, if not necessarily greater, more secure if the lives of their workers were improved.[1]

Nitrate Towns of Chile

Mining, especially of nitrates and copper, has been a major industry in Chile since the early nineteenth century. Without nitrates and copper, the northern third of the country would have little economic importance. With recognition of its value as a fertilizer and ingredient in the manufacture of explosives, nitrate exportation began in the 1830s, and by 1869 a flourishing industry had been established. After 1920, however, the Haber-Bosch process for the manufacture of synthetic nitrate presented a serious competitive threat to the Chilean export.[2] The expansive desert plains of Tarapaca, Antofagasta, Atacama, and Tacma provinces, eighty kilometers east of the Pacific coast, offered substantial deposits of nitrate. The complete absence of rain made possible the working of soluble caliche, a gray, rocklike substance containing sodium chloride, sodium nitrate, and iodine salts. Capitalists who organized the companies and built the towns, known as *oficinas salitreras*, saltpeter or nitrate plants, were mainly from England and the United States; although a few were German and Chilean. Workers were mostly Chilean because they were native to the region and proved stronger than immigrants for mining. By 1910 nearly 435,000 were employed. Between 1830 and 1880, production increased from 14,000 to 300,000 tons.[3] During the 1880s, Colonel T. J. North and Robert Harvey, two Englishmen, organized a company capitalized at more than £5 million to exploit the Tarapaca region. What followed were intensive development and a worldwide advertising campaign to publish the mineral's qualities. By 1910, 2,336,000 metric tons of nitrate had been exported and 50 percent of the nation's income depended on its production.[4]

In 1884, thirty-six of the forty-four operating oficinas were located in the province of Tarapaca, but later mines in Antofagasta proved to be even more important. More than thirty English companies were the principal owners of the oficinas. The Anglo Chilian Nitrate and Railway Company, Ltd., registered in 1888, had laid ninety-six kilometers of railroad track to link the harbor of Tocopilla to inland deposits. The Liverpool Nitrate Company, Ltd., was also mining in this area, but the most important company was the Nitrate Railways Company, Ltd., which had laid 606 kilometers of track to connect oficinas in Tarapaca with the harbors of Iquique and Piragua. The Lautaro Nitrate Company, Ltd., founded in 1889, had 27 oficinas that shipped nitrates to the port cities of Taltal and Iquique as well as Tocopilla.

The system used by nitrate companies to establish a territory involved both company towns placed in the areas of nitrate deposits and the connecting link to the harbor. Many kilometers of railroad track were laid to make this geographical and administrative area, known as a *canton*, work as a unit.[5] The province of Antofagasta contained four *cantones*: Canton Central and the port of Antofagasta, Canton Aguas Blancas and the port of Caletta Colosso, Canton Taltal and the port of Taltal, and Canton El Toco and the port of Tocopilla. Altogether more than seventy oficinas were once in operation. Within the region a few towns were dedicated to commercial activities. Baquedano and Pampa Union were two that supplied the oficinas and their workers. Because of arid conditions, equipment to pump subterranean water and a special solar desalination plant—the first in the world in 1872—were also provided.[6] The nitrate industry thus represented a complete regional system in which railroads provided the network that transformed the desert plains. Only two oficinas remain in operation today, however, and only a portion of the once-extensive railroad system survives to connect the region with northern Argentina and Bolivia.

The layouts of nitrate towns differed, depending on whether they were organized by companies employing the Shanks system of mining (British, German, and Chilean) or the Guggenheim system (American).[7] Certain basic elements of organization were used regardless of the system employed. Four areas or zones were clearly defined: (1) the factory area, including railroad station and workshops; (2) housing for managerial staff, generally placed close to the factory and in relation to it; (3) a plaza with surrounding community buildings; and (4) workers' camp. The oficinas José Santos Ossa, Aconcagua, or Francisco Puelma (Shanks system) are good examples of such zoning. House designs varied according to the status of employees. The better houses were situated near the plaza. In this zone, rows of semidetached houses built of adobe and brick lined the streets with no open spaces in between. On the outskirts of town, a regular grid was laid out to define the workers' camp. Rectangular blocks of different dimensions (30 × 60 meters; 25 × 400 meters) were laid out according to the type of dwelling designed. The Oficina José Santos Ossa of Canton Central (1910–1926) was planned with 50 percent of the town area used for the factory railroad, management housing, and plaza. The remaining 50 percent was taken up by the workers' camp (Fig. 7.2), an area approximately 200 × 250 meters with 368 houses for families and 19 apartment blocks for unmarried people.[8] Chacabuco (1924–1938), with 3,144 workers and their families, was the most important oficina within the Shanks system. Its general plan reveals an organized zoning pattern, including the main plaza, workers' camp, and other areas (Fig. 7.3). The factory and railroad yard formed the southern and southeastern zones, and management housing occupied the northern zone. Community buildings were located around the main plaza (50 × 50 meters), but other public buildings and open spaces, such as the church, baths, market, and soccer field, were distributed throughout the workers' area. This western zone (600 × 600 meters) was organized on a regular grid and, although the streets were of a regular width (13 meters), the size and shape of blocks varied in relation to the house design adopted; 706 houses and 326 single rooms were provided in all.

It is interesting to observe the way the workers' area is confined: two rows of houses form the town's western boundaries, which contrasts with the natural terrain. It should be noted that a similar organization was used in planning Ingenio Santa Ana of Tucuman (pp. 229–30), which had a square at center framed by straight rows of workers' houses. *Tortas*—mountains of mineral residue—and factory smokestacks created a backdrop in the desert landscape for the nitrate company towns. Oficina Maria Elena (1925), in Canton El Toco, one of only two factories still operating, was built by the Guggenheim Brothers after a plan prepared in their New York offices (Fig. 7.4). This industrial plant is four times larger than Chacabuco. It is situated in an area twelve hundred meters square, seventy kilometers inland from Tocopilla harbor.[9] Zoned into three main areas, Maria Elena had a formal plan: (1) its factory, railroad yards, and workshops formed the northern part; (2) housing for the principals—the Barrio americano—formed the northwestern part and was laid out as a garden suburb; and (3) workers' housing followed the geometrical pattern of radial streets in an octagonal plan (800 × 800 meters). The plaza and community buildings define the center of town. The treatment of the plaza and

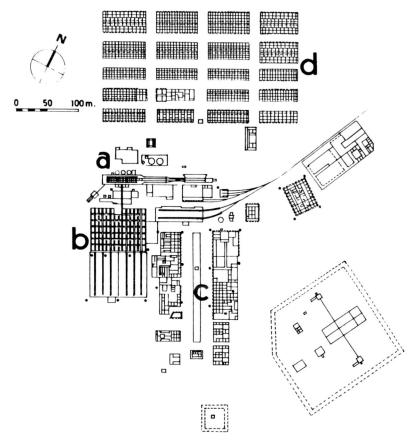

Figure 7.2 Plan of Oficina José Santos Ossa, Canton Central, Chile: a. Industrial area; b. Railroad and workshops; c. Plaza, Community buildings, and Employee housing; d. Workers' camp. (Drawn by Virginia E. de Ledesma from E. Garcés Felin, *Las Ciudades del salitre* [Universidad del Norte, Chile: Editorial Universitaria, 1988].)

street pattern would seem to derive from Vencenzo Scamozzi's ideal city of the Renaissance, minus fortifications.[10]

Tannin, Meat-Packing, and Sugar Towns of Argentina

Settlements along the eastern margin of El Chaco province, which was largely uninhabited before 1860, began as quebracho lumbering centers. The quebracho tree, native to Argentina, was cut and hauled to extracting plants located close to the Parana River. The extract of the quebracho tree, tannin, became a much sought-after product used by pharmacists as an astringent and by distillers for clarification of wine and beer. Quebracho was also used for railway ties (sleepers). In 1895, the German Harteneck brothers organized the first extracting plant in Fives Lilles, Santa

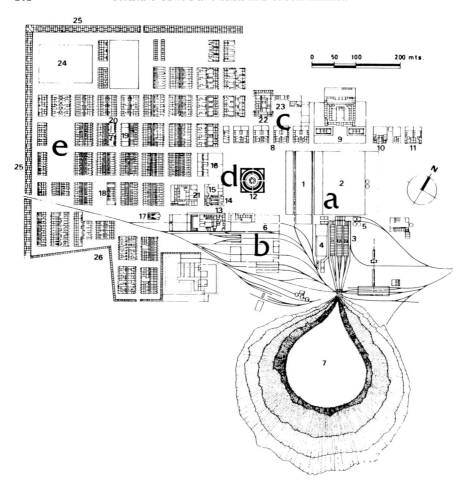

Figure 7.3 Plan of Oficina Chacabuco, Canton Central, Chile: a. Industrial area; b. Railroad and workshops; c. Employee housing; d. Plaza and community buildings; e. Workers' camp. (Drawn by Virginia E. de Ledesma from *Las Ciudades del salitre*.)

Fe.[11] Four years later, they brought modern machinery from Amberes, and their Calchaqui plant was put in operation. The Hartenecks later associated with a Frenchman, the baron Portalis, and together they organized the Forestal Land, Timber and Railway Company, Ltd. Their holdings included more than 600,000 hectares and supported many company towns. In 1902, La Guillermina, located 470 kilometers from Calchagui, produced fourteen thousand tons of tannin per year.[12] By 1910, the Forestal company had monopolized Argentinian production and was exporting its tannin to England, the United States, and Germany. By 1914, it controlled half of all tannin production and virtually all trading. By then, the quebracho cutters had cleared and depleted the forests, in bands running northwestward into the interior of the Chaco, and agricultural settlers were arriving to cultivate small farms along the railroad lines.

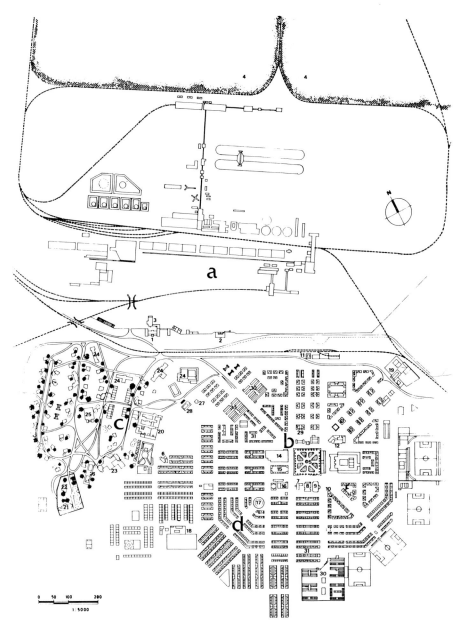

Figure 7.4 Plan of Oficina Maria Elena, Canton El Toco, Chile: A. Industrial area; B. Plaza and community buildings; C. Employees' housing; D. Workers' camp. (Drawn by Virginia E. de Ledesma from *Las Ciudades del salitre*.)

The types of settlements founded by the industry included the *obraje*, or transitory lumber camps, which were situated in the quebracho forests, *picadas*, or permanent storage centers, *pueblos tanineros*, well-organized company towns where quebracho was processed, and the ports from which the tannin was sent to Buenos Aires and Rosario before export to England and the United States. A main railroad line connected important cities such as Reconquista and Resistencia, and smaller ones were extended to serve the eastern forests and the western ports on the Paraguay River.[13]

The pueblos tanineros were always built along the Paraguay River, and Forestal had twenty-five ships waiting in Piracua, Piracuacito, Peguacho, and Ocampo. Railroad lines connected the picadas with the factories and harbors, whereas oxen were used to haul the tree trunks from the forests to the picadas. Quebracho Fusionados was founded in 1906; its factories were in close proximity to Puerto Tirol, Puerto Max, and Puerto Maria on the Paraguay River. The Argentine Quebracho Co. (1904) owned 200,000 hectares and shipped fifty tons of tannin and sixty thousand to seventy thousand trunks daily to the company's warehouses and central offices in New York.[14] By 1920 vast areas of quebracho had been cleared, and because the tree takes a century to reach maturity, no reforestation was attempted. Another tree, the mimosa, eventually replaced the quebracho. Its tannin was inferior, but the tree matured quickly and forests could be replaced in shorter time. Companies bought new land in Brazil and South Africa and abandoned El Chaco and all the equipment and towns built over most of a century. By 1950, El Chaco's former company towns and other small settlements had been largely reclaimed by nature.[15]

In organizing the pueblos tanineros in the quebracho forests, tannin companies adopted town plans in accord with the European origins of their capital investors. Fontana (1915–1931), for example, founded by Spaniards, was planned with four main areas: (1) the factory with its various buildings placed in a straight line to facilitate processing; (2) the workers' housing, organized on a regular grid with dwellings on individual lots; (3) a main plaza with community buildings bordering it and the church (after the Spanish tradition) facing the square; and (4) a restricted area, where the owner lived, with management housing and offices as well as the sports arena. Streets planted with shade trees and named after the trees were paved with the industrial residue of sawdust (Fig. 7.5).

Agriculture and cattle-raising have always dominated the Argentine plains. Leather and beef jerky obtained from rendering plants, or *saladeros*, were the leading income-producing products by the middle of the nineteenth century. Saladero Colon, organized in the 1860s, became one of the most important towns. Twenty years earlier the baron Justus von Liebig had developed in Germany an industrial process to obtain *extractus carnis*, canned meat. In 1861, another German, George Giesbert, realized that it was possible to apply Liebig's procedures to the slaughterhouse industry during a visit to Uruguay. The first industrial plant was installed in Fray Bentos, Uruguay, to produce *extractus Carnis Liebig*; two years later the company was managed by the Societé Fray Bentos Giesbert et Cie. of Amberes. Because of his success, Giesbert decided to expand to Argentina. British

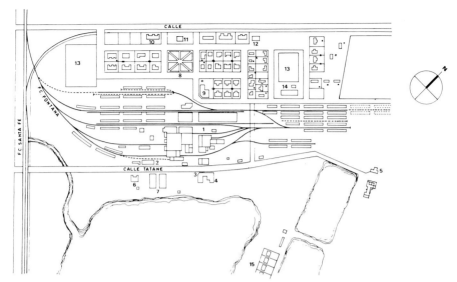

Figure 7.5 Plan of Fontana, El Chaco, Argentina: 1. Factory; 2. Workshops; 3. Administration offices; 4. Grocery store; 5. Manager's house; 6. School; 7. Tennis court; 8. Plaza; 9. Pub; 10. Houses for unmarried workers; 11. Church; 12. Houses for unmarried people; 13. Soccer field; 14. Club. (Drawn by Virginia E. de Ledesma from *Pueblos tanineros del NEA, Fontana.*)

capital was used in 1865 to organize the Liebig's Extract of Meat Company, Ltd., but the Argentine operation was slow to develop until 1903 and the purchase of Saladero Colon.[16] This new industrial plant, around which Liebig's company town ("Pueblo Liebig") developed, became the most modern meat packing factory of South America. Supply of beef depended on vast ranch land and important rural settlements, *estancias*, for cattle breeding. A fleet of steamships transported *extractus carnis* and "corned beef" to European countries, where the products were consumed.

Pueblo Liebig in Entre Ríos, Argentina, followed the pattern of British villages and was laid out without a formal town center. Two main streets, which led straight to the factory at the edge of town on the banks of the Uruguay River, dominated the plan. Without a plaza, Pueblo Liebig's public areas amounted only to informal leftover spaces used by workers for social recreation. The administration offices, the shipping offices, and a group of managers' houses, together with library and tennis courts, were set in line along the northern street. This area also included a house for visitors and the "Mess," a sort of hotel, and was recognized as a complete neighborhood, La Hilera. To the southwest, in a low-lying area, another neighborhood, El Pueblito, was the place where the workers lived and where buildings were of poor quality and densely situated. Three blocks accommodated most of the workers' houses, with another group lined up along the southern street. Back-to-back houses, rooms for unmarried men, and a club were also built in this section of town. A physical barrier, la manga, a wood-fenced stockyard in which animals were kept before rendering, separated both neighborhoods and clearly defined one side of town from the other.

The province of Tucumán contained eighty-two sugar refineries when the first railroad arrived in 1876. President Avellaneda's policies (he was one of three presidents who represented the interior of the country between 1874 and 1890) were designed to encourage development, offering patronage to provincial elites who had been neglected by earlier governments.[17] In 1876 one of Argentina's first railroads was built, from Rosario to Córdoba and then to Tucumán. Railroad development led to a rapid increase in cane growing because of the introduction of modern refining machinery. Thirty-four existing factories were now organized as modern *ingenios*, or refineries. Because of the new machinery and processing capacities, the area of sugar cane plantations in Tucumán expanded from 10,594 hectares in 1880 to 106,800 hectares by 1916.[18] Small settlements, or *colonias*, were organized by the *ingenios*, or refinery towns, to administer these rural areas. Irrigation systems were built as well as a number of private roads to connect the sugar plantations. By the time sugar cane activity had reached maturity in Tucumán, a complete territorial system of settlements had been organized. This agroindustrial activity involved *cañaverales* (sugar cane plantations), *colonias* (rural settlements dedicated to agricultural activities), *cargaderos* (small places in rural areas close to roads or railroad lines where sugar cane was taken to be weighed before it was sent to the *ingenio*), and the *ingenios* as well as railroads and irrigation systems.

Housing

Housing was a social responsibility that had to be fulfilled at low cost and yet be of sufficient quality to protect the health of workers. Different types of houses were adopted according to the status of those who occupied them, and they reveal the socioeconomic stratification that characterized Chilean and Argentine company towns. The maintenance of the dwellings was the responsibility of the companies, which had permanent staffs for this purpose. In none of the houses studied was the number of desired rooms a function of family size. Only one- or two-room houses were provided, together with small areas for a kitchen and latrine. Houses varied in style and decoration, but in every case they represented simple forms. Most were one-story, terraced, back-to-back, or tunnel-back units. The houses built in these towns were neither rural nor urban in character, but rather a mixture of the two. Company housing was something new to these areas but proved to be quite efficient.

Nitrate companies arranged dwellings in rectangular blocks divided into lots. Residential streets varied in width from 13 to 25 meters, although pedestrian passageways were as narrow as 2.5 meters. Rooflines were low (3.5 meters) and emphasized the horizontal plane. In the backyard or patio, protection from the sun was provided by overhanging roofs, and those overhangs eventually led to the advent of front and back galleries. The front galleries became an important element in the urban design of these blocks, offering better climate protection and permitted greater social intercourse. Bathrooms were simple latrines located at the back of the house, and some used collectively. Connections between rooms were made directly without the benefit of a hall. In Oficina Pedro de Valdivia, a special type of dwelling called a *buque*, for boat, formed an entire block and accommodated as many as nineteen rooms on each side of a large central yard. The yard was a common open space with secondary entrances to the rooms leading from it. Collective latrines were placed along one of the shorter sides of this patio and opposite a restricted entrance. Common places for washing and bathing were also provided. In Oficina Maria Elena, Pasajes, Prat y O'Higgins, and Orella, similar *buques* were constructed (Fig. 7.6). Entrances to these larger apartment blocks were given special attention. Neocolonial ornamentation, following the Spanish tradition, was used for the exterior treatment of Prat y O'Higgins. Adobe, the traditional building material, was used in their construction as well as zinc sheet roofing that represented the application of a new industrial product. Spanish Neocolonial styles were also used for management housing that included single- and double-family units with generous floor areas, including a porch, dining room, living room, bedrooms, kitchen, bathrooms, and even maids' rooms (Figs. 7.7 and 7.8).

The Sugar Towns of Tucumán, Argentina: A Case Study

Tucumán, in the northwestern part of Argentina, enjoyed a diversified economy resulting from farms known as *estancias* or *fincas*, and the growing of sugar cane had been included among traditional crops since 1821 when Bishop José Eusebio Colombres reintroduced it to Argentina.[19] Cane was first grown during the eighteenth century in the Mission of Lules, a place close to the capital of the province, but it died out after the Jesuits were expelled from Latin America. These rural farms can be considered the starting point for the development of company towns, widely known as *ingenios*, of the sugar industry. Their organization took place in two stages, the first between 1820 and 1876 and the second between 1876 and 1930. The first began when Bishop Colombres induced farmers to plant sugar cane by convincing them of its economic benefits.[20] When the railroad arrived in Tucumán in 1876, the cultivation of sugar cane had already reached a high level of development. The produce of the eighty-two *estancias* scattered throughout the territory was shipped by cart or wagon to the northwest corner of Argentina and then to Bolivia, but the arrival of a railroad provided the network needed to get the produce to the larger ports of Buenos Aires and Rosario. After 1876 the economy of the entire region changed. Farmers who owned small establishments now had the opportunity of importing new equipment from Europe, especially Europe, France, and Germany, along with skilled technicians to operate it. The federal and provincial governments supported the sugar industry with special credits and lenient tax policies. This second stage marked the arrival of the Industrial Revolution in Tucumán, and by its close the majority of *ingenios* had been built. No substantive changes have occurred since 1930. Only technical improvements have been made to obtain better production, although factory buildings or refineries have largely remained unchanged.

PLAN

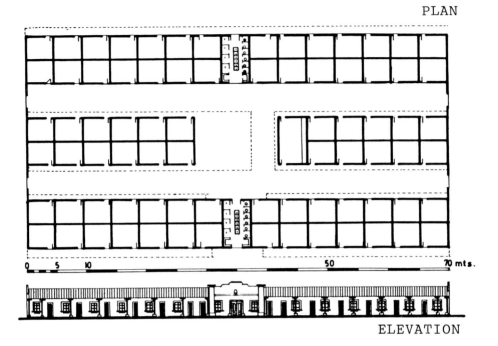

ELEVATION

Figure 7.6 Workers' camps (Pasajes Prat y O'Higgins [above] and Pasaje Orella [right]), Oficina Maria Elena, Canton El Toco, Chile. (Drawn by Virginia E. de Ledesma from *Las Ciudades del salitre*.)

Ingenio San Pablo (Fig. 7.9) and Ingenio Cruz Alta are good examples of the morphology that transformed the appearance of farming settlements. In 1826, Jean Nougués arrived from France to seek his fortune in Tucumán. He bought a few acres of land and began to grow rice, corn, and wheat and also raised cattle. Water from a nearby stream was sufficient to operate a flour mill. The construction of a dam and the channeling of water through a millrace provided turbine power for tanning and refining, and a small sugar cane plantation to produce sugar and strong wine added to the wealth of the farm that eventually came to be known as Ingenio San Pablo. Similar activities occurred in Estancia La Cruz Alta, and by 1830 its owner, Simon Garcia, had constructed a sugar mill in the main patio of his farm. By 1869 he was largely engaged in sugar and alcohol production, and in 1872 he replaced his original mill with one of iron construction. In 1877, making use of the now-completed railroad and special credits, Garcia purchased a steam mill and a sugar kettle from England. That transaction signaled the end of Estancia La Cruz Alta and the beginning of Ingenio Cruz Alta.[21]

At first, all farming activities took place in the same buildings and open spaces.

PLAN

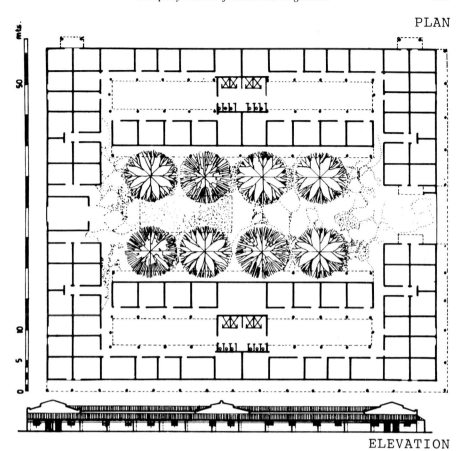

ELEVATION

By 1830, however, those related to sugar cane began to increase in importance and a transformation occurred. The *estancia* owned by Obispo Colombres, Quinta El Bajo, was the first one to undergo such change. Following the vernacular tradition, Colombres's house was the most important building on the farm. A two-story frame house with wide arcades open to the north, it typified the residential architecture of a landowner. It had a private garden complete with gallery and, on either side, two large dependencies, or *galpones*, made of adobe, which contained some of the farm's machinery. The house and dependencies framed a courtyard where the sugar mill and other equipment were kept. This space was first called a "labor patio," but in Cruz Alta and other places it was termed a "laboratory patio." It was also used to stockpile cane harvested from the plantation, or *cañaveral*. The cane was then processed in the mill and the juice taken to sugar evaporators and other pans; the leftover fiber remained in the patio in great quantities, waiting to be used as fuel. This patio area was the origin of the future *ingenios' canchon* and was especially noisy and dirty. Oxen tended by children pulled the heavy wagons of sugar cane and turned the sugar mill in the patio. The mix of raw material, animals, cane, sugar,

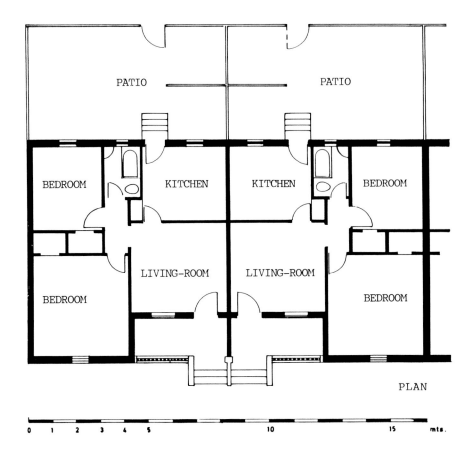

PATIO   PATIO

BEDROOM   KITCHEN   KITCHEN   BEDROOM

LIVING-ROOM   LIVING-ROOM

BEDROOM   BEDROOM

PLAN

0   1   2   3   4   5   10   15   mts.

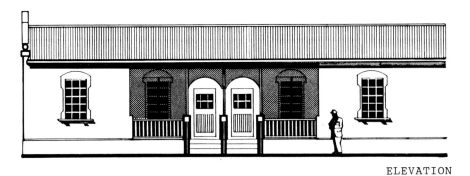

ELEVATION

Figure 7.7 Management housing (Barrio americano), Oficina Maria Elena, Canton El Toco, Chile. (Drawn by Virginia E. de Ledesma from *Las Ciudades del salitre*.)

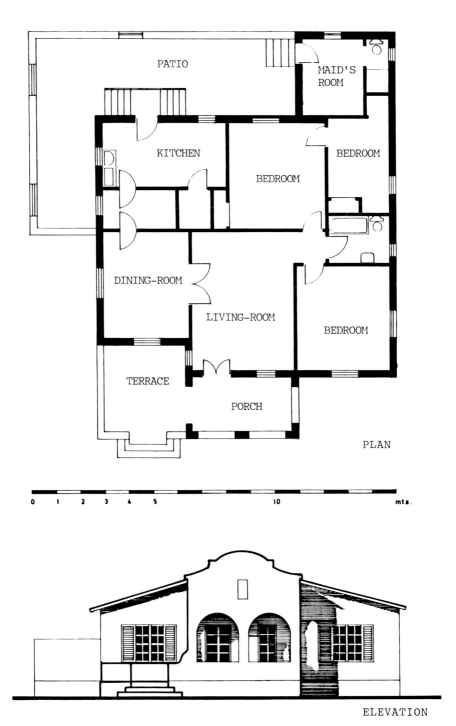

PATIO

MAID'S
ROOM

KITCHEN

BEDROOM

BEDROOM

DINING-ROOM

LIVING-ROOM

BEDROOM

TERRACE

PORCH

PLAN

0 1 2 3 4 5   10   mts.

ELEVATION

Figure 7.8 Management housing (Barrio americano), Oficina Maria Elena, Canton El Toco, Chile. (Drawn by Virginia E. de Ledesma from *Las Ciudades del salitre*.)

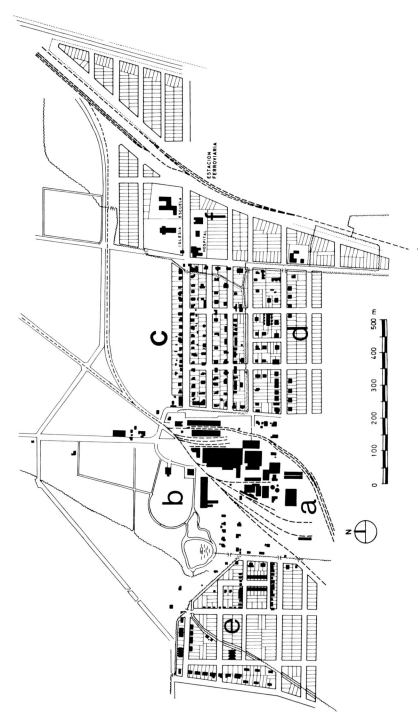

Figure 7.9 Plan of Ingenio San Pablo, Tucumán, Argentina: a. industrial area; b. the chalet and the private park; c. employees' housing; d. permanent workers' housing; e. transitory workers' housing; f. community buildings. (Drawn by Arcadio Kotowicz from O. Paterlini de Koch, *Pueblos Azucareros de Tucumán* [Tucumán, Argentina: Instituto Argentino de Investigaciones de Historia de la Arquitectura y del Urbanismo, 1987].)

and people all moving around would become a fixture of even the most organized *ingenios*.

In addition to the residence and labor patio, the two *galpones*, which at first were used only to store tools and other implements, were the origin of the future factory (Fig. 7.10). As activity increased, their importance within the farm also increased. In this way the factory evolved, and the *galpones* eventually turned into the mill hall or hall of draining molasses. The factories built during the preindustrial era were completely replaced after 1876. Technical changes and innovations rendered obsolete the traditional arrangement and structure of the buildings. Brick, iron, and then steel began to be introduced in large quantities. Entire buildings were framed in steel, permitting the use of large windows to provide natural lighting and ventilation. Building materials used were always imported, usually from Britain and France, as were the factory designs and floor layouts. Factories and warehouses were organized around a large open space, *canchon*, where first wagons and then trains carried cane from the plantations and carried away the sugar to the depots. The industrial areas were especially active, as dust, noise, animals, workers, sugar cane, and sugar bags, together with industrial residues, competed for space.

The character of the *estancia* was shaped by local traditions and practical requirements, and its layout followed no particular pattern. Aesthetic considerations extended only to the family house. Two or three chimneys scattered about the labor

Figure 7.10 Hacienda La Concepcion, Tucumán, Argentina, ca. 1880. (From *Memoria historica y descriptiva de la provincia de Tucumán.*)

patio gave the impression of a factory, but they represented only the beginning of an industrial site. As the settlement evolved from a working farm, each component or area was developed into a zone of the company town. After 1876, the eighty-two *estancias* were transformed into thirty-four organized *ingenios*. Those landowners who could not afford industrialization continued to raise sugar cane and remained *cañeros*.

The landowner (turned industrialist) built a town for workers on his estate, creating a self-sustaining community containing all industrial, residential, and attendant facilities. What it lacked was self-government. Everything was ruled or controlled by the owner of the factory; paternalism predominated. Only after 1945 did industrialists begin to transfer property to the government and the community begin to function as a free town. The period 1876–1930 represents the most vigorous economic growth and exploitation. Many fortunes were made during these years, stemming from a laissez-faire government policy. Engineers, architects, and builders who arrived in Tucumán remained largely anonymous. Most were Spanish and Italian immigrants, although a few lived in the province or were hired in Buenos Aires. General layouts of *ingenios* and architecture reveal two different schools of training, picturesque or contour planning and Beaux Arts symmetry and formality.

Company towns differed in degree. Some *ingenios*, such as Bella Vista, conformed to rectangular layouts as found in colonial towns. Its plan was defined by a system of major and minor streets. The main avenue or boulevard connected the plantations, factory, and railroad station. Secondary streets defined the workers' residential area, and pedestrian paths allowed people to move through various quarters. Because of its functional purpose, the avenue needed to be generous in size. Twenty to thirty meters in width, it permitted wagons, trains, and horses to carry raw material and sugar. The avenue was noisy and dusty, and pedestrians could use only narrow walks on either side. Housing and community buildings were located along the avenue or close to it. Some town plans were dominated by a straight axis (Ingenio La Florida), others adopted the shape of a T (Ingenio San Juan), still others a cross (Ingenio Santa Lucia) or a square (Ingenio Santa Ana). In some instances a curvilinear web of streets, varied paths, and open spaces produced a picturesque or contour plan. Secondary streets were mostly used by workers whose houses lined both sides. Inhabitants created their own pedestrian paths to move easily from one place to another. Most towns did not present the image of well-cared-for places. Visitors rarely departed from the main avenue because the rest of the town was rather unpleasant. Storm water collected in open channels, and in some places it flowed down the streets. There was no paving, and rain, industrial residue, and dust turned the streets into quagmires.

A sugar town was divided into several zones or components that were clearly defined:

> 1. Industrial zone: Factory, depots, workshops, and laboratories situated in a central location. The importance of the buildings made them the focus of the plan.
> 2. Family house and park zone: The owner of the factory lived in a "Chalet" or "La Sala" that could resemble a European villa with an artificial landscape or park borrowed from English or French garden traditions.

3. Community buildings zone: The hospital, church, drugstore (controlled by the owners of the factory), primary school, and sports area were included among these facilities.

4. Housing zone for managerial and technical staff: A special layout was used to accommodate the better paid employees in small houses that reflected the style of the chalet and the administration offices.

5. Workers' housing zone: Small houses and single rooms were provided in regular layouts separated by open spaces.

6. Housing zone for temporary workers: Those who came seasonally for harvesting cane were accommodated in separate areas and given rooms.

The relationship between the various zones was important. The family house or chalet and its park were always located next to the industrial area. Privacy was assured by the park and grounds. Community buildings (Fig. 7.11) were located either near or within the workers' residential quarter, while the administrative staff lived nearer the factory. The zoning and architecture reinforced the image of a centralized and hierarchic settlement with sharply defined districts. The general plan rarely emphasized public open spaces. The Spanish tradition of a central plaza, as adopted by the sixteenth-century "Laws of the Indies," had little but ornamental significance in these industrial towns. Although sometimes streets led to open spaces and people made good use of them, they were small, dispersed, and poorly maintained. Buildings and houses were built as either independent units or blocks of two, four, six, or ten units. They tended to be placed along a common building line parallel to a street but occasionally were grouped in superblocks or followed the

Figure 7.11 Hospital of Ingenio San Pablo, Tucumán, Argentina, ca. 1920. (Archivo general de la nacion, Buenos Aires.)

curve of a contoured street pattern. Existing trees were preserved and new ones planted for protection from the sun. Workers' houses were always one-story units, and each small neighborhood or block was painted in a different color so that it could be easily identified. Flexibility was another feature of these towns: each area could be enlarged without disturbing the overall plan.

Ingenios built and maintained primary schools, and special attention was given to educating the children when they were not employed in harvesting. Adult education was also provided in some *ingenios*, but most adults received training while working in the factories and workshops.[22] For recreation, soccer fields were maintained and good teams and keen competition were much desired. As years passed, these teams turned into the professional soccer clubs of the province. Public baths, including swimming pools, were built in some *ingenios*,[23] although tennis courts and bowling alleys were provided only for the managers and their families. The companies also built Catholic churches. La Trinidad, for example, has a beautiful Renaissance Revival style church where special religious festivities were celebrated each year before the harvest season. Some *ingenios*, such as San Pablo, also maintained a private chapel for the owners and managers. Electricity, a luxury of the period, was the pride of the *ingenio*. Ingenio Lules began to generate electric current as early as 1883, while Buenos Aires was still using gas lighting. Water lines extended to nearly every house during the 1930s, but sewerage was never provided. During the 1930s, the sugar industrialists began to sell company housing to their longtime occupants and transferred the community buildings to the provincial government. Owners of large tracts of land in areas close to the *ingenios* began to sell off subdivisions to create new neighborhoods. One town, La Florida, was planned between two existing *ingenios* to complete the territorial organization of the sugar industry.

Life in a Sugar Town

Living and working in a sugar town were strictly controlled by the policies of the company. In such a community, the industrial owner was at the top of the social and economic pyramid; he owned the town and refinery and managed the workers' lives. Engineers and technicians, always foreigners, belonged to the second economic level, followed by permanent workers, and finally those at the bottom level, migrant or temporary workers. Virtually everything was monitored and each town was physically closed. No one could enter or leave without company permission. Each zone within the town functioned independently, since workers lived in one place and shared their own problems. Owners, managers, and technicians did the same.

The sugar harvesting and refining period lasted from May until October, and during those months thousands of itinerant workers arrived from the northwest— Santiago del Estero, Catamarca, Salta—to work on the plantations or in the factories. In 1881, 11,000 people migrated to the region.[24] Each *ingenio* hired workers according to its size and need (La Esperanza, 600; Concepcion, 420, only 120 of them permanent workers; La Trinidad, 297).[25] Ten years later, Aloi and Fliess cited more than 13,000 workers employed during the sugar-making period. The whole activity may have involved as many as 60,000 people, of whom 15,000 came from Catamarca, Santiago, and Salta,[26] traveling in heavy wagons with their families, animals, and other possessions. The men, women, and children who were temporary laborers worked mostly on the plantations. By 1904, some *ingenios* employed as many as 900 permanent workers and 1,700 temporary ones.[27] It is difficult to arrive at the exact number of migrants because only men were registered and not their families who also worked, but it can be assumed that most *ingenios* doubled in population during harvesting and refining.

Industrialists, who were often elected politicians, attempted to enhance their investments by trying to educate their work forces to the routine of factory life. The people brought to the establishment came from rural areas and had lived in poverty and ignorance for generations. They had no knowledge of industrialization and at the beginning were just unskilled workers, but in time they turned into a stable work force that was well trained in sugar refining. During the 1880s, emigrants from the European countries were encouraged to go to Tucumán, but it was impossible to keep those who arrived on the plantations or in the factories. In 1904 there were 250 native workers, *criollos*, and only 5 foreigners, the technical experts, at Ingenio La Esperanza.[28] Immigrants could not adjust to the weather and difficult working conditions. *Criollos*, even when they drank and gambled, were better able to endure the rain, mud, cold, and sickness. Working conditions were governed by state laws (Codigo de Policia, 1856, and Ley de Conchabos, 1888), but governmental oversight was usually influenced by powerful industrialists.[29] Men, women, and children worked twelve- or thirteen-hour days, and 70 percent were illiterate. No unions protected them until 1904, when the first workers' strike was organized. That event led to provincial and federal intervention, but the situation did not change much after the strike. Those strikes that followed in 1906 and 1907 had little impact. Ignorance and diminished social station acted against material improvements. The situation began to improve only after 1930. Before the first strike, workers' wages included free housing and a certain amount of food (meat and corn). No day of rest was provided on Sunday, and many workers resorted to drink as a pastime. They had little recourse but to accept the conditions and routine that controlled their lives. In 1907 the company stores, where workers had to purchase their goods, were abolished, an important step toward greater economic and personal freedom. In 1919 protestors fought to reduce workdays from twelve to eight hours, and some *ingenios*, such as Bella Vista, adopted the principle before it became law in 1923.

Housing in a Sugar Town

Industrialists had no alternative to providing housing for permanent and temporary workers. *Ingenios'* housing, no matter how spartan, meant a great improvement for the *criollos*. Units were provided free of rent, but considering the small amount of money received for labor, it can be said that housing was a part of wages.[30]

Workers' houses were, at first, small adobe *ranchos* built around the factory, but after 1880, timber framing and tiles were used to improve roofs, replacing the traditional thatch. Units were also placed in a line along the streets to form row houses or terraces. Workers' housing reflected neither urban nor rural building design, perhaps because the labor force was mainly from the countryside and the builders from urban areas. The houses built for the *ingenios* improved on local conditions and created a new style that could be recognized as "sugar industrial housing." Houses for permanent workers were built as independent units or organized into groups of two or four; they generally had one or two rooms as well as a gallery or porch and a small kitchen and bathroom placed away from the other rooms because of poor plumbing. Some *ingenios*, such as San Pablo, built public baths to encourage bathing.

The row houses of permanent workers were offered in a variety of plans, each unit with a separate entry and yard so the family could grow its own vegetables and care for domestic animals. These were not gardens but rather patios, and although trees were grown to provide shade, no other plants, including grass, were cultivated. Rooms had no particular designation, and families made their own decisions about how to use them: if there were two rooms, one was used as a bedroom shared by parents, daughters, sons, and sometimes grandparents; the other served as a living room, used mainly to display furniture. No aisles or halls were provided to lead from one room to another: access was room-to-room or by the gallery. Rural traditions, weather conditions, and cultural habits caused workers to spend much of their time in open spaces, and in that regard, the gallery and patio were used intensively. Kitchens were too small and uncomfortable, and only old furniture was kept there, while most cooking and dining took place in the open air of the semi-enclosed gallery or patio.

Temporary workers' houses were of poorer quality. Units were always organized in groups of eight or ten, the *cuartos*. Families could use a room, part of the common gallery, and the kitchen. Baths and latrines were provided in common spaces. People lived in the temporary housing six to seven months each year, but as years passed and the tenants returned or became permanent workers, they remained in these original units, where such makeshift materials as sugar cane leaves, timber, and discarded sheets of galvanized iron were used to enlarge the small adobe houses.

Much better housing, following in most cases that of European and American company towns, was provided for people coming to the *ingenios* as overseers and technical experts. Their houses were located close to the factory, and each unit had ample space for a well-cared-for garden. One- and two-story houses had sufficient room for different activities, including a hall, living room, bedrooms, kitchen, and bathroom, as well as generous exterior galleries. Their occupants were always foreign-born. William Hill, for example, was from Cornwall, England, where he had trained as an engineer. He first went to Peru to organize *ingenios* Casagrande and Santa Clara,[31] and in 1875 he went to Argentina to prepare Los Ralos, Ledesma, and Concepcion. Afterward, he stayed in Argentina to manage El Manantial, which he finally bought in order to become a sugar industrialist himself.

Managing the factory and overseeing the *criollos* were the main activities of these foreigners. Some organized special schools for workers. As years went by, the *criollos* began to replace them in management positions.

The chalet was the largest and most distinguished residence of the settlement. Special care was given to its design, construction, and landscaping. It was one of only a few structures with any pretense to traditional European styles. The chalets of Ingenio La Trinidad and La Florida exhibited Neoclassical features; Ingenio Mercede, the Beaux Arts style; San Pablo and Santa Ana (Fig. 7.12), eclecticism; and Bella Vista, Neocolonial. The finest and largest residences of the province often borrowed from Andrea Palladio's villa plans. Most were three stories in height with rooms and loggias that opened to a park. The architect Manuel Graña, who had come from Spain, and the engineer Luis F. Nougués, who was one of the owners of Ingenio San Pablo, or builders such as the Venchiarutti, who emigrated from Italy, designed several of these houses. The French architect Charles Thays was hired by Nougués Brothers to design San Pablo's private park. A winding path led down to the chalet and then to the private chapel. Thays laid out the flower gardens and placed statues and rockeries at interesting points. The true beauty of the park was the planting and organization of its terrain; clumps of trees were planted in a picturesque manner. Exotic plants such as *arcodaxias regias*, a gift from President Roca, were included for contrast, but Thays's most important achievement was restoring indigenous plants. Artificial lakes were also created in some *ingenios*, such as Santa Ana and Mercedes. Workers could use the park only when permitted

Figure 7.12 Chalet of Ingenio Santa Ana, Tucumán, Argentina. (Archivo general de la nacion, Buenos Aires.)

Conclusion

Latin American company towns, although strongly influenced by what was happening in Europe and the United States, reveal a character of their own. Their founders traveled to England, France, Germany, or the United States to buy advanced machinery for their factories and sometimes returned with new ideas about town planning. Some towns were even designed abroad. Architects, engineers, and builders who were enticed to these frontier provinces contributed their knowledge of design and construction to indigenous cultural traditions. Of the many investors and businessmen who became involved in town building, the British and French were the most prominent. By the 1880s the British had invested heavily in railroads, public utilities, and government bonds, and soon they were involved in the meatpacking industry. But French, German, Argentine, and some Spanish immigrants also provided investment capital, technology, and industrial expertise. Some became involved in several different ventures at once: the baron Portalis, for example, who arrived from France to organize the tannin industry in the Chaco, became involved in the creation of the Banco Francés del Rio de la Plata and in railroad construction in Santa Fe. He was also an importer of farm equipment, sugar, and alcohol; a salesman for the Fives-Lilles Company of Paris; and one of the owners of Ingenio Santa Ana. Many industrialists were also prominent members of the provincial and federal governments. Their interest in town building went beyond the factory or refinery to include housing. The designs they adopted for workers' housing gave rise in most cases to a new kind of unit adapted to industrial employment. Old vernacular houses were replaced by dwellings that attempted to upgrade and improve living conditions. Design ideas from abroad were transplanted but took form according to local needs. New construction materials were tested. However, the American industrialist Harry F. Guggenheim noted, "The adobe house proved most satisfactory. They blend attractively with the pampa landscape, maintain a more even temperature, and the fact that they can be manufactured locally enables the management to add to the housing facilities as necessity demands without keeping a large stock of building materials continually on hand."[32] Although wood and corrugated iron had first been used, they were less suitable than adobe for housing. Guggenheim and other owners of company towns sought acceptance of their views on industrial development and housing. But as foreign investors in developing countries, they were also forced to compromise.

Notes

1. Colin Bell and Rose Bell, *City Fathers: The Early History of Town Planning, England* (London: Praeger, 1969), 240.

2. *Enciclopaedia Britannica*, vol. 5 (Chicago: William Benton, 1968), 546.

3. W. H. Koebel, ed., *Enciclopedia de la America del Sur*, vol. 4 (London: Anglo and South American Publishing Co., 1911), 4: 1649.

4. Eugenio Garcés Feliu, *Las Ciudades del Salitre: Un estudio de las Officinas Sali-*

treras en la region de Antofagasta, (Universidad del Norte, Chile: Editorial Universitaria, 1988), 19.

5. "'Canton': circunscripciones geografico-administrativas, que organizan a un conjunto de officinas salitreras, relacionadas a un area territorial comun, vinculadas a un ferrocarril y conectadas a un mismo puerto." Ibid., 23.

6. Ibid.

7. The Shanks system, developed by the Englishman James Humberstone for separating nitrate from the caliche, started industrial mining of the mineral. To meet this competition, the Guggenheim process, which used chemical lixiviation, was developed to replace the old Shanks steam coil refining technique. The new system was highly mechanized and reduced labor costs, increased efficiency, and processed ores of lower grade. Garcés Feliu, *Ciudades del Salitre*, 121–22; Enrique Cuevas, *The Nitrate Industry* (New York: William S. Meyers, 1916), 10–11; Belisario Diaz Ossa, *The Chilean Nitrate Industry* (Rome: International Institute of Agriculture, 1925), 15.

8. Garcés Feliu, *Ciudades del Salitre*, 45.

9. Ibid., 69–70.

10. Bell and Bell, *City Fathers*, 72.

11. Graciela Viñuales, "Los Poblados de la Explotacion Forestal," *Construccion de la Ciudad* (La colonizacion del Territorio Argentino, 1875–1925), n. 19 (Barcelona: 1925), 33.

12. Reginald Lloyd, *Impresiones de la Republica Argentina en en Siglo XX* (London: Lloyd's Great Britain Publishing Co., 1911), 463.

13. Viñuales, "Poblados de la Explotacion," 34.

14. Ibid., 446.

15. Teresita Francini y Jorge Rosé, "Pueblos Tenineros del NEA, Fontana," in *Documentos de Arquitectura Nacional y Americana*, n. 4, (Chaco, Argentina: Universidad Nacional del Nordeste, 1976), 60.

16. Carlos Canavessi, et al., "Pueblo Liebig" (Entre Rios, Argentina, 1988).

17. From President Avellaneda's speech, 1874: "We had to bring a festival of work and progress to the center of our interior regions in order to call attention to a new way to revive its activities and its dreams for the future." Donna J. Guy, *Argentina Sugar Politics: Tucuman and the Generation of Eighty* (Tempe: Center for Latin American Studies, Arizona State University, 1980), 28.

18. Olga Paterlini de Koch, *Pueblos Azucareros de Tucumán*, (Tucumán, Argentina: Instituto Argentino de Investigaciones de Historia de la Arquitectura y del Urbanismo, 1987), 26.

19. Emilio Schleh, "La caña de azucar en Tucumán: Memoria de su Introduccion y Propagacion," [Centro Azucarero Argentino] *Revista Azucarera*, año 7, n. 80 (August 1909): 126–27.

20. Guy, *Argentina Sugar Politics*, 16.

21. Paterlini de Koch, *Pueblos Azucareros de Tucumán*, 47.

22. Ibid., 129.

23. Ibid., 130.

24. Paul Groussac et al., *Memoria Historica y Descriptiva de la Provincia de Tucumán* (Buenos Aires: M. Biedma, 1882), 521.

25. Ibid.

26. Juan Bialet-Massé, *El Estado de las clases obreras argentinas a comienzos del siglo*, (Cordoba: Universidad Nacional de Cordoba, 1904), 101.

27. Ibid., 105.

28. Ibid.
29. Guy, *Argentina Sugar Politics*, 35.
30. Paterlini de Koch, *Pueblos Azucareros de Tucumán*, 95.
31. Ibid., 113.
32. "Building American Towns in Chile," *Literary Digest* 60 (September 1920): 117.

Bibliography

For additional reading about the company towns discussed in the preceding chapters, as well as other information on the architecture, landscapes, and social history of the regions or places herein described, the contributors have compiled a brief list of sources.

South Wales

Addis, John. *The Crawshay Dynasty*. Cardiff: University of Wales Press, 1957.

Carter, Harold. "The Growth of Industry, 1750–1850." In *Wales: A Physical, Historical and Regional Geography*. Edited by E. G. Bowen. London: Muthuen, 1957.

Carter, Harold, and Sandra Wheatley. *Merthyr Tydfil in 1851: A Study of the Spatial Structure of a Welsh Industrial Town*. Cardiff: University of Wales Press, 1982.

Clarke, T. E. *Guide to Merthyr Tydfil*. Merthyr Tydfil: London, 1848.

Cliffe, Charles Frederick. *The Book of South Wales*. London: Hamilton, Adams and Co., 1854.

Davis, E. A. "Life in a Nineteenth-Century Iron Town." In *Glamorgan Historian*, edited by Roy Denning, vol. 12, Cowbridge, South Wales: D. Brown, 1977.

de la Beche, Henry. *Report on the State of Bristol, Bath, Frome, Swansea, Merthyr Tydfil and Brecon*. London: W. Clowes, 1845.

Elsas, Madeleine, ed. *Iron in the Making: Dowlais Iron Company Letters 1782–1860*. Cardiff: County Records Committee of the Quarterly Sessions and County Council, 1960.

Evans, The Reverend J. *Letters Written during a Tour through South Wales in the Year 1803 and at Other Times*. London: C. and R. Baldwin, 1804.

Ginswick, Jules, ed. *Labour and the Poor in England and Wales 1849–1851: The Letters to* The Morning Chronicle *from the Correspondents in the Manufacturing and Mining Districts, the Towns of Liverpool and Birmingham and the Rural Districts*. vol. 3, *South Wales–North Wales*. London: Frank Cass, 1983.

Hadfield, Charles. *The Canals of South Wales and the Border*. Cardiff: University of Wales Press, 1967.

Hilling, John B. "The Buildings of Merthyr Tydfil." in *Glamorgan Historian*, edited by Stewart Williams, vol. 8, Cowbridge, South Wales: D. Brown, 1973.

————. *Cardiff and the Valleys: Architecture and Townscape*. London: Lund Humphries, 1973.

Hopkins, T. J., ed. "Robert Clutterbuck's Tour through Glamorgan, 1799." In *Glamorgan Historian*, edited by Stewart Williams, vol. 3, Cowbridge, South Wales: D. Brown, 1968.

John, A[rthur]. H. *The Industrial Development of South Wales 1750–1850*. Cardiff: University of Wales Press, 1950.

————, and Glanmor Williams, eds. *Glamorgan County History*. Vol. 5, *Industrial Glamorgan from 1700 to 1970*. Cardiff: Glamorgan County History Trust Ltd. (distributed by University of Wales Press), 1980.

Jones, Frances M. "The Aesthetics of the Nineteenth-Century Industrial Town." In *The Victorian City: Images and Realities*, edited by H. J. Dyos and Michael Wolff. London: Routledge & Kegan Paul, 1973.

Jones, Ieuan Gwynedd. "Merthyr Tydfil in 1850: Impressions and Contrasts." in *Glamorgan Historian*, edited by Stewart Williams. vol. 10, Cowbridge, South Wales: D. Brown, 1975.

Lewis, Samuel. *Topographical Dictionary of Wales*. London: S. Lewis & Co., 1849.

Lloyd, John. *The Early History of the Old South Wales Iron Works (1760 to 1840)*. London: Bedford Press, 1906.

Lowe, J[eremy]. B. *Welsh Industrial Workers Housing 1775–1875*. Cardiff: National Museum of Wales, 1977.

Malkin, Benjamin Heath. *The Scenery, Antiquities, and Biography of South Wales from Materials Collected during Two Excursions in the Year 1803*. London: T. N. Longman and O. Rees, 1804.

Manby, G. W. *An Historic and Picturesque Guide from Clifton, through the Counties of Monmouth, Glamorgan, and Brecknock*. Bristol: Fenley and Baylis, 1802.

Morgan, Prys. "From a Death to a View: The Hunt for the Welsh Past in the Romantic Period." In *The Invention of Tradition*, edited by Eric Hobsbawm and Terence Ranger, Cambridge: Cambridge University Press, 1983.

Owen, John A. *The History of the Dowlais Iron Works 1759–1970*. Newport, Gwent (South Wales): Starling Press, 1977.

————. "Merthyr Tydfil: Iron Metropolis 1790–1860." In *Merthyr Historian*, vol. 1. Merthyr Tydfil, South Wales: Merthyr Tydfil Historical Society, 1976.

Rammell, Thomas Webster. *Report to the General Board of Health on the Town of Merthyr Tydfil*. London: W. Clowes, 1850.

Rees, D. Morgan. *The Industrial Archaeology of Wales*. Newton Abbot: David and Charles, 1975.

Rees, The Reverend T. *Topographical and Historical Description of South Wales*. London: Sherwood, Neely and Jones, 1819.

Roberts, Edwin F. *A Visit to the Ironworks and Environs of Merthyr-Tydfil in 1852*. Swansea, 1853.

Roberts, R. O. "Industrial Expansion in South Wales." In *Wales in the Eighteenth Century*, edited by Donald Moore. Swansea: C. Davies, 1976.

Taylor, Margaret Stewart. "The Big Houses of Merthyr Tydfil." In *Merthyr Historian*, vol. 1. Merthyr Tydfil, South Wales: Merthyr Tydfil Historical Society, 1976.

Vaughn, F. "Some Aspects of Life in Merthyr Tydfil in the Nineteenth Century." In *Merthyr Historian*, vol. 3. Merthyr Tydfil, South Wales: Merthyr Tydfil Historical Society, 1980.

Wilkins, Charles. *The History of the Iron, Steel and Tinplate Trades.* Merthyr Tydfil, South Wales: J. Williams, 1903.

——. *The History of Merthyr Tydfil.* Merthyr Tydfil, South Wales: J. Williams and Son, 1908.

Williams, Gwyn A. *The Merthyr Rising.* London: Croom Helm, 1978.

——. *The Welsh in Their History.* London: Croom Helm, 1982.

Williams, Moelwyn. *The Making of the South Wales Landscape.* London: Hodder and Stoughton, 1975.

France

Audiganne, A. *Les Populations ouvrières et les industries de la France dans le mouvement social du XIXe siecle.* 2 vols. Paris: Capelle, Libraire-Editeur, 1854.

Benoît-Levy, George. *La Cité-Jardin.* Paris: Henri Jouve, 1904.

Butler, Remy, and Patrice Noisette. *De la Cité ouvrière au grand ensemble: La politique capitaliste du logement social 1815–1975.* Paris: François Maspero, 1977.

Cacheux, Emile. *Habitations ouvrières.* Laval: Imprimerie et stereotypie E. Jamin, 1882.

Challamel, Jules. *Compte rendu et documents du congrés international des habitations à bon marché.* Paris: Secretariat de la Societé française des habitations à bon marché, 1900.

——. *Les Habitations à bon marché en belgique et en france.* Paris: F. Pichon, 1895.

Choay, Françoise. *L'Urbanisme, utopies et réalités, une anthologie.* Paris: Editions du Seuil, 1965.

Clark, George. *Les Habitations des classes ouvrières en France: Nouveau systems de logements garnis pour les celibataires à Paris.* Paris: Chaix, 1854.

——. *Logements modèles: Systeme nouveau pour l'amelioration des habitations ouvrières proposé au gouvernement français.* Paris: Imprimerie de N. Chaix, 1855.

Closson, Prosper. *Etablissements Menier, usine de Noisiel-Sur-Marne.* Paris: E. Plon et Cie., 1878.

Considerant, Victor. *Description du phalanstere et considérations sociales sur l'architectonique.* 2d ed. Paris: Librairie societaire, 1838.

Dameth, H. *Memoire sur la foundation de cités industrielles dites cités de l'Union.* Paris: Imprimerie de Schneider, 1849.

Degrand, E., and Dr. Faucher. *Exposition universelle de 1867: Rapports du jury international, habitations caracterisées par le bon marché uni aux conditions d'hygiene et de bien-être.* Groupe 10, classes 89 à 95, t. 13. Paris: Imprimerie administrative de Paul Dupont, 1868.

Dumont, André-Alfred. *Les Habitations ouvrières: Dans les grands centres industriels et plus particulieremont dans la region du Nord.* Lille: V. A. Masson, 1905.

Duval, Fernand. *J.-B. Andre Godin et le Familistere de Guise.* Paris: V. Giard et E. Briere, 1905.

Fourier, Charles. *Cités ouvrières: Des modifications à introduire dans l'architecture des villes.* Paris: Librarie phalansterienne, 1849.

——. *Le Nouveau Monde industriel et societaire ou invention du procédé d'industrie attrayante et naturelle distribuée en series passionnées.* Paris: Bossange Père, 1829.

Godin, Jean-Baptiste André. *La Richesse au service du peuple: Le Familistere de Guise.* Paris: Librairie de la Bibliotheque democratique, 1874.

——. *Solutions sociales.* Paris: A. Le Chevalier, 1871.

Gosset, Alphonse. "Maisons à bon marché par groupes de quatre pour cités ouvriers." *Encyclopedie d'Architecture*. vol. 8. Paris: A. Morel et cie., 1879.

Guerrand, Roger-H. *Les Origines du logement social en france*. Paris: Les Editions Ouvrières, 1967.

Lavedan, Pierre. *Historie de l'urbanisme: Epoque contemporaine*. Paris: Henri Laurens, Editeur, 1952.

Les Reflexions d'un visiteur curieux devant l'exposition du Chocolat-Menier. Paris: E. Plon, Nourrit, et Cie., 1889.

Markovitch, T. J. *L'Industrie française de 1789 à 1964*. 7 vols. Paris: Cahiers de L'Institute de Science Economique Appliquée, 1966.

Marrey, Bernard. *Un Capitalisme ideal*. Paris: Clancier-Guenaud, 1984.

Menier, Exposition universale de Paris, 1889. Paris: Typographie de E. Plon, Nourrit et Cie., 1889.

Muller, Emile. *Cités ouvrières et agricoles, bains, lavoirs, sechoirs cuisines economiques*. Paris: Carilian-Goeury et V. Dalmont, 1854.

——— and Emile Cacheux. *Les Habitations ouvrières en tous pays*. Paris: Baudry and Cie., 1889.

———. *Les Habitations ouvrières du tous pays: Table des matières des planches*. Paris: Baudry and Cie., 1889.

———. *Habitations ouvrières et agricoles, cités, bains et lavoirs*, planches. Paris: Victor Dalmont, 1855–56.

Murard, Lion, and Patrick Zylberman. *Le Petit Travailleur infatigable*. Paris: Recherches, 1976.

Nansouty, Max. *Les Etablissements Menier à l'exposition de 1889, ler fascicule*. Paris: Publications du Journal Le Genie Civil, 1889.

Penot, A. *Les Cités ouvrières de Mulhouse et du département du Haut-Rhin*. Paris: Librairie de Eugene Lacroix, 1867.

Roulliet, Antony. *Des habitations à bon marché: Legislation*. Paris: Guillaumin, 1889.

———. *Habitations ouvrières à l'exposition universelle de 1889 à Paris*. Paris: Berger-Levrault et Cie., 1889.

Saulnier, Jules. "Habitation pour deux maisons d'ouvriers à Noisiel (Seine-et-Marne)." *Encyclopedie d'architecture: Revue mensuelle des travaux publics et particuliers*, vol. 4. Paris: A. Morel et Cie., 1875.

———. "Usine Menier, à Noisiel (Seine-et-Marne)." *Encyclopedie d'architecture: Revue mensuelle des travaux public et particuliers*. vol. 3. Paris: A. Morel et Cie., 1874.

Siegfried, Jules. *Les Cités ouvrières*. Le Havre: Imprimerie du journal Le Havre, 1877.

Villermé, Louis René. *Sur les cités ouvrières*. Paris: J.-B. Bailliere, 1850.

———. *Tableau de l'état physique et moral des ouvrières employés dans les manufacturers de coton, de laine et de soie*. 2 vols. Paris: J. Renouard, 1840.

Scandinavia

Ahnlund, M., and L. Brunnström. "Från Dawson till Pullman: Nordamerikanska bolagssamhällen - en översikt" (with captions in English and a summary: From Dawson to Pullman: North American company towns—an overview). *Bebyggelsehistorisk tidskrift* 13 (1987): 9–59.

———. "Bolagsbyggandet—ett försummat kapitel i arkitektur—och stadsplanehistoria" (with a German summary: Aktiengesellschaftliches Bauen—ein vernachlässigtes

Kapitel der Architektur—und Stadtplangeschichte). *Taidehistoriallisa Tutkimuksia/Konsthistoriska Studier* 9 (1986): 13–27.

———, Karin Eriksson, and Eva Vikstrom. "Aldre industrier och industriminnen vid Umeälvens nedre del" (with an English summary: Older industries and industrial monuments in the lower part of the Ume River valley). *Norrländska städer och kulturmiljöer.* nr 6. Umeå: Department of Art History, Umeå University, 1980.

Ahnlund, M. "Norrbyskär—om tillkomsten av ett norrländskt sågverkssamhälle på 1890-talet" (with an English summary: Norrbyskär—the birth of a Swedish sawmill community in the 1890s). *Norrländska städer och kulturmiljöer,* nr. 1. Umeå: Department of Art History, Umeå University, 1978.

Bedoire, F., ed. "Textilindustrins miljöer" (with an English summary: Environments of the textile industries: an introduction). *Bebyggelsehistorisk tidskrift,* nr. 15. Stockholm, 1988.

Björklund, J. "From the Gulf of Bothnia to the White Sea—Swedish Direct Investments in the Sawmill Industry of Tsarist Russia," *Scandinavian Economic History Review* 1 (1984): 17–41.

Brunnström, L. "Järnväg och gruvindustri skapar nya urbana förutsättningar i sekelskiftets Norrbotten," *Bebyggelsehistorisk tidskrift* 1 (1981): 24–48.

———. "KIRUNA—ett samhällsbygge i sekelskiftets Sverige: Del I. En bebyggelsehistorisk studie av anläggningsskedet fram till 1910" (with an English summary: KIRUNA—a Swedish mining city from the turn of the century). *Norrländska städer och kulturmiljöer* , nr 3. Umeå: Dokuma, 1981.

Linnés. Dalaresa, *Iter Dalecarlium.* Uppsala: Hugo Gebers förlag, 1953.

Ericsson, B. *Bergsstaden Falun 1720–1769.* Uppsala: Department of History, Stockholm University, 1970.

Lundkvist, K. A. "Den malmcolmska verkstaden i Norrköping 1836–1868." *Daedalus.* Stockholm: Sveriges Tekniska Museum, Stockholm, 1976.

Mikkola, K. "Alvar Aalto som industrins arkitekt," *Arkitektur* nr 4 (1969): 14–17.

Naucler, O. *Stora Kopparbergs gruva och kopparverk: Två akademiska avhandlingar vid Uppsala universitet år 1702 och 1703.* Uppsala: Almqvist & Wiksell, 1941.

Douhan, B. and O. Hirn. *Smedernas Lövsta: Lövstabruk: En guide till herrgårdens och brukets historia.* Lövstabruk: Stiftelsen Leufsta, 1987.

Norlin, E. *Stenkol: Kort handbok om stenkol med särskild hänsyn till svensk upphandling och förbrukning.* Stockholm: Sveriges Industriförbund, 1927.

Sahlström, N. *Stadsplaner och stadsbild i Falun 1628–1850.* Falun: Stadsfullmäktige i Falun, 1953.

Selling, G. "Herrgårdarna och bebyggelsen." *Forsmarks bruk—en uppländsk herrgårdsmiljö.* Stockholm: Forsmarks Kraftgrupp A B, 1984.

Sestoft, J. "Arbejdets bygninger" (with captions in English). *Danmarks arkitektur.* Copenhagen: Nordisk Forlag A/S, 1979.

New England

Bahr, Betsy W. *New England Mill Engineering: Rationalization and Reform in Textile Mill Design, 1790–1920.* Ph.D. diss., University of Delaware, 1987.

Beaudry, Mary C., and Stephen A. Mrozowski. "The Archeology of Work and Home Life in Lowell, Massachusetts: An Interdisciplinary Study of the Boott Cotton Mills Corporation." *IA, Journal of the Society for Industrial Archeology* 14 no. 2 (1988): 1–22.

————, eds. *Interdisciplinary Investigations of the Boott Mills, Lowell, Massachusetts*. 3 vols. Cultural Resource Management Study nos. 18–20. Boston: Department of the Interior, National Park Service, North Atlantic Regional Office, 1987–91.

Candee, Richard M. "The 1822 Allendale Mill and Slow-Burning Construction: A Case Study in the Transmission of an Architectural Technology." *IA, The Journal of the Society of Industrial Archeology* 15, no. 1 (1989): 21–34.

————. "Architecture and Corporate Planning in the Early Waltham System." In *Essays from the Lowell Conference on Industrial History 1982 and 1983*, edited by Robert Weible, 17–43. North Andover, Mass.: Museum of American Textile History, 1985.

————. "New Towns of the Early New England Textile Industry." In *Perspectives in Vernacular Architecture*, edited by Camille Wells. Vol. 1, *Vernacular Architecture Forum*, 31–51, Columbia: University of Missouri, 1981.

Clark, Victor S. *History of Manufactures in the United States*. vol. 1, *1607–1860*. 1929. Reprint. New York: Peter Smith, 1949.

Coolidge, John. *Mill and Mansion: A Study of Architecture and Society in Lowell, Massachusetts, 1820–1865*. New York: Columbia University Press, 1942.

Dalzell, Robert F., Jr. *Enterprising Elite: The Boston Associates and the World They Made*. Cambridge and London: Harvard University Press, 1987.

Dunwell, Steve *The Run of the Mill*. Boston: David R. Godine, 1978.

Dublin, Thomas *Women at Work: The Transformation of Work and Community in Lowell, Massachusetts, 1826–1860*. New York: Columbia University Press, 1979.

————, ed. *Farm to Factory: Women's Letters, 1830–1860*. New York: Columbia University Press, 1981.

Garner, John S. *The Model Company Town: Urban Design through Private Enterprise in Nineteenth-Century New England*. Amherst: University of Massachusetts Press, 1984.

Garvin, James L. *Academic Architecture and the Building Trades in the Piscataqua Region of New Hampshire and Southern Maine, 1715–1815*. Ph.D. diss., Boston University, 1983.

Hay, Duncan Erroll. "The New City on the Merrimack: The Essex Company and Its Role in the Creation of Lawrence, Massachusetts." Ph.D. diss., University of Delaware, 1986.

Jeremy, David. *Transatlantic Industrial Revolution: The Diffusion of Textile Technologies between Britain and America, 1790–1830s*. Cambridge: MIT Press, 1981.

Kulik, Gary, Roger Parks, and Theodore Penn. *The New England Mill Village, 1790–1860*. In *Documents in American Industrial History*, edited by Michael B. Folson, vol. 2. Cambridge and London: MIT Press and Merrimack Valley Textile Museum, 1982.

Lubar, Steven David. *Corporate and Urban Contexts of Textile Technology in Nineteenth-Century Lowell, Massachusetts: A Study of the Social Nature of Technological Knowledge*. Ph.D. diss., University of Chicago, 1983.

Montgomery, James. *A Practical Detail of Cotton Manufacture or the United States of America and the State of the Cotton Manufacture of That Country Contrasted and Compared with That of Great Britain*. Glasgow, 1840.

Pierson, William H., Jr. *American Buildings and Their Architects: Technology and the Picturesque, the Corporate and the Early Gothic Styles*. New York: Doubleday & Co., 1978.

Prude, Jonathan. *The Coming of Industrial Order: Town and Factory Life in Rural Massachusetts, 1810–1860*. Cambridge: Cambridge University Press, 1983.

Ware, Caroline F. *The Early New England Cotton Manufacture: A Study in Industrial Beginnings*. Boston: Houghton-Mifflin, 1933.

American South

Comey, Arthur, and Max S. Wehrly. "Planned Communities." *The Supplementary Report of the Urbanism Committee: Urban Planning and Land Policies*, pt. 1, vol. 2. Washington, D.C.: Government Printing Office, 1939.

Draper, Earle S. "Southern Textile Village Planning," *Landscape Architecture* 18 (October 1927): 1–28.

Glass, Brent. "Southern Mill Hills: Design in a 'Public Place.'" In *Carolina Dwelling: Towards Preservation of Place: In Celebration of the North Carolina Vernacular Landscape*, edited by Doug Swaim, 138–49. Raleigh: School of Design, North Carolina State University, 1978.

Hall, Jacquelyn Dowd, James Leloudis, Robert Korstad, Mary Murphy, Lu Ann Jones, and Christopher B. Daly. *Like A Family: The Making of a Southern Cotton Mill World*. Chapel Hill: University of North Carolina Press, 1987.

Hanchett, Thomas. "Earle Sumner Draper: City Planner of the New South." In *Early Twentieth-Century Suburbs in North Carolina*, edited by Catherine Bishir and Lawrence S. Early, 79–82. Raleigh: North Carolina Department of Cultural Resources, 1985.

Magnussen, Leifur. "Southern Cotton Mill Villages." In *Housing by Employers in the United States*, 139–60. Bulletin no. 263, U.S. Department of Labor, Bureau of Labor Statistics. Washington, D.C.: Government Printing Office, 1920.

Rhyne, Jennings. *Some Southern Textile Workers and Their Villages*. Chapel Hill: University of North Carolina Press, 1930.

American West

Allen, James B. *The Company Town in the American West*. Norman, Okla., 1966.

Allen, Ruth. *The Great Southwest Strike*. Austin, 1942.

Allis, S. *As Seen in a Logging Camp*. N.p., 1900.

Andrews, Ralph. *Timber, Toil, and Trouble in the Big Woods*. Seattle, 1968.

Binns, Archie. *Sea in the Forest*. New York, 1953.

Chaplin, Ralph. *Wobbly*. Chicago, 1948.

Coman, Edwin T., and Helen Gibbs. *Time, Tide, and Timber: A Century of Pope and Talbot*. Stanford, 1950.

Cox, John. *Random Lengths: Forty Years with Timber Beasts and Sawdust Savages*. Eugene, Oreg., 1949.

Cox, Thomas R. *Mills and Markets: A History of the Pacific Coast Lumber Industry to 1900*. Seattle, 1974.

Ellis, Lucia. *Head Rig: Story of the West Coast Lumber Industry*. Portland, Oreg., 1965.

Enerson, Irma Lee. *The Woods Were Full of Men*. N.p., 1963.

Engstrom, Emil. *The Vanishing Logger*. New York, 1956.

Erickson, Kenneth A. "The Morphology of Lumber Settlements in Western Oregon and Washington." Ph.D. diss., University of California-Berkeley, 1965.

Greever, William S. *The Bonanza West: The Story of the Western Mining Rushes, 1848–1900*. Norman, Okla., 1963.

Hempstead, A. G. *History of Snohomish County, Washington*. Everett, Wash., 1931.

Hidy, Ralph. *Timber and Men: The Weyerhauser Story*. New York, 1963.

Holbrook, Stewart. *Green Commonwealth*. Seattle, 1944.

Hughson, Oliver. "When We Logged the Columbia." *Oregon Historical Quarterly* 60 (1959): 173–209.

Knight, Rolf. *Work Camps and Company Towns in Canada and the United States: An Annotated Bibliography*. Vancouver, B.C., 1975.

Jensen, Vernon. *Lumber and Labor*. New York, 1945.

Lewis, Marvin. *The Mining Frontier: Contemporary Accounts from the American West*. Norman, Okla., 1967.

"Life in a Company Town." *New Republic*, 82 (September 1937): 171.

Louis, Loretta. "History of Ruby City: The Life and Death of a Mining Town." *Pacific Northwest Quarterly* 32 (January 1941): 61–78.

Mason, Gregory. "A Summer in an Oregon Lumber Camp." *Oregon Historical Quarterly* 1 (1909): 613–14.

Magnusson, Leifer. "Company Housing in the Bituminous Coal Fields." U.S. Bureau of Labor, *Monthly Labor Review* 10, no. 4 (April 1920): 1045–52.

———. *Housing by Employers in the United States*. Washington, D.C., 1920.

McGovern, George S. "The Colorado Coal Strike, 1913–14." Ph.D. diss., Northwestern University, 1953.

Morgan, Murray. *The Last Wilderness*. New York, 1955.

Paul, Rodman W. *Mining Frontiers of the Far West, 1848–1880*. New York, 1963.

Reps, John W. *Cities of the American West: A History of Frontier Urban Planning*. Princeton, 1979.

Roth, Leland M. *Concise History of American Architecture*. New York, 1979.

———. "Three Industrial Towns by McKim, Mead & White." *Journal, Society of Architectural Historians* 38 (December 1979): 317–47.

Tyler, Robert. *Rebels in the Woods: The I.W.W. in the Pacific Northwest*. Eugene, Oreg., 1967.

South America

Provincia de Tucumán. *Anuario de Estadisticas de la Provincia de Tucumán*, vols. 1 y 2. Tucuman, Argentina: Director Paulino Rodriguez Marquina, 1895.

Avila, Julio P. *Noticias Historicas: la caña de azucar de las Indias Occidentales. Refutaciones*. Tucumán, Argentina, 1923.

Bialet-Massé, Juan. *El estado de las clases obreras argentinas a comienzos del siglo*, 2d ed. Cordoba: Universidad Nacional de Cordoba, 1904.

Centro Azucarero Argentino. *Cincuentenario del Centro Azucarero Argentino: Desarrollo de la industria en medio siglo, 1880–1944*. Buenos Aires: E. Echleh, 1944.

Koebel, W. E., ed. *Enciclopedia de la America del Sur*, vol. 4. London: Anglo and South American Publishing Co., 1911.

Franchini, Teresita y Jorge Rosé. "Pueblos Tanineros del NEA, Fontana." In *Documentos de Arquitectura Nacional y Americana*, no. 4. Chaco, Argentina: Universidad Nacional del Nordeste, 1976.

Garcés Feliu, Eugenio. *Las Ciudades del Salitre: Un estudio de las Officinas Salitreras en la region de Antofagasta.* Universidad del Norte, Chile: Editorial Universitaria, 1988.

Granillo, Arsenio. Provincia de Tucuman, 1872, 2d ed., serie 5, vol. 1. Tucuman, Argentina: Archivo Historico de Tucuman, 1947.

Groussac, Paul, Alfredo Bousquet, Inocencio Liberani. *Memoria Historica y Descriptiva de la Provincia de Tucuman.* Buenos Aires: M. Biedma, 1882.

Guy, Donna J. *Argentine Sugar Politics: Tucuman and the Generation of Eighty.* Tempe: Arizona State University, Center for Latin American Studies, 1980.

Hardoy, J. Enrique and Maria Elena Langdon. "El pensamiento regional en Argentina y Chile entre 1850 y 1930." In *El Proceso de Urbanizacion de las Americas desde sus origenes hasta nuestros dias.* Ediciones SIAP, 1979.

Hardoy, J. Enrique, Richard Schaendel, and Richard Morse. *Coloquios sobre Urbanizacion en America desde Sus Origenes hasta nuestros dias.* Ediciones SIAP, Tomo IV.

Llanes, Lilian. *Apuntes para una Historia sobre los constructores cubanos.* Havana, Cuba: Ediciones Letras Cubanas, 1985.

Nougués, Miguel Alfredo. *Los fundadores, los propulsores, los realizadores de San Pablo.* Buenos Aires, 1976.

Paterlini de Koch, Olga. *Pueblos Azucareros de Tucumán.* Serie Tipologias Arquitectonicas, Poblados Industriales. Tucumán, Argentina: Instituto Argentino de Investigaciones de Historia de la Arquitectura y del Urbanismo, 1987.

Scobie, James. "Changing Urban Patterns: The Porteño Case 1880–1920." In *El Proceso de Urbanizacion en America desde sus Origenes hasta nuestros dias.* Buenos Aires: Instituto Torcuato di Tella, 1969.

Index

Page numbers in italics refer to figures.